# THE IDEA OF POLITICS

## The Uses of Power in Society

# THE
# IDEA OF POLITICS

*The Uses of Power in Society*

## MAURICE DUVERGER

*Institut d'Études Politiques de l'Université de Paris*

*translated by*
## ROBERT NORTH & RUTH MURPHY

METHUEN & CO LTD
11 NEW FETTER LANE   LONDON EC4

*First published in Paris, 1964, under
the title Introduction à la Politique, by Éditions
Gallimard. © 1964 by Éditions Gallimard*

*First English language edition published
1966 by Methuen & Co Ltd*

*Reprinted 1967*

*Printed in Great Britain by
Ebenezer Baylis & Son Ltd
The Trinity Press, Worcester, and London*

# Foreword

In the eighteenth century it was easy to write an introduction to politics. Today it is easy in the Soviet Union. However, in western Europe in the year 1964 it is a very difficult task, because here and now there is no generally accepted overall theory of politics such as existed in the eighteenth century or exists today in the Communist world. Any attempt to write one must therefore be based on a personal approach.

None the less this essay follows a line of thought common to many contemporary sociologists. The problem we face is not to construct a new western theory in opposition to the Marxist theory, but to consider our ideas and those opposed to them as relative and partial views which should be integrated into a general synthesis. That can only be achieved in time and no claim is made that it has been accomplished in these few pages. This essay is not a theory of politics but the sketch of an introduction to such a theory. Its general trend is more important than the detail which includes a good many theories, as yet unverified.

The decision to publish such a sketch is based on the belief that an effort of this kind is of importance to all citizens in a democracy. One of the obstacles which prevents them from fully exercising their rights in the western world today is that they are distracted by individual political problems which they cannot set in an overall context. There is an abundance of information about each and every question, but this is accompanied by an almost complete absence of a general view which alone would make it possible to understand the importance and significance of each individual problem. Any contribution to the filling of so fundamental a gap is useful, even if this attempt proves inadequate. Of its inadequacies the author himself is well aware.

# Contents

# Introduction

Littré in his 1870 dictionary defined politics as 'the science of government of states'. Robert in 1962 defined it as 'the art and practice of government of human societies'. The comparison between the two definitions, given almost a century apart, is not without interest. Both make government the object of politics. Today, however, the government of states is related to that of other human societies, the term government thus meaning, in any society, organized power, the institutions of command and control. The issue is the subject of debate among specialists: some still consider politics as the science of the state, of organized power in the national community; the majority see it as the science of organized power in all communities.

This difference of opinion is unimportant. In fact, even those who define politics as the science of power in general recognize that it is in the state that power finds its most developed and most highly organized form, and hence it is in this context that it should mainly be studied; in other human societies it remains embryonic. However, the concept of politics as the science of power has one basic superiority: it is more operational because it alone allows verification of the hypothesis on which it is based. A comparative study of power in every kind of community may reveal the existence of differences between power in the state and power in other communities. On the other hand, to study power only within the framework of the state without comparing it with power elsewhere is restrictive, making it impossible to verify whether the difference of kind posited *a priori* exists or not.

It has been suggested that a distinction be made between large and small communities. In the latter, competition for power is between individuals, power itself being weakly organized; the situation roughly corresponds to the elementary distinction between the 'rulers' and 'ruled', between leaders and members. In large communities, on the other hand, political conflict involves social categories, intermediate groups set up within the total society, as well as individuals; power is organized structurally and hierarchically. Some sociologists limit politics to the study of this complex power which operates in large communities and exclude the analysis of leadership in small groupings.

The two phenomena are too closely linked to be studied separately. In ministerial committees, in administrative committees, in the executive committees of political parties, at every level of government in large communities, there are to be found small groups in which the political nature of authority is indisputable. The more valid distinction is between two levels of analysis: the micropolitical dealing with relations on the individual plane, based upon personal contact; the macropolitical dealing with group relationships where direct contact does not exist or is replaced by indirect contact between intermediaries, by administrative relationships or by artificial, theatrical contacts (the minister's handshake, the television appearance of the head of state). Research must be pursued simultaneously on both levels, but the passage from one to the other, the change in scale, raises an important problem.

The definitions of Littré and Robert differ on another point: the first speaks of politics as a science, the latter considers it simply as an art and an activity. *A priori*, the inverse would appear more natural. Today political science is recognized in almost every university in the world; it has its chairs, its professors and teachers, its students and its research funds. Every year several thousand books and articles are published in the field. A century ago it was scarcely being talked of. It was only between 1859 and 1872 that Paul Janet changed the title of his great work *Histoire de la philosophie politique dans ses rapports avec la morale*, replacing *philosophie politique* by *science politique*. At that time no university post catered for the subject; it had no official place in the Pantheon of knowledge. Linguistic development seems here to have run counter to scientific development.

Yet the two really go hand in hand. Littré was writing at the end of the nineteenth century, when it was thought that science would make possible the study of all human relations and not physical or biological phenomena only, when the coming of the 'Positive age' announced by Auguste Comte was expected. The very development of the social sciences has led to a restriction of these ambitions. Today we have at our disposal very many much improved modes of investigation of social and political life, but at the same time we are more conscious of the narrowness of the limits within which they can be used. Politics is much more scientific in 1964 than in Littré's day. Statesmen can and do effectively use statistics, electronic computers, public opinion polls, techniques for the manipulation of the masses, and so on. However, we now know that the area covered by this scientific kind of politics is much smaller than that of politics as an art, based upon imprecise material that is not measurable but is intuitive and irrational.

It would be vain to hope that the two will ever entirely coincide, that politics can become entirely scientific. Political decisions bring into play not only objective data but also value-judgements about man and society. The fact that these value-judgements are not unrelated to the situation of those who formulate them, that indeed they in part reflect social class and personal interests, makes no difference. Liberty never exists *in vacuo*; it is always exercised by men who are conditioned by their experience. The disparity between the aims stated and those actually pursued, the masking of the one by the other, does not change the fact that political choice is dominated by aims. Political science is of major importance because it removes the masks, it demystifies. It can make clear the real terms of choice, but it cannot choose.

In so far as politics is based, then, on choices and commitments, its concepts are relative; definable in relation to particular sets of values and differing in significance. We can describe the Marxist, the Liberal, the Conservative, the Fascist view of politics, but there is no totally 'objective' view of politics, because there is no totally objective politics. Political science can separate the objective elements from those which are not so, and thus critically assess each view. It is capable of determining the depth to which at a given period the particular view has penetrated, as well as its evolution. It is capable also, by confronting those views, of complementing them and of assessing them one against the others, in just the same way as different photographs of the same object taken from different points of view may be brought together in order to give a more complete picture of the object which cannot be seen directly in the round.

Behind all the systems of values and all individual judgements there are generally to be found two basic attitudes. Ever since men have been reflecting on politics they have oscillated between two dramatically opposed interpretations. According to one, politics is conflict, a struggle in which power allows those who possess it to ensure their hold on society and to profit by it. According to the other view, politics is an effort to bring about the rule of order and justice, in which power guarantees the general interest and the common good against the pressures of private interests. In the first case, politics serves to maintain the privileges of a minority against the majority. In the second, it is a means of realizing the integration of all citizens into the community and of creating the just state of which Aristotle spoke so long ago.

The acceptance of one or other of these theses is in part determined by social situation. The oppressed, the unsatisfied, the poor, the wretched, whether as individuals or as a class, cannot see power as assuring a real order, but only a caricature of it behind which is hidden the domination of privilege; for them politics means conflict. Those who are rich, well provided for, satisfied, find society harmonious and see power as maintaining an authentic order; for them politics means integration. It often happens that the latter succeed to some extent in persuading the former that political strife is dishonest, unhealthy, sordid, and that those who engage in it seek their own selfish interests by dubious means. To disarm opponents in such a way is to secure a considerable personal advantage. 'Depolitization' always favours the established order, immobility and conservatism.

The two attitudes express only a part of the truth, of course. The most optimistic of Conservatives cannot deny that even if the aim of politics is to bring about social integration it rarely achieves it in a satisfactory way. They describe politics idealistically, as it ought to be. Their opponents describe it more realistically, as it is. But in their turn they can scarcely deny that they paint too black a picture. The most oppressive and unjust of governments fulfil some functions that are in the general interest, if only in the technical field, in regulating motor traffic, for example, in running the postal services or in arranging for the collection of household refuse.

In the last resort, the essence of politics, its real nature and true significance, is to be found in the fact that it is always and at all times ambivalent. The statue of Janus, the two-faced god, is the true image of the state and expresses the most profound of political realities. The state – and in a more general way, organized power in any society – is always and at all times both the instrument by which certain groups dominate others, an instrument used in the interest of the rulers and to the disadvantage of the ruled, and also a means of ensuring a particular social order, of achieving some integration of the individual into the collectivity for the general good. The two elements always co-exist, though the importance of each varies with the period, the circumstances and the country concerned. The relations between conflict and integration are, moreover, complex. Every attack on the existing social order implies the image and anticipation of a superior, more authentic order. Every conflict implies a dream of integration and represents an effort to bring it into being. Many thinkers maintain that conflict and integration are not two opposed faces but one and the same overall process in which conflict naturally produces integration, and divisions, by their development, tend naturally towards their own suppression leading to the coming of the city of harmony.

For classical liberal thinkers integration is produced by conflict as this develops, the two phenomena being concomitant.

Competition produces the maximum increase in production and the best division of its proceeds, thus leading at any given moment to the best possible economic situation. Political competition is said to produce similar effects: as a result of it, the best, the most fitted, the *élite*, govern for the benefit of all. Political harmony, disturbed only by those who are abnormal, perverse or sick, thus parallels economic harmony. Marxist thinkers also see conflict as the driving force in the evolution of societies, leading necessarily to an ending of divisions and the coming of a society without conflict. However, this integration appears only as the last phase in a very long-term process, only in the distant future. A partial integration or synthesis is achieved at each stage and this immediately becomes a new source of contradiction and strife. Political harmony, it is said, will develop rhythmically until that end point in history which is the 'higher phase of Communism'.

## Part I

# The Elements of Conflict

In all human communities, and even in animal societies, power confers certain advantages and privileges, such as honour, prestige, material benefits and pleasures. As a result, there is a bitter struggle for power, taking place on two different planes. The first, which could be called *horizontal*, opposes man to man, group to group, or class to class, in the struggle to attain, share or influence power. Individuals compete for a parliamentary seat, an appointment as prefect, a ministerial portfolio, the general's insignia, a cardinal's hat. In large communities these individual conflicts are paralleled by group rivalries within the society, whether parish, regional or national, by conflicts of class, race and ideology.

The second type of political conflict takes place on a *vertical* plane, opposing power, the government which commands, to the citizens who resist, the rulers to the ruled, the members of the community to the whole apparatus of social control. Not that the opposition is between the citizens on one side and an abstract 'power' on the other; rather, it is between some citizens, who hold power, and others, who are subject to it. Power always works to the benefit of one group, one clan, one class; the opposition to it comes from other groups, clans, or classes, who wish to take the place of those in power. Nevertheless, within the dominant class there is a minority which controls the apparatus of government, and between this minority and the majority of the ruling class there arise conflicts which are quite distinct from the clashes between the ruling class and the rest of the population. These divergences between rulers and ruled, between those who command and those who must obey, between the holders of power and the other citizens, can be seen in all human society.

The various political ideologies differ not only in the relative importance they give to conflict and integration but also in their conception of the conflict and its causes. For Marxists, political disagreement is caused by the socio-economic structures. The modes of production, such as ancient or medieval agriculture, or modern industry, are determined by the state of technical development, and in their turn they give rise to social classes, which either rule or are ruled, and therefore conflict. The ruling classes use the state to maintain their power over the other classes, which naturally resist. Political strife thus reflects the class struggle, and is therefore essentially collective, setting group against group within the community. Competition between individuals is only of secondary importance to Marxists, who also neglect the clash between citizens and state, except in so far as it coincides with the conflict between the dominated classes and the dominant class which rules the state. However, the experience of Stalinism has made them aware of the problem.

Liberal philosophies, on the other hand, mainly consider the other two forms of political strife, that is, competition between individuals to obtain the best position in society, and the struggle of citizens against power, which is by nature oppressive. Western thinkers hold that both these forms of strife are caused by factors which are essentially psychological. Power corrupts because it allows those who rule to indulge their passions to the detriment of those they rule over. 'All power corrupts, and absolute power corrupts absolutely.' Power is a permanent temptation, and as Alain says, 'there is no man who, if he had total power and were quite free to exercise it, would not sacrifice justice to his passions'. Furthermore, in a society where needs outstrip the goods available to satisfy them, every man strives to obtain for himself the maximum advantage over his fellows and holding power is an effective means to this end. This elementary psychological portrait of *homo politicus*, motivated like *homo economicus* by personal interest, is today being enriched and complicated by the findings of psychoanalysis, which attributes more complex motivational forces to political strife.

The evolution of the highly developed nations towards an affluent society is leading western thinkers to recognize the importance of socio-economic factors, such as technical progress and economic scarcity, in political conflict, and this recognition is bringing them closer to Marxism. The concepts of affluence and poverty are allowing rediscovery of some other causes of political strife that were pointed out by older writers and then to some extent neglected by the two main doctrines of today. Analysis of the underdeveloped countries is bringing the influence of population factors back into the limelight. It is also focusing attention on the influence of geography, which was stressed by all the classical writers, from Herodotus to Montesquieu, and, nearer our own day, by the geopoliticians who were writing at the beginning of the twentieth century.

Political conflicts thus emerge as the result of many factors, which react one on the other. We shall now attempt to draw an overall picture of them, and to determine their reciprocal connections and their respective importance.

# 1. Biological Factors

There are two theories which make biological factors the most important elements in political strife: the 'struggle for life' theory, and the racialist theory. The former transfers to human society Darwin's doctrine of the evolution of species, according to which each individual has to fight the rest in order to survive, and only the fittest do so successfully. The mechanism of natural selection ensures the conservation and development of the best adapted. Darwin's theory is a biological version of bourgeois philosophy which is expressed in economic terms by the doctrine of free enterprise: to the struggle for life corresponds the struggle to satisfy needs. In the political sphere, this becomes Mosca's 'struggle for pre-eminence', on which theories of the *élite* are based. In the struggle for power, stimulated by the advantages power confers, there emerge the best, the most able, those best fitted to govern.

Racialism removes these ideas from the individual sphere to the collective one. Here, differences of aptitude between individuals are less important than differences of aptitude between races. Whereas some races are more suited to command, and are naturally born to dominate, others are born to obey, though they do not accept this of their own accord. In this theory, the combat between inferior and superior races is the essence of political strife.

In fact, neither of these theories has any scientific validity. But this does not mean that we should totally reject the idea that politics is founded in biology. A study of animal societies reveals the existence therein of authority and organized power comparable in some ways to similar phenomena in human societies. Politics existed before man. Aristotle's famous definition of man as a 'political animal' is not valid, for there are other political animals besides man. Needless to say, there are great differences between politics in human societies and politics in animal societies; and though exaggerated comparisons of the two may make for good fiction, they do not correspond to the facts. Nevertheless, politics has some biological foundation.

## POLITICS IN ANIMAL SOCIETIES

As well as limited or fragmentary social phenomena such as temporary groupings, parasitism and group feeding, there are real communities to be found among animals, some of a small, family nature, and other much bigger ones which bring together a large number of individuals of the same species. Some have a highly developed and complex form of organization. Animal societies have long been known, and to compare them with human societies is by no means new: beehives, anthills and termitaries have been the subject of countless dissertations. But it is interesting to note the 'homocentric' tendency of comparisons with human society. Animal societies are judged favourably or unfavourably according to whether the animals being studied are useful or harmful to man. It is flattering to compare a human group to a hive, which is composed of useful bees; to compare it to a termitary, which is composed of harmful animals, is pejorative; while comparison with an anthill, made up of animals which are generally neither useful nor harmful, is neutral or at least ambivalent.

Social phenomena among animals bear only a sporadic, erratic relation to biological evolution. They will be found in some species, while a closely related species shows no sign of them. There is no correlation with zoological classes. Social animals are neither more nor less evolved than solitary ones. For example, there are animals, like some insects, which show a relatively low level of evolution biologically, but which show high social evolution, while others, like some mammals, are highly evolved biologically, but are asocial. Even within the same category of animals, we find the same lack of correlation between social and organic evolution: biologically, termites are much less evolved than bees or ants, but termitaries are much more highly organized than hives or anthills. Socialization appears to be a way in which species evolve that is different from organic evolution. It is as if, at every level of biological evolution, some species entered on the path of socialization, for reasons unknown to us, and found there a new way of evolving which has brought some of them to a high degree of perfection.

There seems to be a fundamental difference between two kinds of animal society: insect societies and vertebrate societies. The latter only can be compared to human societies. The others are organisms rather than societies. A student of termites, E. Marais, wrote in 1953: 'A termitary is a composite animal which has reached a certain phase of its development, and can only be differentiated from other animals of the same kind by its inability to move.' Termites in a termitary, ants in an anthill and bees in a hive have a much greater resemblance to the cells which make up the human organism or that of the higher animals than they have to citizens in a state, or a beaver in a community of beavers.

The basic factor underlying the organization of insects in termitary, anthill or beehive seems to be material, physical *stimuli*: tropisms and reflexes based on form, movement, contact and so on. The insects are categorized and allocated different tasks according to organic differences: 'kings' and 'queens', workers, drones, warriors and reproducers are physiologically as different from one another as muscle, bone and nerve cells in a vertebrate. The whole organism is co-ordinated and regulated almost automatically. If the queen bee dies or disappears, the female workers will pay particular attention to feeding some of the larvae to turn them into queens and replace the old one. It has been shown that they behave in this way, not because they have noted the death or disappearance of the queen, but because an 'external hormone', secreted by the queen, is lacking. In a hive where the queen, though alive and visible, is isolated in a transparent envelope, the workers will begin to give special treatment to larvae, as if there were no queen; whereas if the queen has disappeared, but a bit of cloth soaked in her 'external hormone' is introduced into the hive, the workers do not start the special treatment, but continue to act just as if the queen were still there. Similarly, in a human or vertebrate organism, internal hormones regulate and co-ordinate the cells and organs.

However, this view of insect societies as a collective organism should not be exaggerated. First, the automatic regulation mechanisms are not as rigid as they are in man or the other vertebrates: sometimes, despite the presence of the queen and her hormone, the workers will produce other queens, which causes social conflict. More important, the basic elements of the collective organism, the individual insects, are much more complex and autonomous in structure than are the cells of a human body. This necessarily means that the whole is different in character. In fact, these collective insect organisms stand half-way between organisms properly so called, and real societies, i.e. vertebrate societies.

In vertebrate societies the individual's existence is much more independent of the collectivity. Division of functions, if it occurs, is based on psychological and not on physiological factors. Thus some vertebrates at the bottom of the social scale are, in fact, deprived of the chance to reproduce, and become, as it were, psychological castrates, condemned to forced continence; but there is an essential difference between them and the 'workers' or 'warriors' of insect societies, which is that the latter are physiologically asexual. Again, in vertebrate societies, it is the existence of 'leaders' whom the group obeys, rather than any automatic mechanisms, which ensures the proper functioning of the whole. The social order is political, not biological. In a termitary, beehive or anthill there are no leaders; the anthropomorphic expressions used, 'king' or 'queen', are misleading, as the constituent elements of such 'composite animals' obey no one; the very notion of obedience is just as meaningless to them as it is to the cells of a human organism. (Cancerous cells are not 'disobedient'; an automatic regulation mechanism has gone wrong, that is all.)

In higher vertebrate societies politics appear, in their most elementary form, with the emergence of hierarchies. These are usually linear: *a* dominates all the others; *b* dominates all the others except *a*; *c* dominates all the rest except *a* and *b*, and so on. Sometimes they are three-sided: *a* dominates *b*, who dominates *c*, who dominates *a*. These hierarchies only benefit the higher ranks, and do not seem to serve the interests of the group as a whole. However, among some kinds of fish the poor wretch who has the lowest rank fulfils an important social function, that of scapegoat or butt. The attacks of the others all converge on him, which helps to lessen tensions within the group. Often, hiding behind a stone or the aquarium thermostat, he will humbly die from this ostracism. On the other hand, higher-ranking individuals will sometimes intervene to defend the weaker when they are under attack; this happens among jackdaws, where the powerful protect the powerless and so maintain social order. This brings us to the idea of leaders in the strict sense of the term.

In some animal societies the leader is not only the highest-placed member of a hierarchy, with advantages over the other members, but he is also a ruler commanding the whole of the group for its collective good. He may be the herd leader, who takes the group to feed, brings it back, guides it. He may be the war leader, directing attack and defence. Sometimes a leader only emerges in the mating season, usually from among the males. In some family societies both male and female have power over the offspring, but neither one really commands the other; there is simply division of labour. Elsewhere, the organization of government is more complicated, with sentinels, skirmishers, frontier guards, and so on.

Hierarchies bring great advantages for animals who are highly placed, and leadership confers proportional advantages. These advantages are very similar to those that power confers in human society. Sometimes no more is concerned than the right to attack, to bully, or to insult, just as some animals peck, paw or scratch. Or it may be made more complex by a territorial advantage; among some aquarium fish the leader will occupy a large area which the others do not venture into; the second-in-command will have a smaller area, and so on down the scale. In other cases hierarchy and authority give priority in food, a pecking order: the leaders keep the choicest morsels for themselves, and reduce the lowest to subsistence level, if not starvation. Frequently sexual relations are determined by hierarchy and authority. Studies of the Wyoming grouse have shown that the leading cock alone is responsible for 74 per cent of sexual relations, all his deputies together for 13 per cent, and his 'guards', of whom he has three to six, for 3 per cent. Cocks of lower rank are reduced to forced continence, which they obviously find difficult. Many animal leaders have a positive harem, unlike the other members of their society.

In higher vertebrate society hierarchy and power are never conferred by birth. They can depend on age, with the oldest animal leading the herd, or on sex, with the males occupying the higher ranks (though the reverse is possible). Sometimes there are separate male and female hierarchies; then if a female mates with a high-ranking male it gives her a high place in the female hierarchy. This happens among jackdaws, some rabbits and some hens. Usually, access to the higher ranks or to power is the outcome of a struggle between several candidates; the means used are fairly similar to those used in human society: physical strength, energy, wiles, boldness, and even bluff (those who shout the loudest and make most fuss get the highest positions). This struggle for power is continuous; the hierarchies are often challenged, and the leaders overthrown frequently. There is great 'social mobility' among animals, and political conflict is lively.

Clearly, analogies with human society should not be taken too far. In the latter, images of the collectivity are much richer and much more complex; awareness and beliefs play a much more important part in human society, whereas images of the collectivity, awareness and belief are embryonic among animals, even the higher vertebrates, who probably have no value systems. Nevertheless, four essential facts should be retained. First, the distinction between rulers and ruled, between leaders and members of the group, exists in some animal societies; political phenomena appear in the evolutionary scale before man. Second, animal leaders gain personal advantages from power, which is therefore the object of permanent and usually lively competition. Third, power acts as an integrating force, for the common good; this happens in some animal societies, but not in others, where the hierarchy only benefits individuals in the higher ranks; the first face of Janus is always present, but not the second. Fourth, individual qualities alone confer power or a high place in the hierarchy; birth does not count at all. These four facts shed light on some aspects of human politics.

### RACIALIST THEORIES

Racialist theories which give primacy to real or supposed biological factors in political conflict are condemned both by Marxism and by western thinking: Christian doctrine, nineteenth-century Liberal principles, and socialist theory alike condemn them. Hostility towards them has increased since the Nazis massacred six million Jews, in the name of antisemitism, between 1942 and 1945, and also since many Asian and African countries achieved independence, and with it, international influence.

Very few people, with the exception of some Fascists, and whites living in countries with a colonial structure, like South Africa or the 'Deep South', will dare admit to being racialists. But many people are so, in their heart of hearts, often quite unconsciously. Although racialist theories are false and have no scientific value, their influence is still great, and this is a factor in political antagonism. Biologically, race has no political significance, but because of the collective images it provokes it is sociologically of political significance. However, this is a convenient place at which to examine the racialist theories, since the claims they make force us to look at the biological aspects of the problem, too.

The idea common to all racialist theories is that some races are inferior to others in ability and, in particular, are incapable of organizing and maintaining modern forms of society. Left to their own devices, they would only reach a fairly low level of social evolution. However, some races would reach a higher level than others; there are degrees of inferiority. Negroes would scarcely rise above primitive tribal structures. The yellow races would develop complex states, but would be incapable of democracy; at the most, they would reach the level of seventeenth- or eighteenth-century European nations. The

Jews, despite their outstanding intelligence, and gifted as they are for commerce, banking, the arts and destructive criticism, would be incapable of exercising authority or command, and of organizing effective political power. In fact, according to racialist theories, only the non-Jewish white race can create modern states and make them work. The other races, however, do not of their own accord recognize their inferiority, so that between them and the non-Jewish white race there is a fundamental enmity which is the basic driving force in political struggles.

Racialist theories originated in the Middle Ages, when Christian sovereigns wanted to seize the property of the Jewish bankers. (Only the Jews could lend at interest, as the Catholic church forbade usury.) They spread during the sixteenth century, when the Spanish and Portuguese used African slaves to develop their American colonies, but they only became really important politically in the nineteenth century. The French historian, Augustin Thierry, struck by the violence, the depth and the irreducibility of the political struggles that had been rending the country since 1789, giving rise first to the Red Terror and then to the White Terror, put forward in his *Lettres sur l'Histoire de France* (1827) a racialist hypothesis to explain the strife. The French Revolution and its consequences were for Thierry the end of a struggle which had gone on through the ages, since the barbarian invasions, between two races: the Gallo-Romans, who were the original inhabitants, and the Franks, the Germanic conquerors. The former now constituted the peasantry and the third estate; the latter were the aristocracy. The bitter fight between Conservatives and Liberals since 1789 was but another form of this age-old rivalry, with the Gallo-Romans naturally favouring liberty and democracy and the Franks preferring an authoritarian, community system.

It was probably this historical theory of Thierry's which inspired another Frenchman, Arthur de Gobineau, who gave a generalized version of it in his *Essai sur l'inégalité des races humaines* (1853–5). He combined it with the myth of the 'Aryan' race which was just beginning to spread. In 1788, the philologist, Jones, forcefully struck by the similarities between Sanskrit, Greek, Latin, German and Celtic, had put forward the idea that these tongues all derived from a common origin. In 1813, Thomas Young gave the name 'Indo-European' to this original language. Next, the people who spoke it were called 'Aryan', and in 1861 this appellation received official consecration, as it were, at the hands of the great German philologist Max Müller. Then, one after another, a host of pseudo-scholars set to work to try to place this hypothetical race characterized by its no less hypothetical language; their total lack of agreement shows clearly the absurdity of the conclusions they reached. In 1840, Pott had the Aryans come from the Indian valleys of Amou-Daria and Syr-Daria; in 1868, for Benfrey, they came from north of the Black Sea, between the Danube and the Caspian; in 1871, J. C. Cunok found them between the North Sea and the Urals; in 1890, for D. C. Brinton, they originated in North Africa; in 1892, V. Gordon Childe traced them to southern Russia. At the beginning of the twentieth century K. F. Johansson placed them on the shores of the Baltic; in 1921, Kossina, with less precision, just speaks of northern Europe; in 1922, Peter Giles put Hungary as their place of origin; and so on . . .

Arthur de Gobineau, the anti-liberal, aristocratic supporter of the 'legitimate' Bourbon monarchy, made use of this hypothetical Aryan race to justify the aristocracy's privileges and explain the antagonism between the aristocracy and the mass of the people, arguing that the aristocracy descended from the 'Aryans', who brought political organization, philosophy, the arts, culture, civilization and progress to Europe; while the rest of the people were descendants of the original, primitive inhabitants, of naturally inferior race, who owed everything to their Aryan conquerors and, without them, would still be living in the barbarian state they would relapse into should the Aryan aristocracy cease to rule. Gobineau's Aryan conquest, it will be noted, differs from the barbarian invasions which Thierry saw as the beginnings of the racial struggle. For Gobineau, the Greeks, Romans and the Germanic people were already 'Aryanized'; their civilization was, in fact, Aryan.

Aryan theories have the advantage of being vague, which enables them to escape critical examination and proof. Nevertheless Gobineau's disciples, Vacher de Lapouge and Ammon, systematically measured skulls in cemeteries, equating the dolichocephalics with the Aryans. This led Ammon to formulate as a sociological law that the dolichocephalics were more frequently found in towns than in the country; this supported Gobineau's conclusions, since conquerors will naturally tend to settle in towns. Later, it was realized that Ammon's law was totally false.

Gobineau's theories were twisted by the Nazis, who turned the opposition between the Aryan aristocracy and the non-Aryan populace into opposition between non-Jew and Jew, considering the latter, in any society, to be a disruptive element which must be eradicated. This Nazi theory reverses the quantitative terms of the racial antagonism; instead of a racially superior governing minority in conflict with a racially inferior majority, it has a racially superior majority and an inferior minority which is a factor of discord. The government then used racialism to blame all the ills of society on to the minority, an ancient and well-known 'scapegoat' technique.

In colonial-type states, despite appearances, racialism is truer to Gobineau's theory, with the superior white minority in the Aryan role, carrying the torch of civilization and bearing the burden of power, to the benefit of the inferior coloured races who would otherwise return to their natural savage state.

Other racialist theories set out to explain conflict between nations rather than between classes within one country. It was the English writer Houston Stewart Chamberlain, son of an admiral, friend and son-in-law of Wagner, a neurotic passionate admirer of the Germanic people who took German nationality in 1916 in the very middle of the war, who transposed the theory to the international plane. In his *Foundations of the Twentieth Century* (1899), a vast work of twelve hundred pages, he used the myth of the Aryan people to the glorification of the Germans. Instead of assimilating the Aryans to one class, the aristocracy, he equates them with one nation, Germany. 'The

Teuton [he writes] is the very soul of our civilisation. The importance of any nation as a living power today is in proportion to the amount of pure teutonic blood in its population.' He tries, moreover, to show that all great geniuses were of Teutonic blood, including Julius Caesar, Alexander the Great, Giotto, Leonardo da Vinci, Galileo, Voltaire, Lavoisier. For him, even Christ was a Teuton: 'Whoever claimed that Jesus was a Jew, was either stupid or a liar . . . Jesus was not a Jew.' The Germans enthusiastically adopted Chamberlain's theories which justified their expansionist aims. William II invited Chamberlain to Potsdam several times, wrote to him often, and conferred the Iron Cross on him. Adolf Hitler visited the aged Chamberlain in 1923, that is, shortly before he wrote *Mein Kampf*. He was the only politician to attend Chamberlain's funeral in 1927. National-Socialism took over Chamberlain's theories as one of the bases of its doctrine.

Racialist theories are scientifically false. Certainly, there are races which have been defined, biologically, according to the statistical predominance among their constituent members of some genetic factors such as skin colour, hair texture, blood group and so on. There is general agreement that there exist five major races determined by the relative frequency of a number of genes, usually eight: they are (1) the European or Caucasian race; (2) the African or Negroid race; (3) the Amerindian race: (4) the Asiatic or Mongoloid race; (5) the Australian race. Some biologists think it possible to subdivide these major races, again according to gene frequency, and as many as thirty races have been so defined, though there is disagreement on this point. However, this debate is irrelevant here. We need only point out that some of the races which figure largely in racialist theories are scientifically non-existent. No biologist has ever spoken of an Aryan race. Nor has any biologist spoken of a Jewish race; on the contrary, it has been shown that there is a greater correspondence in frequency of genetic characteristics between Jew and non-Jew of one nation than between Jews of different nationality.

As for the true races (black, yellow, white, etc.), science knows no differences between them except biological ones:

pigmentation, eye and hair colour, stature, shape of the skull, blood group, and so on. It has never been proved that these genetic differences give rise to differences in intellectual capacity or in social and political ability. In the United States some sociologists have claimed to prove the superiority of the white over the coloured race by means of intelligence and aptitude tests. But it has been shown that the tests used were based on white civilization, so that it was hardly surprising if people brought up in another civilization did less well in them. In 1931, therefore, American scientists used on babies tests which did not use any intellectual elements, and, age for age, detected some superiority among the whites. It was pointed out, however, that of the babies tested the black were poorer and so less well fed, and in the early months this makes for a considerable difference in development. This explanation received experimental confirmation during the war, when experiments on babies of both races, fed in the same way, produced the same results for black and for white.

Racialist arguments based on differences in the level of development attained by various races are just as invalid. Some yellow, Amerindian and black civilizations were superior to the white civilizations of their time. Differences in development and behaviour are the result of the material and sociological conditions of life, and not of any so-called inferiority. For example, the character traits for which racialists criticize negroes are exactly the same as those that the European working classes were reproached with fifty years ago: laziness, thriftlessness, lying. They are connected with economic underdevelopment, and disappear gradually from among black workers with a rising standard of living, just as they do from among white workers. The American or South African negroes' outlook is explained, not by their genes, but by the fact that they have always been treated as different from, and inferior to, the whites, and have therefore developed inferiority complexes (which they connect more or less with the colour of their skin) and feelings of resentment. Similarly, the way Jews have been treated for centuries, the physical or moral ghetto into which they have been shut, and the sense of persecution that has been developed among them, explain why their behaviour is different from that of non-Jews.

Race distinction is undeniably a major cause of political strife. In some countries, such as the 'Deep South', South Africa and various Latin-American countries, they dominate the whole of political life. But the conflict is caused, not by biological factors, not by the physiological nature of the different races, but by the public 'images' attached to these races and by the kinds of behaviour thus provoked. These 'images' are themselves the result of psychological or sociological situations, and are attributable either to the political device of camouflage, or to psychological transfer mechanisms. In order to gloss over their pillaging of Jewish banks, medieval Christian rulers developed the idea of the accursed race responsible for the death of Christ.

Faced with the rise of Socialism in nineteenth-century Europe, the middle classes used the same technique: by their denunciations of Jewish bankers, of Jewish industrialists, of Jewish businessmen the *Christian* bankers and industrialists and businessmen hoped to distract attention from the capitalistic exploitation which they practised no less than did their Jewish counterparts. Elsewhere, antisemitism has allowed governments to lay the blame for their own mistakes on the Jews: it happened in Germany between 1933 and 1945, as it had happened in Czarist Russia and is happening today in the Middle East. Thus did the Roman emperors throw Christians to the lions – to distract attention from their own mistakes.

Montesquieu fully understood that the theory of negro inferiority could be used to justify the exploitation of black by white. This theory first appeared during the sixteenth century, at the time of the first wave of colonization; it reappeared with the second wave, in the nineteenth and twentieth centuries. Slavery, forced labour or sub-proletarian conditions, which shock when considered in the light of the principle that all men are equal, become permissible when the people who are condemned to such conditions are not considered as men like others, but as 'inferior brethren'. In the United States racialist theories grew out of the expansion of cotton-planting, which was impossible without slave labour. The whole of South Africa's economy depends today on keeping the negroes in a state of underdevelopment. White racialism naturally provokes a counter-racialism, which can now be seen in the United States, in the form of extremist negro movements like the 'Black Muslims', and in some African countries, whose governments blame all their difficulties on to their old colonial rulers.

In societies where racialism exists, and creates social inequalities, it offers some individuals the possibility of resolving their psychological problems by transfer or compensation. Thus, in the colonies and in the 'Deep South', anti-negro racialism is deeper and more aggressive among the 'poor whites' of the poverty-stricken lower classes than among more educated whites in higher positions. There is a simple explanation for this: the fact that there are 'blacks' beneath them gives these poor folk the impression that they are in some way superior. Thanks to the negro, they have some importance, some prestige, and are not right at the bottom of the social ladder. Were the racial inferiority of the negro to disappear, they would become what they are, and what in their heart of hearts they know they are: failures. This brings us to the psychological elements of political conflict.

# 2. Psychological Factors

For Marxist thinkers, political conflict is basically a struggle between groups – the class war – and psychological factors are of only secondary importance in their view. Western thinkers, however, see it as a struggle primarily between individuals who fight for power or who resist those in power; therefore psychological factors are of prime importance in their eyes. The first attempts to describe these factors were coloured by moral considerations, inspired to a greater or less extent by the theology of the Middle Ages, which viewed the desire for domination as a basic human appetite like sexual desire or the desire for knowledge, and consequently denounced the three concupiscences of the flesh, of the mind and of dominion. *Concupiscentia dominandi*, the third of these, was the basic factor in political conflict. Subsequently, liberal thinkers adopted an even more simplified psychological system, basing social divisions upon the individual quest for maximum advantage at the cost of minimum effort, a principle which was held to be fundamental to political conflict just as it was to economic competition. The development of modern psychology, and in particular of psychoanalysis, has given western political theory a firmer foundation in spite of some excesses. In using Freud as an antidote to Marx, there has been some exaggeration of the significance of his conclusions, especially in the United States, where it is sometimes claimed that all political conflict can be explained by psychological frustrations. A healthy reaction against such excesses is beginning to develop.

### PSYCHOANALYSIS AND POLITICS

Space precludes us here from giving anything more than a brief and simplified, and therefore somewhat distorted, account of the psychoanalytical explanations offered for political divisions. The findings of psychoanalysis are complex and involved; they vary, moreover, from author to author, as happens in so many other fields. We shall confine ourselves to a statement of the most important and best founded of them. In its attempt to elucidate the mystery of man, psychoanalysis necessarily departs from the misleadingly clear and so the strange and sometimes paradoxical nature of its findings should not surprise us. Its fundamental and best-established principle is that the period of early infancy plays a decisive part in the psychological formation of the individual. In this period the parents' role is all-important; it is through them that the individual first defines himself in relation to society. These early relations with parents will influence the individual, though unconsciously, in all other subsequent social relationships and particularly in his relations with authority.

The theories dealing with the importance of early infancy have a biological foundation that Freud did not emphasize. As Aldous Huxley put it, man is 'in embryo a monkey'; the baby is born at a far less advanced stage of development than any other mammal. This means that he comes that much sooner into contact with the external world instead of remaining sheltered in the mother's womb; his intelligence must therefore function earlier. At the same time, he is also at a much earlier stage a social animal. The mother-child relationship is in mankind a social relationship, whereas amongst other animals it is for a much longer period purely a physiological relationship. Whatever may be the full consequences of the earlier birth of the human infant, we must note the capital importance which psycho-analysis attributes to the first years and even the earliest months of the individual's life.

At this stage of its existence the child lives in a situation in which freedom and pleasure are dominant. The whole of his existence is based upon the seeking of pleasure. Freud has given an excellent description of what he calls infantile sexuality; it is diffused and not concentrated upon particular organs of the body; it is polymorphous and expressed in many different ways. This quest of pleasure is for the child unhindered by any prohibition or rule. He may not always be able to compel others to give him pleasure, to feed, carry, nurse or cuddle him, but others cannot compel him to deny himself any pleasure that is available; he cries, moves, sleeps, yells, evacuates as he pleases. The life of the child is thus dominated by the pleasure principle and man always retains a certain nostalgia for the lost paradise of infancy.

When he finds himself obliged to quit this state he suffers his first shock, the first traumatic experience which marks him for the rest of his life. To integrate himself into the life of society he has to replace the pleasure-principle by the reality-principle, that is to say he has to give up pleasure or considerably restrict its role. He has to comply with a whole series of constricting rules, duties and prohibitions. He has to cease obeying his instincts, his whims, his tastes, his own wishes. But the need for pleasure is too strong to be thus stifled; it still remains. The conflict between society and the individual appetite for pleasure leads to frustrations which are the basic cause of social conflicts. Either the need for pleasure – the libido – may be repressed into the unconscious and so produce dreams and neuroses or alternatively it may be transformed into a need of a different kind, by transference, substitution or sublimation. For example, inability to satisfy sexual desires may lead to competitiveness in business or sport, to activity in politics or the arts.

Some psychoanalysts argue similarly that industrial civilization which tends to the construction of a rational, mechanical, aseptic and conformist world is in fundamental opposition to the instinctive tendencies and basic desires of man. The reality-principle tends to stifle, completely and utterly, the pleasure-principle. The inhumanity of the setting is alleged to produce, by compensation, a development of aggressiveness and violence. As Norman Brown puts it, 'aggression results from the revolt of the frustrated instincts against a desexualised and inadequate world'. This interpretation is in direct conflict with those theories which view technical development and the resulting improvement in the standard of living as factors in decreasing tension and so as aids to integration. Here, on the other hand, technical progress, which constructs a world in which the instincts have no place, is seen as a factor in the increase of aggressiveness, authoritarianism and violence and consequently as leading to the development of divisions and conflicts.

The frustration theory is one of the principal foundations of the psychoanalytical explanation of political strife, but it seemed inadequate even to Freud himself and he subsequently complemented it. In the latter part of his life he took the view that aggressiveness and violence, in particular, were also the product of a 'death wish' which he defined as in conflict with the libido. This struggle in the heart of every human being between Eros and Thanatos is one of the most impressive but also one of the most disconcerting and obscure of the doctrines of psychoanalytic theory. The argument is that every man is impelled to seek a life of pleasure and at the same time to seek his own destruction as though overcome by vertigo. No man, however, dare look his own death in the face; it repels and also fascinates. Thus, the individual transfers to others the wish for self-destruction: aggressiveness, that is the tendency to destroy others, is then a transference of the death instinct which is made by those in whom it is powerful, in whom Thanatos is stronger than Eros.

Aggressiveness, violence, domination, authoritarianism – these obvious constituents of political conflict – may also be the result of the phenomenon of compensation. Psychoanalysis lays great emphasis on the ambivalence of feelings and attitudes and on their contradictory character. It sees in a tendency to eroticism, for example, the consequence either of considerable sexual powers or alternatively of impotence which impels the victim to assert himself in this respect in order to conceal his deficiencies. In the same way, the desire to dominate, which is an authoritarian attitude, may result either from a real urge for power in a strong and energetic individual or from a psychological weakness: an inner confusion and an inability to achieve self-control and to gain the respect of others which the individual conceals by the adoption of the opposite attitude. In this connection, a well-known inquiry conducted in 1950 by T. Adorno in the United States on 'the authoritarian personality' is of some interest. It showed a relationship between conservative attitudes in politics and a particular type of psychological make-up. The authoritarian personality is defined by his strict conformism, by blind acceptance of traditional patterns of value, by faithful obedience to authority and by a simplified view of the world of social and moral values as divided into well-defined categories (good and evil, black and white, virtue and vice) in which everything is clear, patterned and circumscribed, in which the powerful are held to deserve their position because they are the best while the weak merit their subordination because in every respect they are inferior; that is to say a world in which the value of the individual is determined solely by external criteria, based upon social position.

This pattern of political behaviour is characteristic principally of those who are unsure of themselves and who have never succeeded in building up and stabilizing their own personality – men who are assailed by doubts about their 'ego' and their own identity. Because they have nothing within themselves on which to lay hold, they cling to external props and stays. Thus the stability of the social order becomes the foundation on which they stabilize their own personality. When they defend the social order, it is themselves, their own psychological balance, that they are defending. This explains their aggressiveness and their hate for their opponents, and especially for those who are 'different', for those whose pattern of behaviour and code of values are in contradiction with the social order, and thus threaten its basis and its universality. In periods of peace when the social order is not in peril authoritarian personalities belong to conservative parties; when it is under attack, their aggressive tendencies naturally grow and drive them towards Fascist movements. In this way, those who are inwardly least assured show externally the greatest assurance and parties based upon force are for the most part made up of the weak.

The phenomena of authoritarianism, violence and domination have yet other psychological explanations. Sometimes they are due to compensation for individual failures. The individual may seek revenge upon other people because they do not love him, because they make fun of him, because they consider him inferior. The weak, the stupid and the failure try to assert themselves by humiliating those who are superior to them, by trying to bring others down below their own level. The dissident psychoanalyst, Adler, has observed that brutality and despotism are often due to overcompensation for the pain suffered by men who are below average height or who have some physical defect: most of the dictators were small (cf. Caesar, Napoleon, Hitler, Stalin, Mussolini, Franco). Adler also considers that authoritarian tendencies are fundamental. For him, the instinct to dominate is the mainspring of the psyche, replacing Freud's concept of the libido or the need for pleasure. The similarity of this theory to the medieval concept of *concupiscentia dominandi* is not without interest.

It is not only on the question of political divisions that psychoanalytic theory sheds light. It offers an interesting explanation of the ambivalence that men have always recognized in politics: conflict and integration. The two aspects of power, oppression and benefaction, exploitation and harmonization, are interpreted as reflecting the ambivalence of the child's feelings towards his parents. In the human unconscious, that is to say, power is based upon the father and mother images. Everyday language does indeed reflect this phenomenon. We talk of the colonel as the 'father of his regiment', of the 'paternalism' of industrial leaders, of 'patronage', of the Pope as the 'father' of the faithful, of the 'metropolis' (from the Greek mother), of 'patricians', and so on. In the same way, patriotism is a transposition of the relations between children and parents, for the 'fatherland' or 'motherland' is not only the land of our ancestors, it is an entity of a parental kind. France is seen by the French as their 'mother' and the head of the state who represents France as the 'father' of the French. All political ideologies, all beliefs concerning power thus show traces of 'paternalism' in this sense.

During the first painful transformation that takes place in human life, the changeover from the pleasure-principle to the reality-principle, parents play a fundamental part. They are the first to formulate the rules of duty and prohibition to which the child must henceforward adapt himself. In a sense they represent the Angel with the fiery sword driving man from the earthly Paradise and prohibiting access to it where once they had been the angel guiding man in this Paradise and showing him the fruits to be enjoyed. The change in the parents' role creates in the mind of the child a conflict in his attitude towards them. Till now he had received from them, and especially from the mother, nothing but joy and pleasure. Now they become an obstacle to his enjoyment and his pleasure, although he still has need of them and is still dependent on them in his weakness. This gives rise to a basic ambivalence of feeling towards them: love along with hate; gratitude as well as rancour.

An ambivalent attitude to all authority, viewed both as protective and unendurable, as beneficial but oppressive, is thus to be explained not only as arising from experience which teaches us that power is both useful and hampering, necessary as well as constricting, but also from the most secret and inmost sources of the self. It is the unconscious reproduction, to a greater or less degree, of the ambivalence of the child's feelings for his parents which, in its turn, arises from conflict between the pleasure-principle and the reality-principle. However, the paternalist aspect of power is not to be exaggerated. Some forms of authority seem to bear no relationship to unconscious memories of parental power, as witness bureaucratic authority founded in Max Weber's sense on ability, efficiency and techniques. In the same way, leadership in small groups seems to be unrelated to patterns of parental authority.

All these psychological phenomena are in part the product of the forms of social organization. Ethnologists have shown that the œdipus complex, which Freud thought universal, does not exist in some kinds of society where family relationships are organized in a different way. Many frustrations are similarly produced by the form of society. Anxieties relating to castration or impotence do not exist amongst the men of a society in which the absence of sexual relations does not imply privation. The intensity of the conflict between the pleasure-principle and the reality-principle varies with the kind of culture and in some it is relatively minor. It may be that the libido occupies a central place in human psychology only in contemporary western cultures, where, in fact, it has been most studied. In any event, psychological explanations of political divisions must always be limited in their scope. In any given society the number of frustrated, repressed, aggressive or authoritarian individuals is relatively constant over long periods of history during which political conflicts are, however, sometimes violent, sometimes mild. The psychological germ is of much less importance than the sociological culture in which it grows. If circumstances and social factors had not brought Adolf Hitler to power in Germany in 1933 there is every reason to believe that there would today be living in some small corner of Germany, basking in the affection of their grandchildren and the respect of their neighbours, two peaceful, punctual, serious-minded bourgeois, Adolf Eichmann and Heinrich Himmler.

## POLITICAL TEMPERAMENT

The concept of temperaments or personality is to be found as early as Hippocrates. It is based upon the idea that individuals can be classified according to behaviour and attitudes that are in the main the product of innate aptitudes, more or less biologically determined. The temperament concept is the contrary of the class concept which classifies behaviour and attitudes according to social structures.

In politics, the temperament theory seeks to explain divisions on a basis of individual dispositions which are largely congenital. According to this view, some types of men are driven by their personal tendencies towards particular political attitudes and this brings them into conflict with other men whose temperament drives them to take up opposing attitudes. Some attempt has been made to discover possible correlations between political behaviour and recognized types of temperament, but unfortunately there is no agreement among psychologists as to the definition of these types. We must therefore confine ourselves to examples drawn from the most widespread classifications.

Let us first consider possible correlations between political attitudes and the Heymans-Wiesma classification of character, which was introduced into France by René Le Senne and Gaston Berger. It is based upon three principal criteria: (*a*) emotivity, (*b*) activity, (*c*) resonance, that is the degree to which mental events persist. (On this last criterion, a distinction is drawn between the 'primary' who live in the present not in the past and the 'secondary' in whom the resonance of the past is prolonged for some time.) In politics the 'amorphous' (unemotive, inactive, primary) and the 'phlegmatic' (unemotive, active, secondary) would naturally be unconcerned with strife, little given to seeking power, respectful of the freedom of other men, that is to say they would be moderates and peacemakers. On the other hand, the 'passionate' (emotive, active, secondary) and the 'choleric' (emotive, active, primary) would be attracted towards political conflict and towards power, the former being by nature authoritarian leaders, the latter rabblerousers, orators or journalists, who in the last resort are unlikely to try to be dictators (Danton, Jaurès). The 'nervous' (emotive, inactive, primary) and the 'sentimental' (emotive, inactive, secondary) would be the natural revolutionaries, the former tending towards anarchism, the latter not always far from authoritarianism (Robespierre). The 'apathetic' (unemotive, inactive, secondary) would be natural conservatives and the 'sanguine' (unemotive, active, primary) would be primarily the opportunist (Talleyrand). However, the whole of this pattern is somewhat vague and superficial.

A further correlation has been noted by Emmanuel Mounier between political attitudes and the psychosomatic classification of Kretschmer, who modernized the ancient ideas of Hippocrates by distinguishing three essential human types: the broad or 'pyknic', the long or 'leptosomatic' and the 'athletic' or robust in whom tranquil viscosity goes hand in hand with a certain explosiveness. Mirabeau, who was both flexible and fiery, brilliant and popular, would be the exact illustration of the 'pyknic' and cyclothymic politician. Leptosomatics with schizoid tendencies, on the other hand, would be detached, calculating and unscrupulous, either sectarian idealists or insensitive tyrants 'to whom all that is moderate in man seems alien'. Correlations of this kind are as tenuous as those previously described. Nor are the relationships between political attitudes and the Jungian classification into introvert and extrovert any less so. The introvert is in essence the man turned in upon himself, upon his inner world, towards ideas. He cares little for the opinion of others and, naturally anti-conformist, he is unsociable. The extrovert, on the other hand, concerns himself primarily with what is external to himself: wealth, prestige, social approval; he is conformist and active. The democratic politician, the member of parliament, the councillor or the local notability would seem to correspond to the extrovert type, the technocrat or the Jacobin to the introvert.

There is more interest to be found in the attempts made to establish a direct classification of political temperaments, especially those of the English social psychologist Eysenck. Starting from a factorial analysis of replies to attitude question-naires, he has defined two basic polarities, two co-ordinates, which make it possible to distinguish four main types of political attitude or temperament and to plot with some precision actual behaviour in accordance with these types. The axes concerned are Radical/Conservative and Tough minded/Tender minded. Radical is here used in its English sense of favourable to change and reform, i.e. 'progressive', and this first axis corresponds approximately to the traditional distinction between Left and Right. The other axis is deduced from the fact that within these two groups (Left and Right) there co-exist very different attitudes. On the Right we have Conservatives proper and also Fascists; on the Left, Democratic Socialists as well as Com-munists. For Eysenck these differences are to be explained by the second axis (Tough minded/Tender minded); at one end there are to be found both the Fascists and the Communists, at the other, the traditional Conservatives and Social Democrats. The juxtaposition of the axes, one as abscissa, the other as ord-inate, is the only suitable way of representing the different types of political temperament.

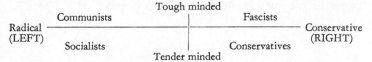

Eysenck's theories are very useful in explaining political divisions, but they raise two sets of objections. First of all, it is not at all clear that the distinctions Radical/Conservative and Tough minded/Tender minded do not, in fact, correspond to sociological rather than psychological differences. Eysenck's inquiries show that the distribution of individuals amongst the four types he has defined do not exactly correspond with their distribution by class, income level or by other social classifications, but that there do exist some correlations in these respects. It cannot then be affirmed that these four types correspond to innate psychological patterns, to 'temperaments', rather than to sociological situations. In the second place, the definition of each type is open to certain objections. The distinction between Radical and Conservative is fairly clear and can, it seems, be used with some generality. However, the distinction between Tough minded and Tender minded is a great deal more vague and its use more debatable.

When we look more carefully at the questions which Eysenck has used to identify the Tough and the Tender, we have the impression that the distinction being made is moral rather than political. Toughness seems to be defined to some extent by what might be called strong-mindedness or free thinking, independence of traditional morality, whereas Tenderness seems to be related to a moral and religious cast of mind in the Protestant tradition, highly individualistic and based upon the will of each man to do his duty without external constraint. It corresponds to faith in God, vague piety and strict sexual morality, belief in the equality of men, in gentleness and non-violence, in Christian charity and the freedom of each man from the interference of state though not from the dictates of religion and morality. It is not possible to assimilate Eysenck's classification Tough minded/Tender minded to an Authoritarian/Democratic division, as French thinkers have too often done. The Eysenck division is quite different and does not seem to be applicable outside the Anglo-Saxon context.

# 3. Demographic Factors

The notion that demography influences political conflicts has long been widespread. The public readily accepts population pressure as an explanation of wars and revolutions. This explanation was thought out several centuries ago, long before Hitler used it as the basis for his 'lebensraum' propaganda, or contemporary sociologists took it up. Nevertheless, the main political theories give scarcely any importance to demographic factors. Liberals and Marxists alike scarcely touch on the question. Catholics, nationalists and Communists agree in their criticism of the Malthusian theses and in their opposition to birth control. Nevertheless, the quickening rate of population growth in underdeveloped countries is a vital factor in political conflict.

## POPULATION PRESSURE

For a long time some thinkers have been of the opinion that demographic pressure was the essential factor in the most serious conflicts. It is an age-old idea that, in overpopulated countries, there are violent social tensions and frequent revolutions and wars. In less densely populated countries, on the other hand, political conflict is reputed to be less bitter, the rulers less frequently challenged, and peace more assured. In antiquity, Aristotle and Plato thought that excessive increase in population brought political disturbance in its wake. Montaigne, in chapter XXIII of book II of his *Essays*, speaks of war in the medical terms of his age, describing it as the 'blood-letting of the commonwealth' which purges the organism of the state and keeps it from being disrupted by an excess of youthful blood. This was a familiar theme in Montaigne's day, and many Renaissance writers explained the upheavals of the age by the increase of population. 'War is necessary so that young men may leave the country and the population may decrease', wrote Ulrich von Hutten in 1518. 'If war and death do not come to our aid, we will have to leave our land and wander like gypsies', added Sebastian Franck in 1538. In the eighteenth century the idea that demographic pressure aggravated political conflict directly inspired the theses of Malthus, who feared that population increase among the poor, who would be condemned to greater poverty by such an increase, would intensify their envy of the estates of the rich and destroy the social order.

These theories of population pressure rest on an impressive array of facts. Between 1814 and 1914 the population of Europe·doubled, and this rapid growth was followed by the outbreak of the major conflicts of the first half of the twentieth century. At the end of the eighteenth century France was probably overpopulated in relation to the natural resources and the techniques of the age: then there occurred the 1789 Revolution and the wars of 1792–1815. In underdeveloped countries today overpopulation coincides with many revolutionary movements, and often with an attitude of belligerency. In the thirties Germany and Japan were manifestly overpopulated; their expansionist policies and the wars they started were aimed at obtaining the territory they lacked. Inversely, the underpopulation of the United States in the nineteenth century, and the possibility that malcontents had of going westwards, eased social tensions and in particular lessened the intensity of the class war. It is quite understandable therefore· that Gaston Bouthoul should conclude that in our day wars fulfil the regulatory function that big epidemics fulfilled in the past, since they lead to a slackening of demographic pressure, acting like safety-valves. Such, more or less, was Montaigne's idea.

Nevertheless, these population-pressure theories can be criticized for oversimplifying the problem. The most densely populated countries are not the most belligerent, otherwise Holland would be the most warlike country in Europe, given the density of its population. Though overpopulated, China was peaceable for centuries, while the Red Indian tribes of North America, though scattered over vast tracts of land, were continually engaged in war. Many factors besides overpopulation accounted for the French Revolution; moreover, the Russian revolutions of 1905 and 1917 occurred in an underpopulated country, to which the notion of population pressure is totally inapplicable.

The idea is, in fact, very vague. It cannot be defined solely by density of population. The age of the population, which rises as the economy expands, and thereby diminishes pressure, must also be taken into account. Collective images are important, too: the idea of the 'yellow peril', which has been fashionable since the end of the last century, rests not so much on a realistic assessment of Chinese and Japanese strength as on a vague picture of teeming slant-eyed hordes pouring over the white man's land.

It is very important, too, to consider natural resources and the possibilities of exploiting them. The population pressure theory is a scarcity theory: it is economic rather than demographic. Malthus was considering it from this point of view in 1798 when he formulated his famous law: 'Population tends naturally to increase in geometric progression, while the means of subsistence tend naturally to increase in arithmetical progression.' The disparity between the two becomes greater and greater, since population expands in the ratio 2, 4, 8, 16, 32, 64, 128 . . . whereas the increase in the means of subsistence follows the ratio 2, 4, 6, 8, 10, 12, 14. . . . This meant that unless the number of births was voluntarily restricted mankind was doomed to famine, and famine would cause very serious conflict.

Formulated mathematically, as it was by its author, Malthus's law has never been verified and, in fact, cannot be verified: what is meant by the 'natural' increase in population or means of subsistence? But the idea that the former increase more rapidly than the latter took a firm and lasting hold on men's minds. In our day the acceleration in the rate of population expansion has given it a new lease of life and Malthusianism is undergoing a positive renaissance, particularly in the United States. There is an obvious contrast between the almost unlimited possibilities of population expansion and the limited nature of resources.

Moreover, some people consider that intensive cultivation tends to exhaust the soil, so that food is in danger of becoming scarcer. The most optimistic thinkers estimate that rational exploitation would make the earth capable of feeding more than six thousand million men; but this number will probably be exceeded by the year 2000. Even if one admits the possibility of feeding ten thousand million people this absolute ceiling will have been reached in less than seventy-five years from now. The blind optimism of the expansionist theories will not solve such a problem.

At the present moment the theory of demographic pressure expresses the situation of the underdeveloped countries, where the population is increasing at an extraordinary rate, which considerably aggravates political conflicts. Two kinds of demographic equilibrium tend to come about naturally, through the interplay of physiological and sociological factors: one in primitive countries, and one in highly developed industrial countries. In primitive countries the equilibrium which develops is similar to that which is found among many species of animal. It is based on the combination of a high birth-rate and a high death-rate. It could be called the 'sturgeon equilibrium'.

The female sturgeon lays tens of thousands of eggs. If they all reached maturity, and if all the eggs of these new sturgeons had the same good fortune, all other species of animals would very rapidly be wiped out, and the whole earth would be given over to sturgeons. However, thousands of eggs do not reach maturity, and thousands of young fish are also destroyed, with the result that a relative demographic balance is achieved among sturgeons. The demographic equilibrium to be found in primitive human society is similar: the high natural fertility and the lack of birth-control bring about a very high birth-rate, while lack of hygiene, difficulties of nutrition, disease and premature ageing cause an equally high death-rate.

In highly developed industrial countries, the situation differs in two ways. Better hygiene, more plentiful and better-balanced food and the development of medical care lower the death-rate. The birth-rate also drops, as a result in the first place of biological factors about which little is known as yet, but whose effect is fairly certain. Contrary to common opinion, under-nutrition and physiological weakness result in a high natural fertility, which appears to diminish when food is better and general vitality is higher. Furthermore, rising standards of comfort and the development of education and individualism increase voluntary birth-control, so that in the end a demographic equilibrium is established, based on a low birth-rate coinciding with a low death-rate. The population increases, but slowly.

In underdeveloped countries the primitive equilibrium has been lost, while that of the highly industrialized countries has not yet been attained. The introduction of some elementary rules of hygiene and medicine, of easy and inexpensive ways of tackling endemic disease, such as the regular use of D.D.T. in large quantities, rapidly bring down the infantile mortality rate, which is of prime importance from the point of view of population increase. (In this respect, extension of life among the old, after the faculty of reproduction has been lost, is of no significance.) The birth-rate, on the other hand, tends to remain at the same high level for a long time, first because the way of life and feeding habits scarcely change, and the natural fecundity remains unmodified, and next because traditional moral behaviour and general outlook are very slow in evolving, and continue to oppose voluntary birth-control for a long time. In these conditions, the population tends to increase very rapidly.

The resultant demographic imbalance is all the more serious, since it occurs at a time when the need to speed up economic growth makes it very difficult to maintain the supply of food at its usual level. Workers have to be transferred from the production of ordinary consumer goods to the construction of factories, roads, and dams, that is, to the investments necessary for creating the infrastructure of a modern country. During this intermediate period food supplies tend to diminish, while the population tends to large and rapid increase. In this way the underdeveloped countries find themselves in an explosive situation. Political conflicts develop with great violence because of the population pressure, and are likely to result in revolution, war and dictatorship, unless the harshest measures are taken to spread the use of contraceptives.

## THE COMPOSITION OF THE POPULATION

The composition of the population by age and sex, and its geographical distribution, have a part to play in political conflicts. In developed countries, where life is long and the birth-rate low, the proportion of old to young is high, whereas in underdeveloped countries there are few old people. It is generally admitted that the old are more conservative, more attached to the existing order, while the young are more revolutionary. Nevertheless, the preference for novelty found among the young is easily diverted to false novelty which by its shocking, provoking and apparently violent nature corresponds fairly closely to the psychological manifestations of the desire for novelty among the young. In the middle classes this crisis frequently gives rise to a conflict between the need for change that it provokes and the deep instinctive attachment to a privileged social situation; this conflict may lead to Fascism and to the various movements of the *jeunesse dorée* type. All in all, a nation of young people is more inclined to revolutions and profound changes, which are highly repugnant to a nation of older people.

Various studies have shown that young people vote less for moderate and conservative parties, and more for parties which propose change, be they Left-wing or extreme Right-wing; though, except in special circumstances, they tend on the whole to the Left rather than to the extreme Right. The average age of the population is reflected, too, in the age of its leaders: the youth of the leaders of present-day underdeveloped countries mirrors the average age in their countries just as the youth of the men who effected the French Revolution did. These demographic phenomena partially explain why industrialized nations, with a higher average age, become more and more conservative, and why, in contrast, underdeveloped countries, with a low average age, are more revolutionary.

Moreover, in a young population of the underdeveloped type the proportion of old people to be supported is relatively small, while in industrialized countries with a high average age the proportion is high. It has been forecast that the proportion could rise to 25 per cent (at the present moment it is 16 per cent in France and Great Britain, 12 per cent in Italy, 10 per cent in Spain). The heavy burden which is thus laid on the working population causes a real clash between generations. Finally, the higher the proportion of old people in a state, the less dynamic it becomes, with an increasing tendency to immobilism. These ideas are very imprecise, but they do nevertheless correspond in some degree to the facts. The clichés—clinging to established values, security before all else, 'pensioner mentality'—do illustrate a whole way of life which comes to predominate as the average age of the population rises, and which is naturally reflected in political activity.

Differences in the distribution of the sexes have less influence on politics. The myth of the rape of the Sabine women has perpetuated the memory of the wars fought for women which were probably quite frequent at one stage of civilization. It is not certain that demographic scarcity was their only cause, and that a desire for change was not a contributory factor. Folk stories about American pioneer communities or colonists in various countries have also popularized the picture of scarcity of women causing internal strife. Such conflicts provoked by frustration are real, but their import should not be exaggerated.

Of much more importance are the consequences that an original scarcity of women can have in the formation of certain institutions and types of behaviour which persist long after the scarcity has disappeared. The lack of white women and the original attitude of colonists towards coloured women played a part in the development of racialist (or, sometimes, non-racialist) feelings. The Brazilian sociologist Gilberto Freyre has made some very penetrating if somewhat exaggerated remarks on this topic. The scarcity of women in the United States, during the 'heroic' period of its history, led to women being highly valued, so that a moral matriarchy, which the law more or less sanctioned, was established and it still persists strongly in American society today. The importance of this phenomenon cannot be doubted: the major part of American wealth is in the hands of women, who have an influence on the Press, radio, television. It is well known, too, that women's clubs play a great part in social and political life.

A predominance of women in the population seems to strengthen conservatism in developed western societies, where women tend on the whole to vote for Right-wing parties more than men do. However, the difference is very small, and some writers attribute it to age rather than sex, arguing that since women live longer on average than men the number of old women, which is much higher than the number of men of the same generations, weights the overall female vote towards the Right, for old people of both sexes are more conservative in the way they vote. The fact that a large number of old women are widows, bound up in their past, is said to accentuate this general tendency.

This theory is most interesting. However, various studies have shown that younger women, too, are more conservative than men in their voting, particularly among the working classes. Some thinkers consider that this tendency reflects the influence of sentimental women's magazines and of a general outlook that girls derive from literature, television and cinema. The best way for them to escape from their position and rise in the social scale is presented as being the discovery of a Prince Charming, and a rich marriage. This prospect makes them adopt middle-class values and robs them of all revolutionary urge. Provided its importance is not exaggerated, this explanation is of some interest.

In underdeveloped countries the political influence of women seems to be exerted in the opposite direction, working against the established order, in favour of change, and towards a worsening of conflict. In general, their social situation is worse than that of the men, particularly in Moslem countries, in Asia, in Latin America, and so on. Women compose the most oppressed social group, so it is natural that they should also be the most revolutionary. Nevertheless, the idea of the emancipation of women can also be used to camouflage refusal of a real transformation in the structure of society. We have seen this happen in North Africa, with the campaign against the veil, among those who wished Algeria to remain French; and we have seen it in South Vietnam, with the propaganda of the too famous Mrs Nhu.

Uneven geographical distribution of population engenders political antagonism. In some regions underpopulation makes economic life difficult, and so causes frustrations which may express themselves in rebellions of a *poujadist* type. Inversely, conflict is aggravated in other regions by overpopulation. In nineteenth-century western Europe mass migration to the towns, causing concentrations of wretched, ill-housed, ill-fed people subjected to terrible conditions of work, most certainly played a leading part in the revolutionary movements. The formation of shanty-towns round urban agglomerations in underdeveloped countries produces the same results. Here the density of population is but one element of a complex situation, in which low standard of living, exploitation by capital, the political framework and ideologies all mingle.

In nearly all countries uneven distribution of population causes inequality in political representation. In depopulated regions, the proportion of M.P.s is higher than the proportion of inhabitants in relation to the whole population; they are therefore overrepresented. In densely populated regions, on the other hand, the proportion of M.P.s is lower than that of the population; they are therefore underrepresented. Technically, these inequalities of representation could be very small. Even if one posits the principle of one representative per X inhabitants, in vast areas constituency boundaries cannot be altered to achieve this minimum figure. Some very scarcely populated regions will thus have one representative for a number of inhabitants below X, but the disparity could be very small. In fact, one finds the contrary, and inequalities in representation are usually considerable, for political reasons.

In most western European countries, in the nineteenth century, the conservative aristocracy relied on the support of the peasantry, in its struggle against the liberal middle classes, and as it was gradually forced to give way on the extension of suffrage, it tended to favour agricultural regions to the detriment of the towns, in order to maintain its dominion. In the twentieth century the middle classes realized that the Socialists and Communists who were threatening them drew most of their support from the towns and that the conservative agricultural areas could help them in their turn to keep power. So they followed the aristocracy in creating inequalities of representation which favoured less-populated rural areas without the peasants benefiting from the arrangement. In both cases the peasantry played a supporting role for another class.

# 4. Geographical Factors

'The policy of a state depends on its geography,' said Napoleon, giving new expression to an old idea that was already in germ in Hippocrates' *Treatise on Air, Waters, Places* written in the fifth century B.C. Herodotus applies the idea in his *Histories*. Aristotle, in the seventh book of the *Politics*, formulated a theory on the relationships between climate and liberty which was to be often taken up by other writers in succeeding centuries, and in particular by Jean Bodin in the sixteenth century, before being developed by Montesquieu in Books XIV–XVII of *De l'Esprit des Lois*. At the end of the nineteenth century and at the beginning of the twentieth these ideas were elaborated by a whole school of geographers. In 1897 a German, Frederick Ratzel, published a *Political Geography* and later his disciples gave the name Geo-politics to this new subject. The French school of Human Geography, founded by Vidal de la Blache and Jean Brunhes, has proved less deterministic and less fanciful in its concepts.

No thinker, whether he be Conservative or Liberal, Fascist or Marxist, denies that politics is, in fact, dependent on geography, but there is no agreement on the degree of dependence. Conservatives tend to exaggerate the influence, progressives incline to minimize it. Barrès took the view that politics was based upon 'the earth and the dead buried in it', that is to say upon geography and history, with the latter largely determined by the former. The German school of geo-politics was closely connected first with the Pan-Germanists and later with the Nazis. In fact, the very basis of Right-wing philosophy is that man is strictly determined by the land and his environment and cannot escape the bonds of nature. The Left wing by contrast considers that man is free, that he can escape from the conditioning effects of nature and that he tends to do so.

The influence of geography is inseparable from that of techniques which, in fact, allow man to overcome the difficulties of his natural environment. Geographical factors are consequently as much sociological as geographical and as technical progress advances the sociological becomes more important than the purely geographical. In archaic societies political conflict is much affected by geography, in modern societies it is relatively unaffected.

## CLIMATE AND NATURAL RESOURCES

The ancients from Herodotus to Montesquieu stressed the importance of the direct influence of climate on human behaviour. Their theories are psychogeographical. 'Great heat is inimical to human strength and determination,' we read in Book XVII of *De L'Esprit des Lois*, 'whereas in cold climes there is a certain strength of body and mind which makes men capable of sustained, arduous, great and bold actions.' The conclusion is 'that it is not astonishing that the cowardice of peoples in hot climes has almost always made them slaves, and that the courage of peoples in cold climes has preserved their freedom'. 'Civil servitude' – that is slavery – is linked in the same way with climate. In hot countries 'men are only induced to perform a painful duty through fear of punishment, and there, in consequence, slavery is less offensive to reason'. These theories of Montesquieu repeat those of Aristotle. Having established that a cold climate is conducive to liberty, and a hot climate to servitude, Aristotle examines the problem of the temperate climate, which clearly troubles him. Without really explaining why, he considers that men there are free, but that they also know how to govern. Jean Bodin takes up the same theme. But Bodin, a native of Anjou, appears more concerned to defend southerners than Montesquieu, a native of the Gironde. He thinks that their intellectual qualities compensate for their lack of energy, and that both depend on climate.

Current ideas on the political influence of climate are not far removed from these traditional theories. In the nineteenth century Michelet stressed the influence of summer heat on the revolutionary days of 1789 (which occurred mainly between May and September). His theory would cover the revolutions of 1830 (July) and the June Days of 1848, but not the outbreak, in February, of the 1848 revolution. Moreover, the Russian revolutions of 1905 and 1917 both took place in October in a country that is already cold at this time of year. Forty years ago the fashion was to explain wars and revolutions in terms of 'sun-spots', an equally implausible theory. The effect of climate is sociological rather than psychological: it influences the general way of life, institutions and social customs. Ancient Mediterranean democracy, centred round the agora or the forum, is obviously bound up with life in the open air, as are the 'Palavers' of Africa and the 'Djemaas' of the Berbers.

Climate exercises its greatest influence through the animal and vegetable resources. It is a factor in the fertility of the land; like the composition of the soil, its configuration, and its mineral content, climate is a factor in determining the productivity of the land. Here Geography and Economics meet. In archaic societies the latter depends very closely upon the former, but this dependence diminishes with the growth of technical progress. The political theory of natural resources, like that of climate, has for a long time been psychological. In this respect one basic contradiction has proved a stumbling-block. On the one hand wealth seems to be a source of power, and therefore a means of social and political development; on the other, it dissipates energy, weakens courage and thus leads to stagnation and decadence.

The ancients tended rather towards the second interpretation. Montesquieu, for example, regards the fertility of the soil and the abundance of wealth as conducive to servitude; on the other hand, a lack of natural resources favours civil liberty and independence of foreign powers. In fertile countries 'the country people, the largest section of the population, are not jealous of their freedom; they are too busy and too occupied with their own private concerns. A countryside which is over-flowing with wealth fears looting and fears the military.' On the other hand, in poor countries 'liberty is the only possession worth defending'. Then again, 'the sterility of the soil makes men industrious, sober, inured to labour, courageous and fit for war; they must needs obtain what the land refuses them. A fertile country imparts along with security indolence and a certain care for self-preservation.' In this argument are to be found once again the moralizing theses linking frugality with democracy much developed in antiquity by thinkers like Cato.

Modern theories on the parallel development of democracy and affluence are directly opposed to such views. They regard poverty as a factor in aggravating political differences, making it more difficult for democracies to function. Wealth, on the contrary, would tend to reduce political conflict and favour liberty. Nevertheless, international competition interferes with internal rivalry and in this respect a certain type of wealth may promote discord rather than reduce it. The competition for raw materials is very important in this connection: it breeds conflict between states and also internal disorder. Many of the struggles in the Belgian Congo and particularly in Katanga arise from the mineral resources in the district. For example, some revolutions in oil-producing countries and certain authoritarian régimes entrusted with the maintenance of 'order' are directly linked with pressure from the purchasing states. Nevertheless we must be careful not to exaggerate: today there is a myth attached to oil and its political influence as there was in the nineteenth century attaching to coal and steel.

The old theories of the political influence of climate and natural resources ought to be reconsidered. Brought up to date, they would probably provide the best explanation of the present inequality of development between different nations. Racialists claim that this is due to the inequality of race. But all experiments show that Africans, Asiatics and American Indians under the same living conditions as whites have the same aptitudes and the same intellectual level. If we compare a map of the levels of social and economic development with a map of the great climatic and botanical zones, the results are striking. Areas of maximum underdevelopment correspond with the northern and southern glacial regions, the equatorial regions and the subtropical desert zones. Maximum development corresponds with temperate zones, i.e. in the northern hemisphere, North America, Europe, Russia, the fringe of North Africa; in the southern hemisphere, Australia, New Zealand, parts of Chile and the Argentine, the fringe of South Africa. Steppe zones result in a sort of middle stage of development based on patriarchal societies which form the nucleus of conquering peoples. Local circumstances which improve the climatic and botanical conditions (river valleys – Nile, Tigris, Euphrates; the monsoon areas of Asia; altitude in the case of the Inca and Aztec empires) give rise to a level of development higher than that of the surrounding regions.

Today, compared with the effect of technical development, climatic and botanical influences are secondary, but for centuries they played a fundamental role. Handicapped by their geographical position, the countries in glacial, equatorial and tropical regions have developed at a considerably slower rate and may find it difficult to catch up. If they were industrialized, the effect of climate and natural resources would be reduced. However, precisely because of this age-old influence of climate and natural resources, they had not the knowledge to become industrialized. Technology enables nations which have been able to develop their industry to accelerate their rate of development considerably, and consequently the gap between them and the underdeveloped countries is widening more quickly. The curse of geography still lies over the peoples of non-temperate zones, and perhaps more heavily than before.

## SPACE

Space, which is a recent field of study, is another geographical factor inseparable from climate and natural resources. Its importance and its relation to these two can be demonstrated by the concrete example of ancient Egypt. The Nile valley, cut off by deserts, constitutes a natural region. Because of the regular flooding of the river, its lands are enormously rich. To use this natural phenomenon the development of a system of dams and the permanent upkeep of canals and pumps is necessary and all this requires an extremely developed and centralized social organization. From antiquity onwards we find both the urgent need of a highly organized state and all the factors favourable to the development of such a state, such as wealth, ease of communication along the Nile and no near-by refuge for rebels. In the Tigris and Euphrates valleys the combination of climate, resources and position afforded the same possibilities of civilization, but because there was no regular flooding centralization did not develop to the same degree. This notion of the importance of space was perceived by Montesquieu when he was studying islands. He said: 'Island peoples are more disposed to liberty than continental peoples. They are separated from great empires by the sea and foreign tyranny cannot bolster internal tyranny. Conquerors are stopped by the sea; the islanders are not enveloped by conquest and therefore they preserve their laws the more easily.' We must extend this notion of islands and consider it in a broader sense. Together with islands in the sea (the strict definition of insularity) we must consider oases, which are islands in the desert; the valleys of certain rivers like the Nile, which are surrounded by desert expanses; and clearings, which are islands in the forest, and so on. Island peoples have no neighbours; they are separated from other peoples by 'a vacuum', and this gives them greater security. Conversely, where there are no natural obstacles, conditions favour invasion, and states are more vulnerable and less stable. The immense plain of northern Europe was much more liable to invasion than the central mountainous regions. The unstable and fluctuating nature of the nations which developed there, the uncertainty about their boundaries, the changes they underwent in the course of history, all are political phenomena closely linked with geography.

The geographical distribution of population is of great political importance. In his study of western France in 1913, André Siegfried established that sparsely populated areas tended to be conservative while more densely populated areas were more disposed to change. This phenomenon he explained in the first case in terms of isolation, which causes the inhabitants of such a community to turn all their attention inwards on to themselves and the traditions of their community. In the second case the greater number of contacts enables the easy and rapid spread of new ideas. This analysis seems valid, even though villagers' unceasing concern with each other's business means that social pressure also is a factor in village conservatism. The size of the rural agglomeration is also important: when it really forms a town, as in southern Italy and Sicily, for example, the atmosphere is completely different from the atmosphere of a tiny country market town. Be that as it may, the degree of concentration or dispersion in a rural area is essentially dependent upon geographical factors, notably the availability of water and the permeability of the ground, which thus exercise political influence.

In this respect the concentration of population in towns is even more important. In the difference between town and country Marx saw an essential political opposition. Democracy was born in towns, at the time of the Ancient City States. At the end of the Middle Ages and the beginning of the Renaissance the development of towns favoured the spread of new ideas. In modern industrial towns Socialism has spread. Revolutions are essentially urban phenomena (peasant risings are rare, and even more rarely constructive). The political influence of towns is not only direct, through the contacts that towns promote between men and the opportunities they provide for political activity (e.g. the right of public meeting, and especially the right to demonstrate, which are essentially urban rights), but their influence works indirectly, too, through the fact that towns are the essential element in civilization and material and intellectual progress. Language has accepted this in regarding 'urbane' as synonymous with 'civilized'.

The planning of the geographical space inside towns also has political consequences. It has been said – with some exaggeration perhaps – that the introduction of the lift has aggravated the class struggle by emphasizing the segregation of classes. Previously the aristocracy and the bourgeoisie inhabited the lower floors of the building above the mezzanine (the first floor being 'genteel', the second a little less so, and the third less still), while the lower orders would live in the upper storeys and the mezzanines of the same building, with the result that there was daily contact between the classes. The lift, on the other hand, made the upper floors desirable once more, so increasing the tendency for the formation of separate working-class districts. Laws on low-rent housing reinforced the same trend. Town planners now tend, however, to create mixed districts, often for political reasons, for example to diminish working-class grievances. In these mixed districts the workers' votes show less support for the Left than they do in purely working-class areas.

The political importance of lines of communication is evident. The routes followed by trade, pilgrims and invaders all establish contacts as they carry goods, armies, illnesses and ideas along their path. Electoral geography shows them to be routes for the spread of new doctrines. They also promote contact between populace and authority, between rulers and ruled. Police and soldiers make use of them to repress revolt; pockets of resistance are sited well away from them in areas of difficult access. 'Civilization follows the road', said Kipling. So, too, does centralization; and this ever-present ambivalence of lines of communication precludes any political determinism. The fact that some river valleys, surrounded by desert, were politically privileged in antiquity when the first great states developed (Tigris, Euphrates, Nile) can perhaps be explained by the two contradictory advantages they enjoyed: isolation by the desert and contact via the waterway.

There is a similar advantage in being situated by the sea. The sea is both a protective barrier and a means of communication; indeed, in antiquity it was the only long-distance route for any considerable trade in heavy goods. Upon it were built up the Greek and Roman maritime empires. In a political context a contrast has often been noted between peoples of the hinterland, who are farmers living in some isolation and thrown upon their own resources, and coastal peoples, who are traders and sailors, with access to communications and living by them. It is the contrast between autocratic Sparta and democratic Athens, between autocratic central Europe and democratic Great Britain. Nevertheless some consider that a settled agricultural population is more inclined towards democracy than nomadic peoples, who tend to authoritarianism.

Means of communication are only one part of a wider notion which we might call 'position'. Let us take present-day France, with her population of 48 millions, her towns, factories, universities, her technical and intellectual equipment, and transport her to the Pacific, setting her where New Zealand now lies; her political importance in the world would be greatly reduced (let us, for the sake of argument, say by three-quarters). Then it becomes true that 75 per cent of political importance is dependent on geographical position. Such a supposition is, of course, absurd: if France were situated where New Zealand lies she would be very different from the France we know. This in itself shows the importance of position. We could multiply similar examples: Swiss neutrality is evidently linked with Switzerland's position in Europe; the possible development of Communism in Cuba is only important because of the island's proximity to the U.S.A. Position can be regarded from different points of view: in relation to other states, to main communication routes, and to raw materials and natural resources in general, etc. It is also linked with history. The transfer of politically important centres from the Mediterranean to the Atlantic changed the conditions of the people living on the shores of these seas.

In short, like all other geographical factors, position is dependent on the idea we have of it, as much as on material factors. The great American geographer Bowman wrote at the end of his career that all his life had been a struggle to explain to people that natural environment had no significance for them beyond the significance they chose to give it. The statement is something of an exaggeration; natural environment has its own reality, independent of the collective image we have of it. But this plays a very important part. Thus, the idea of natural frontiers, false from the geographical point of view (rivers and mountains unite rather than divide) has bred much political discord. The example of systems of map projection is even more striking. The technique used to portray the terrestrial globe as a planisphere has a considerable influence on certain political attitudes. The place of western Europe in the struggle between the U.S.A. and the U.S.S.R. changes according to whether we look at a planisphere based on the traditional equatorial projection or a planisphere using polar projection, a method which has become popular in the last twenty years. In the first case, Europe lies between the two great powers and seems the very object of the conflict; then the idea of a 'non-aligned' Europe seems absurd. In the second case, the United States and Russia lie in close proximity, facing one another across the North Pole, while Europe lies abandoned on the side-lines; European neutrality then seems possible.

Geography has been used as a pretext to elaborate fanciful theories in order to justify national demands. We have just cited the myth of natural frontiers, which has been very widely used. The myth of 'Lebensraum', both geographical and democratic, has been much less invoked; it was used primarily by Nazi Germany and by Japan. Other myths have only served among diplomats and staff officers to bring some fame to their authors. The strangest of these myths is that of the 'heartland', formulated in 1919 by the English geographer Mackinder. He simplifies the interpretation of the planisphere and treats Europe, Asia and Africa as a single unit, the centre of world political life, which he calls 'The World-Island'. It is composed of highly developed, well-populated maritime countries on the periphery, with emptier and less civilized areas inland. In this huge continental mass one region occupies the key position from which the whole can be dominated. Mackinder calls this region 'the heartland' and situates it on Russian soil, in the Ukraine. On the basis of these divisions and this terminology, he sums up his theory in one lapidary and often-quoted sentence: 'He who holds eastern Europe governs the Heartland; he who holds the Heartland governs the World-Island; he who holds the World-Island governs the world.' The poetic value of this theory is certain, but on the level of reality it remains a fantasy.

# 5. Socio-economic Factors

Socio-economic elements are probably the most important factor in political conflict. Throughout history, right up to the present day, all human societies have been characterized by penury, that is, by an insufficient supply of goods in relation to the needs to be satisfied. In industrial countries today we are beginning to witness the advent of affluent societies, in which men's needs will to some extent be fulfilled, not only their basic needs, like food, clothing and shelter, but also such secondary needs as comfort, leisure and culture. Some thinkers question whether this is possible, arguing that there is no limit to the extension of human needs, which grow as fast as they are satisfied. However, no country has yet reached such a stage of development. There is penury everywhere. In France today, despite the rapidly expanding economy, two out of three industrial workers are unable to take a holiday away from home as they would like, because they lack the material means to do so.

It could be imagined that in such a situation of overall penury every member of the social body would undergo the same degree of privation as the others, so that all suffer equally. In fact, this hypothesis is scarcely ever fulfilled. Some ancient agrarian communities, and some socialist countries today, have come near to achieving it. But usually penury engenders inequality, so that some classes or categories can obtain all that they desire, while others suffer more than their share of privation. In a word, there are the privileged and the oppressed, and the inequality between them fosters a deep-rooted antagonism which is the essential basis of political strife. The oppressed struggle to improve their condition, and the privileged fight to retain their privileges. The main stake in the battle is power, since holding power confers vital advantages.

### SOCIAL CLASS

'The whole history of society so far is the history of the class war': this famous opening sentence of the 1848 *Communist Manifesto* does not express so novel an idea as people think. Before Marx, many thinkers had considered that political antagonisms were engendered by inequality between social groups – which groups constituted social classes in the broadest meaning of the term. Marx's originality lay in the fact that he made class warfare the fundamental element in political conflict, and in particular, that he gave a restricted and precise definition of class. Previously, the generally accepted notion of class corresponded approximately to that held by present-day American sociologists, who split society up into vertical 'strata' determined by the average standard of living: this is really a more detailed restatement of the old opposition between rich and poor, between the 'haves' and the 'have nots', the privileged and the exploited.

Thus summarily defined, class plays a vital part in political life. Opinion polls and analyses of elections and parties all show that there is a fairly close correlation between political choice and standard of living, and while there is no rigid division between all the 'rich' on one side and all the 'poor' on the other, nevertheless the rich align themselves for the most part on one side, while most of the poor are on the other. In any society there is a fundamental opposition between the privileged, who can satisfy their desires and enjoy life to the full, and the oppressed, who suffer varying degrees of privation, and strive to replace the rich, who struggle to keep their position. This conflict is political in so far as it is concerned with power: which it always is, since holding power is one of the most effective ways of enjoying and keeping privilege.

Nevertheless, the 'strata' of society only constitute classes in so far as they have some measure of stability and permanence. If all the members of a society were born with equal opportunities, the diversity in standards of living brought about by diversity in individual achievement would not produce classes properly so-called. In this hypothetical situation political conflicts would remain on the individual level, with antagonisms caused mainly by psychological factors. The notion of class is based both on inequality in social situation and on the collective nature of this inequality: that is, it is based on the fact that people are born into a social category, even if they can later escape from it. The concept of class cannot be separated from the concept of hereditary privilege. This is the basis on which we shall attempt to give a fuller and more workable definition of class than is provided by Marxism.

For determining class, collective images of living standards are just as important as their material definition. The image which members of a society have of the different rungs on the social scale, the way in which each member places himself on this scale, in a word the feeling of belonging to a class, 'class-consciousness', play an important part in fostering political conflicts. In the United States many interesting studies have been made of this phenomenon since the 'Middletown' inquiry on which was based the famous differentiation of six classes: upper-upper, lower-upper, upper-middle, lower-middle, upper-lower, lower-lower. These studies are more or less based on theories elaborated by French sociologists of the Durkheim school, according to whom the members of a society evaluate their own positions and distribute themselves into several categories, each with its levels and different forms of prestige.

In 1925, Emile Goblot studied in this way the 'barriers' and 'levels' of the different classes. Maurice Halbwachs worked out an overall theory of class considered as a collective psychological phenomenon. The problem is to determine the criteria of the sense of belonging to a class. Material living standards are the fundamental criterion, but many people place themselves above or below their real class level. This phenomenon has a great influence on the development of political conflict.

With different living standards go differences in way of life, that is, in behaviour, morals, habits and mentality, which reinforce the sense of class. But one's way of life does not depend solely on one's standard of living. For instance, a grocer and a teacher or a popular singer and a banker with the same income will not live in the same way. This influences

political behaviour, and in particular fosters corporative antagonisms. A more profound difference, which frequently leads
to conflict, separates town-dwellers and country-dwellers, and
one sometimes hears talk of a 'peasant class', defined basically
by its way of life. Marx himself was struck by this difference
between town and country, but he linked it with his general
conception of class as defined by means of production, as a very
interesting passage of his *German Ideology* shows: 'the greatest
distinction between physical work and intellectual work is to
be found in the separation between town and country. The
opposition between town and country begins with the change
from a state of savagery to one of civilisation, from a tribal
regime to the State, from locality to nation, and can be found
throughout the history of civilisation until our day. . . . Here
for the first time we find the population splitting into two
major classes, based directly on the division of labour and the
instruments of production.'

Marxism does not ignore the notions of way of life, sense of
belonging, and standard of living. Marx protested against
the common belief which made degree of wealth or poverty
the basic criterion: 'Ordinary common sense transforms the
distinction between classes into difference in size of purse.
Purse-size is a purely qualitative difference, which can always
be used to set one against the other two members of the same
class.' But Lenin brings into his definition of class 'the share
in the social wealth' of which one can dispose (*La Grande
Initiative*, 1919). This does not, however, contradict Marx. For
a Marxist, standard of living, sense of belonging and way of
life are secondary and derivative elements in the definition of
class. They are the consequence and the reflection of a primary
element, which is the private ownership of the means of production. There are, according to Marxism, two opposing
classes: one which owns the instruments of production and
one which has no resources except its labour. From this difference arise divergences in standard of living, way of life and
sense of belonging which themselves engender political conflict.
Private ownership of the means of production is the cause of
all these differences: it is this private ownership that gives rise

to the existence of two classes with opposing interests, which are at war with one another.

The antagonism between these two classes, the essential motive force in political life, arises from the fact that private ownership of the means of production allows the owner to appropriate part of the labour of the non-owner. When one subtracts from the value of a man-made object everything which has helped to produce it (including the necessary means of subsistence of the producer) something is left over, the added value. The capitalist retains this added value, and only gives the proletarian what he needs in order to live. Of course, in modern capitalist societies the pressure of trade unions and workers' parties prevents confiscation of all the added value. But exploitation will continue as long as private ownership of the means of production. Moreover, it is very striking that in the West the owners of the means of production have higher incomes than salaried workers of an equivalent cultural and technical level doing equivalent work.

For Marxists, this class struggle between owners and non-owners is the vital cause of political antagonism, which reflects it. Classes themselves are determined by the system of production and the mode of ownership, which in turn are engendered by the state of techniques (or 'productive forces'). Thus the following pattern of dependent relationships between political phenomena and systems of production emerges: techniques (productive forces) → systems of production and mode of ownership → social classes → class warfare → political strife. Thus, primitive techniques caused the system of production and the mode of ownership of antiquity, with its conflict between masters and slaves, and the slave state; medieval agricultural techniques gave rise to the feudal system of production and mode of ownership, with its conflict between lords and serfs, and the *ancien régime* type of state; industrial techniques caused the capitalist system of production and mode of ownership, with its struggle between the middle classes and the proletariat, and the western democratic state. The very evolution of industrial techniques is tending towards the suppression of private ownership, which was the basis of previous systems of production, and towards the Socialist system of production which, according to Marxist doctrine, puts an end to class warfare and finally causes the state to wither away, after an intermediate phase of proletarian dictatorship.

Every system of production (or mode of ownership) produces several varieties of political régime, that is, several forms of class struggle. In antiquity the slave state varied in form, being now an Egyptian or Persian-type despotate, now a tyranny of the Greek type, now Athenian-style democracy, now an empire on the Roman model. The feudal state developed from an uncentralized régime based on a collection of independent fiefs, towards a centralized monarchy like that of Louis XIV. The bourgeois state may be a western democracy or a Fascist régime. Socialist states based on proletarian dictatorship may be of the Soviet type or 'people's democracies'. To sum up, contemporary Marxist theorists thus distinguish between 'state types' and 'state forms'. State 'types' correspond to a particular class system and are four in number: the slave state, the feudal state, the bourgeois state and the Socialist state. Within each *type* there are several possible *forms*, that is, political régimes.

Nevertheless, within each type of state political conflict is basically always the same, according to the Marxists. In the ancient slave state, the feudal state, and the capitalist state respectively, there is a basic conflict between masters and slaves, lords and serfs, bourgeois and workers. In every case there is opposition between the private owners of the means of production and those who have to rely on their labour to earn a living. Within each state type, however, this fundamental conflict manifests itself in different ways, according to the form of state. Thus, in the medieval state the serfs struggled individually, and usually without support from elsewhere, against their lord. In the centralized monarchy they sometimes relied on the support of the urban middle classes, or of the king, in their struggle against the nobility. In this way their struggle became more general and came to operate on a broader scale. In a capitalist state the opposition between bourgeois and workers is manifested differently in western democracies, where it operates through parties and where the workers are free to develop their own organizations, and in Fascist régimes, where middle-class domination is violent and implacable, and proletarian resistance is clandestine and brutal.

Furthermore, there are always secondary clashes operating in conjunction with the basic conflict, founded on class warfare. The class struggle is never simply a clash between two classes; the reality never corresponds to the ideal. Alongside the two main classes which reflect the existing systems of production there are nearly always survivals of classes corresponding to the previous system which has not entirely disappeared: in a capitalist régime, for example, one finds landowning aristocrats and peasants. There are, also, classes which correspond to the future system of production, which is gradually beginning to emerge; in feudal society, for example, there were some bourgeois. These rising and declining classes maintain a variety of alliances with the main classes, joining forces now with one side and now with the other, as best suits their own interests. Moreover, a class is never entirely homogeneous; it is always composed of quite varied elements, which often conflict with one another: small shopkeepers versus department stores, industrialists versus bankers, white-collar workers versus manual workers, and so on. Within any class there are contradictions.

The great political struggles of the nineteenth and the early twentieth centuries were basically class wars in the Marxist sense of the term class. The opposition between Conservatives and (political) Liberals primarily represented the struggle between aristocracy and bourgeoisie, with the peasantry in the role of supporting class to the former. Similarly, the clash of (economic) Liberals and Socialists was really the struggle between the middle classes (in alliance with the declining aristocracy) and the proletariat. Doubtless, there were other factors involved, of a religious, national, or racial nature, but in relation to class they were of secondary importance, and were usually a disguise for class interests. When Marx was writing, and when his ideas were undergoing development, his theory constituted a fairly accurate description of the basic tendencies of political conflict. It is less certain that it can be applied to all other periods of history.

The Marxist view can be criticized from two standpoints. First, it overestimates the part played by class conflict in the formation of political differences. Second, it gives too narrow a definition of class. It is true that traces of the class struggle can be found in any age, but whether its role is as vital, as all-important and as decisive as the Marxists suggest is debatable. Before the nineteenth century the mass of the people were usually allowed no part in political life. They were exploited, but they had neither the intellectual means of understanding that they were being exploited and of envisaging the possibility of changing their situation nor the material means of fighting against it. Political conflicts took place within a limited *élite*, among whom class differences were fairly small. The rival factions which competed for power had no class basis; national or dynastic rivalries, religious or ideological conflicts, disputes among clans, and competition between individuals were more important than the class struggle, with which they had very little connection.

Secondly, the Marxist conception of class is too narrow. Private ownership of the means of production represents one kind of privilege transmitted by heredity; history has other examples to offer. In aristocratic societies legal status was a privilege transmitted by inheritance; in pre-revolutionary France noble birth conferred the right to be an officer in the army, to an ecclesiastical benefice or a bishopric, to presentation at court, enjoyment of prerogatives, donations or pension, to receive feudal dues, and to exercise seigneurial powers. In ancient societies the status of citizen, pilgrim, half-caste, freed-man or slave, transmitted by heredity, produced a variety of ranks of which the Indian caste system is a hypertrophied example. If these facts are taken into account, one reaches a more workable definition of class than the Marxist concept. In general, a class is a category of men who are born into conditions which are relatively homogeneous, but different from and unequal to the conditions found in other categories. Social classes result from the inequality of opportunity that society offers its members at birth, and from the fact that this inequality determines some major types of basic situation. Classes can be defined by their degree of wealth, by what they own, by their legal privileges, or by cultural advantages. The forms that inequality at birth takes are of little importance; the essential fact is that these inequalities exist, and that by producing a variety of ways of life and senses of belonging they constitute categories which men instinctively recognize as such.

Capitalism marked a stage in the progress towards equality, by allowing the individual, through his work, intelligence, and abilities, to acquire freely advantages and privileges and to bequeath them to his descendants, even if he received none from his ancestors. This was much more difficult, if not impossible, in aristocratic or caste systems. An untouchable cannot become a Brahman; a slave could not easily become a citizen; a serf found access to nobility difficult. It was easier to become a capitalist in Europe or America in the nineteenth century. There was some truth in the myth of the self-made man and in Guizot's 'get rich', however exaggerated they were. Nevertheless, the accumulation of capital in some hands finally gave rise to considerable hereditary inequalities.

In the most highly developed western societies the importance of these inequalities is diminishing, while others, which are to be found also in Socialist states, are beginning to appear. Quite apart from any private appropriation of the means of production, inequality of salaries and of social situations has certain hereditary consequences. The son of a senior civil servant, or of a well-known doctor, a famous barrister, the salaried director of a large company, a high-level engineer, has a better start in life than the son of a manual worker, a peasant or an artisan. First of all, he will enjoy better material facilities for study; second, he will receive from his milieu a very important education by osmosis; finally, family connections will help to establish him in his career. These phenomena occur even in Socialist countries, where some types of class redevelop in this way.

They are, however, much more restricted than the hereditary advantages previously discussed, first of all because suitable development of the education system and of the machinery for recruitment and promotion in careers can lessen their effect, and secondly because hereditary transmission is more limited in both scope and duration. Whereas nobility was transmitted in its entirety from father to son, and the owner of a firm can hand on to his son the whole enterprise, a highly paid executive cannot hand down a high salary; he can only give his son the chance of a better education, of social backing, and of indirect material advantages, by handing on personal belongings. If this latter type of inheritance is restricted, as it is in Socialist countries, the chance of classes developing with their consequent inequalities is very limited.

Strangely enough, the situation that then arises is similar to the one that Vilfredo Pareto describes in his theory of *élites*. '*Élites*' are the most able individuals in every branch of human activity. They struggle against the mass – that is, against the less able – in order to attain a position of power. In their struggle they encounter resistance from the *élite* already in power, who tend to form an oligarchy and perpetuate themselves through heredity. This tendency is an obstacle to the 'circulation of *élites*', that is to freedom for the best and most able to rise unhampered in the social scale. This pattern corresponds more or less to that of Socialist societies, where the tendency of the ruling *élites* to become an hereditary class is controlled. The resemblance was not, however, intentional, for Pareto had very little sympathy for Socialism, but acted rather as a theorist of Conservatism.

Under the aristocratic societies of antiquity and of the *ancien régime*, and in nineteenth- and twentieth-century capitalist societies, inheritance of noble status or of the ownership of the means of production generally gave the advantage to the existing *élites* and enabled them to prevent the rise of new *élites*. What is more, these existing *élites* were not *élites* in Pareto's sense of the word, for they had not obtained their position by exercising their own abilities, but had, in most cases, inherited it. In those days, then, the class struggle was certainly the main factor in political strife. Conflict between individuals played a relatively unimportant part, occurring mainly within the ruling classes to decide which of their members should hold more or less direct power. The most highly developed western societies are now in an intermediate situation. The high standard of living is making the defects of capitalism bearable. High salaries, material comfort and relative security are weakening the class struggle and making it assume less violent forms. But private ownership of the means of production still gives rise to extensive hereditary privileges which sustain the class struggle. Only the abolition of this private ownership can reduce antagonism between classes to its simplest form.

## TECHNICAL PROGRESS

The distinction between industrial or developed or highly developed societies on the one hand, and underdeveloped or developing societies on the other, is today one of the bases of western political thinking. On this point, though there are differences of terminology, western thought coincides with Marxist thinking, according to which 'productive forces', that is techniques, are the foundation of the means of production and of all social relationships. 'Social relationships are closely connected to productive forces. When men obtain new productive forces, methods of production change, ways of earning a living change, and all social relationships change. The windmill will give you a society ruled by a sovereign; the steam-powered mill, a society dominated by industrial capitalism' (Karl Marx, *The Poverty of Philosophy*, 1847).

Western and Marxist thinkers agree therefore in recognizing that technical progress is the major influence on society in general, and on political strife in particular, but they do not agree on how this influence works nor on the nature of its effect. According to some western thinkers, technical progress creates a world which is not adapted to human needs and desires, so that tension, opposition and conflict are aggravated. The fundamental incompatibility between man's instincts and the artificial universe in which technical development places him is reputed to be the cause of the wars, the revolutions, the dictatorships, the resurgence of massacre and torture, and the increase in violence that the twentieth century is witnessing. Some Cato-like Conservatives, advocates of a return to the land, the simple life, austerity, and vegetarianism accord with a few moralists and psychoanalysts in holding these conclusions.

However, this pessimistic attitude to technical progress is rare in the West, where optimism is much more common, and is indeed stronger and less discriminating than Marxist optimism. Both East and West believe that technical progress will lead one day to a strifeless, united and harmonious society; Marxism's future paradise, the 'higher phase of Communism', has profound similarities to the western Utopia, the 'affluent society'. But the roads leading to this Eldorado are different. Marxists do not envisage the total disappearance of conflict as the result of a gradual diminution in antagonism, taking place hand in hand with technical development; for them, full possession of paradise is not preceded by partial glimpses of it. Rather, by modifying the means of production and the consequent social relationships, technical progress will go on intensifying the class struggle, which is aggravated by exploitation, revolt and repression, until the outbreak of revolution. The proletariat will then assume power; but there will be a long phase of proletarian dictatorship to be traversed before the higher phase of Communism is reached. The end of conflict will thus only come about after a period of worsening conflict, and will indeed, by a dialectic process, be the result of this very worsening.

Most western thinkers, on the other hand, consider that conflict is gradually reduced while technical progress is taking place, because the latter gradually lessens the scarcity of available goods, which is the main cause of strife. We have said that mankind has never known anything but scarcity, with needs constantly outstripping supply. The expression 'underdeveloped' seems to imply an unusual situation in relation to a state of 'development', which is thought to define what is normal. In fact, the opposite is true: until the twentieth century, all human societies, everywhere, were 'underdeveloped', in the sense that none of them ever managed to ensure satisfaction of the purely basic needs of all their members: food, clothing and shelter.

This situation is only just starting to change. Industrial societies are more or less guaranteeing the essential minimum to all their citizens, and it will not be long before they can provide also for their 'secondary' needs (comfort, leisure, culture). But these industrial societies are still very much in a minority; they do not yet constitute one-third of the human race, and the proportion is tending to decrease rather than to increase, since population increase is much more rapid in the underdeveloped countries.

The scarcity situation usually causes inequality, with a privileged minority enjoying plenty while the masses suffer serious privation. Frequently, the greater the general poverty, the more ostentatious the oligarchies are. In countries where there is continuous famine, fatness is a sign of power. When the populace wears rags, the privileged wear brocade and gold; when the populace lives in wretched slums or sleeps in the open air, the wealthy build rich palaces. This situation, whereby a small number of people enjoy wealth and luxury in the midst of a starving crowd, is of its nature explosive. The inequality causes profound antagonism. The populace hate the privileged classes, who in their turn fear the masses. Political activity takes the form of violence: on the one hand, of the violence of the masses, who are in a state of endemic revolt, and on the other, of the violence of the privileged, protecting themselves against the masses. Furthermore, a result of scarcity is that civilization can only be developed by exploitation of the masses by the privileged. If there were equality in a society where scarcity rules, all the members would have to work all day to barely survive. At this stage, thought, art and culture are only possible if some men enjoy the necessary leisure, thereby imposing an added burden of work on the others.

Technical progress does not suppress inequalities, but it makes them less noticeable. In modern societies differences of occupation, varying in importance, bring with them inequalities in income and working conditions. But here we must be clear what we mean. Two contrasting pictures of the evolution of industrial societies can be given. From one point of view, it can be shown that they tend to complex social stratification, to a diversifying of status. From another point of view, the opposite process can be shown. Many Americans say that the United States is a classless society, and there is indeed a marked similarity in the ways of life to be observed there. Economic development tends to narrow the gap between standards of living and to shorten the scale of incomes. There is less difference between Rockefeller and an American workman than there was between a medieval baron and his serf. The evolution of industrial societies seems to be leading towards the disappearance of extremes of wealth and poverty, and working towards relative equality in living conditions.

Moreover, in modern societies the sources of inequality are different. In underdeveloped societies privilege basically depends on birth; in highly developed countries it is coming more and more to depend on ability. From a philosophic point of view, this difference is not very great, since one is profiting from an innate advantage whether one is born intelligent or born into the aristocracy. The weak-minded, too, have to bear the burden of chance. The same argument is applicable to physical strength and weakness, health and sickness, beauty and ugliness, talent and lack of talent. In practice, the sort of inequality of birth which affects individual aptitudes is more easily accepted than inherited advantages of social position which distribute men in antagonistic classes. Subjective inequalities give rise to more conflict than objective inequalities. Public opinion will usually accept that the cleverest, the most gifted, the most intelligent should achieve more success than the others, and it also understands that this rule is necessary if collective progress is to be ensured.

Most of all, the general rise in living standards, improvements in material well-being and comfort, and developments in leisure and amenities for it, which are all characteristic of economic affluence deriving from technical progress, are diminishing the importance attached to inequalities and their resultant conflicts. When a starving, ragged and slum-dwelling populace is splashed by the carriages of the rich as they drive up to their palaces, injustice is felt strongly, and envy is great; violence alone, or the resignation that comes from great poverty and ignorance, can maintain this situation. But when the worker's tiny car is overtaken by the industrialist's Cadillac or Jaguar, then envy is still aroused, but it is more superficial and secondary. Tensions are lessened, a '*modus vivendi*' is reached, and political struggles lose their violence.

It can scarcely be disputed that, generally speaking, technical progress lessens political antagonism. A comparison between the highly developed and the underdeveloped societies of today will, on the whole, confirm this conclusion. In the former, revolutionary feelings weaken, the wish to destroy the whole established system disappears, and opposition develops within the structure of the régime rather than against it. In the latter, on the other hand, one finds an explosive situation in which irreducible antagonisms give rise to violence. But the rate of development is probably just as important as the level of development. Rapid development increases tension, whereas slow development tends to diminish it. The distinction between stable societies and societies undergoing rapid change is probably as important as the distinction between highly developed and underdeveloped societies. In stable societies the existing order is usually accepted, however unjust it may be. It is considered natural. From a sociological point of view, 'natural' means whatever has been in existence over a long period, so that generations now living, and preceding ones, have known nothing else. It does not occur to anyone that the ancestral order can be overthrown. Moreover, people are used to it, as they are used to an old coat which is no longer uncomfortable, even if it was so originally. Injustice and inequality, arbitrariness and domination, become relatively bearable in the end, so that there is no need to use violence to maintain them. In stable societies, even if they are very inegalitarian, social tensions are weak. Antagonism still exists, but it is dormant.

Rapid development has the opposite effects. Brutal changes in social structure tend to prevent the established order from seeming natural. The changes that evolution brings show that change is possible, since change is actually taking place. As a result, the inequality and injustice that were previously thought to be unavoidable now become unacceptable. Conflict between the poverty-stricken masses and the privileged minority increases. Moreover, rapid development tends to overthrow the traditional structures, so that many people are uprooted, dispossessed. They feel that they are outsiders in their own society, alienated in the true sense of the word. This break-up of the traditional framework makes people more aware of poverty and injustice, and more ready to revolt. Only very strong government can compel the obedience of the masses once they have realized that disobedience is possible and that it opens the door to hope. Moreover, technical progress is not achieved without difficulty or mishap, or without contradictions. We must stress the difficulties of the first period of development, which most of the underdeveloped nations are now going through, having emerged from a long period of torpor, a thousand years of stability, into an age of rapid evolution. On the material level their efforts at transformation are forcing them to impose new sacrifices on their populations, throughout the intermediate phase during which the infrastructure of a modern society is built up. During the primary accumulation of capital penury grows worse rather than better. At the same time, a decrease in the death-rate, but not in the birth-rate, causes tremendous demographic pressure which increases the number of mouths to feed. In this way the mass of the people become slightly more wretched at the very moment when they are becoming aware of their poverty and of the possibility of escaping from it. Obviously, political conflict increases considerably in tension. The situation is similar to that of the European nations in the nineteenth century, when Karl Marx observed the development of the class struggle.

At the same time, contact with modern techniques causes the traditional civilization to dissolve. Societies that rested on a system of balanced human relationships which had grown up slowly over the years, and that often had a very deep-rooted culture and civilization, are brutally destroyed by the sudden introduction of a technical civilization. The old ways of life disappear, and the old values are rejected, without being replaced by new values or an acceptable way of life. Germaine Tillon has invented a very graphic term in French to describe the situation into which these societies find themselves plunged: *clochardisation*. They literally become *clochards*, that is homeless vagrants and beggars, rejected both by the old community which they no longer accept and by the new community which is far above their level of life and culture.

Later, a new balance will be attained; a new type of community life will emerge within the framework of a technical civilization. But a long time must pass before that stage is reached, because the development of a technical civilization runs into the difficulties we have just indicated. The 'intermediate period' is likely to be a long one. Throughout it there will naturally be lively tension between the uprooted masses and the limited *élites* with a much higher living standard. Whence the tendency to authoritarian and even dictatorial régimes. Whence the bitterness towards developed countries. Phenomena analogous to this, with the same tensions and the same political implications, occurred in nineteenth-century Europe, in societies that were rapidly being industrialized; the breakdown of traditional peasant civilizations, under the impact of technology, showed similar characteristics.

# 6. Cultural Factors

For Marxists, there are no strictly cultural factors in political phenomena. Ideologies, beliefs, collective images, institutions and culture are only the reflection of the class system and belong in the superstructure of society. The superstructure undoubtedly influences the base, but only in a secondary and limited fashion. For western thinkers, however, cultural factors are of prime importance. In the eyes of Conservatives, it is nations – that is, the most important cultural units in the present-day world – which beget the fundamental political controversies. For Liberals, 'politics are ideas', and controversies are primarily conflicts of doctrine. Institutions play an important part for all western thinkers.

All these attitudes are too drastic and uncompromising. Western idealism is often only a screen for camouflaging the defence of particular material interests. But institutions, cultures, ideologies and value-systems are not simply the by-products of socio-economic conditions. Rather, not only do they determine the form and context of the political struggle, but also they help to bring these conflicts into being, to aggravate and to attenuate them. There are cultural factors involved in all political differences. Furthermore, all the factors studied so far are cultural in some sense: beliefs concerning individual ability or the struggle for survival, or race, or demographic pressure, geographical position or class are just as important as the material factors, which themselves cannot be isolated from their culture. Except for a few deserts or virgin forests, geographical surroundings are moulded by man. Race is an historical rather than a biological phenomenon. Religions and beliefs affect population growth. Psychology deals not with individuals but with individual men in communication with other men living in a given society at a given time and place. Personality is affected by the status accorded to the self by other men and by the role the self plays in relation to them: status and role are the means by which the individual is involved in his cultural context. Class consciousness and views about the class struggle intensify or diminish that struggle. Technical progress and culture are closely connected; so, too, are class and culture.

## INSTITUTIONS

Human societies are structured; they resemble a building rather than a pile of stones, and the architecture of the building is determined by institutions, which Robert's dictionary defines as 'a set of fundamental forms or structures of social organisation, as established by the law or customs of a group of men'. Seen in this light, institutions have an unquestionable influence on political controversies. Even matrimonial régimes, school systems and the style of social relations have some political effect. Many conservative sociologists and historians, such as Le Play and Fustel de Coulanges, have attempted to explain political life in terms of the family as an institution. Marxists consider the property system to be of fundamental importance; so, too, do some western authors who see in the notion of private property the very foundation of democracy. Finally, strictly political institutions, in the narrow sense, that is the machinery and structure of power, clearly affect the development of political antagonisms.

The problem is whether institutions have political influence in their own right, or whether they simply transmit the influence of other factors. Marxists support the second theory. For them it is the state of productive forces, that is of techniques, which determines the mode of production, that is to say the institutions related to production and to ownership in particular. The modes of production in their turn determine other institutions such as family, sexual, religious and political institutions. Thus there is, as it were, a two-tiered structure, with socio-economic institutions, that is modes of production and the class relationships they engender, on the lower tier, and other institutions on the upper tier. The institutions of the second tier are dependent on those of the first, and both groups result from the state of techniques. Clearly the influences do not operate in one direction only; the upper levels react on the lower, the super-structure reacts on the base. But this interaction is minor when compared with the direct influence of the forces of production.

This Marxist analysis is far too narrow. That institutions depend on the level of technical development and that socio-economic institutions control the others is not in dispute, but at no stage do we find institutions being absolutely determined; all we find is greater or lesser degrees of conditioning. At every level of technical development a wide variety of socio-economic institutions – in Marxist terms, of modes of production and class relationships – is possible. Similarly, to every type of socio-economic institution there may correspond a wide variety of family, religious, political and other institutions.

Marxists do not deny the possibility of a variety of super-structures for one type of base, but they claim that there is always a link between the sort of superstructure which does, in fact, grow up and the nature of the base. We shall examine this argument later, in connection with the relationships between political régimes and systems of production. Here it is sufficient to say that the argument is greatly exaggerated. The conditioning of social and economic institutions by the level of technical development, and of the other institutions by the system of production, is much less rigorous. The same level of development can lead to several kinds of production system without any one specific kind being connected with a specific level of development. The same system of production can lead to very great differences in family, school, cultural, political and religious institutions, without the development of one type rather than another being linked to a particular mode of production.

The differences between the school systems of the United States, England, Germany and France no more correspond to differences in their systems of production than do the differ-ences between the presidential system of the U.S.A. and the British parliamentary system, or the régimes of northern Europe, of France and of Italy. The differences in the sexual behaviour of Catholics and Protestants in the West do not appear to be linked in any way with the different systems of production and levels of technology. The differences between the flexible two-party system of the U.S.A. and the rigid two-party system of Great Britain, or the disciplined multi-partism of the Scandinavian countries and the anarchic multi-partism of France are not based on differences in the modes of production and the state of productive forces. Many more examples could be quoted. Institutions have a certain autonomy within the social and economic structures. As far as their autonomy goes, and this autonomy is fairly extensive, institutions are factors in political controversy, not as intermediaries but in their own right.

Their influence is primarily direct. Later we shall see that political institutions determine the framework within which political battles are fought. Here, as everywhere, form and context are inseparable. The framework in which conflict develops is also a factor in the conflict, increasing or diminishing it. In a democratic system, in which political struggles are carried on freely and openly through elections, parliamentary debates and the Press, conflicts seem from one point of view to be exacerbated. Opinions are reinforced by expression and repetition. From another point of view political differences are lessened by the very fact that they can be expressed and thus have a safety valve. In authoritarian systems the opposite occurs.

The party system provides a good example of the autonomy of institutions and their influence on political conflict. In western democracies we find both the two-party system (Great Britain and U.S.A.) and the multi-party system (Continental Europe), and political conflicts develop accordingly in very different ways. The two-party system suppresses minor conflicts and obliges all opposition to find expression within the framework of major issues. Multi-partism, on the other hand, favours the expression of minor issues and tends to fragment major issues into minor ones. People generally conclude that the multi-party system reduces the importance of political differences by dividing them into several fractions, whereas the two-party system leads to two 'blocks', that is to maximum opposition. This is to confuse the numerical differences in parliamentary representation with the fervour of political dissent. In fact, the respective effects of bi-partism and multi-partism are diametrically opposed to this current belief.

Under the dual system, the parties tend to become alike. The factors affecting their resemblance are fairly simple to define. Let us consider the specific example of Britain at the present day, leaving out the Liberal party, which is of little importance. Who decides whether the Conservative or the Labour party will win the general election? Not their fanatical supporters, who naturally vote for them whatever they do and who are unable to give their vote to a party either more Right wing or more to the Left, but the floating voters, the one or two million moderates, politically in the centre between the two parties, who vote sometimes Conservative and sometimes Labour. To gain their votes, the Conservative party must damp its conservatism and the Labour party its socialism. They must both speak in calm tones and adopt a reassuring air. They must both develop policies clearly tending towards the centre, and therefore extremely similar. In this way the conflict tends to diminish, and the myth of the two 'blocks' which has such a firm hold in France does not correspond to the facts.

Multi-partism produces the opposite results. Each party can only increase its numbers in parliament at the expense of its closest neighbours, so each party endeavours to stress the differences of detail which exist between itself and its closest rival, instead of highlighting their deep similarities. Thus, between parties with similar leanings the rift is deepened, at least when the issue is minor. Major differences are not intensified, but at the same time they are not attenuated by any need for moderation, as in the two-party system. Rather, these major differences are disguised, and this contributes to the somewhat artificial character of political life. Alliances between parties, which are necessary in a multi-party system, only add to the confusion, the parties of the centre sometimes joining with the Right and sometimes with the Left, the flitter-mouse tactic.

Bi-partism and multi-partism are to a large extent a consequence of social and economic factors, for the parties reflect classes and social categories in conflict. Historical development, traditions and circumstances peculiar to each country have their part in this, for conflicts between classes and social groups exist within this cultural context. But another purely technical and institutional factor is involved: the electoral system. We shall show later how the Anglo-Saxon single-ballot majority system leads to bi-partism, and how proportional representation or the French two-ballot system tend towards multi-partism, and that this factor aids or hinders the influence of social, economic and cultural factors.

The relation between electoral systems and party systems shows the autonomy of institutions very clearly. A technical procedure (the electoral system) gives to an institution (the party system) a certain structure which itself influences political conflicts, strengthening or limiting them. The influence of such technical phenomena is limited compared with that of other factors in the conflict, but nevertheless it is often considerable.

Another important consideration is social inertia. Institutions remain long after the forces that created them have disappeared. The survival of these organizations affects political conflicts. For example, the French Radical Socialist party is an historical relic. Several decades ago it corresponded to a social reality, when it embodied the opposition of the die-hard Liberals against the moderate Liberals and the Conservatives. Now the basis of this struggle has practically disappeared, and yet some Radical organizations remain and a certain ideology lives on: Radicalism still survives as an institution. These organizations which outlive the factors which gave them birth tend themselves to become factors in political conflict. Today, the Radical party does not exist as a result of certain political problems; these problems persist because the Radical party persists. Thus some conflicts are based solely on history. The time lapse between the development of some institutions and the evolution of their sociological bases can sometimes create violent political clashes. When institutional reform is not accomplished in time, social inertia can lead to outbreaks of revolution.

The continuation of institutions long after the disappearance of their socio-economic justification can often be of great political importance. The most striking example of this is the survival of the organizations of Imperial Rome largely through the Church, long after the barbarian invasions and the fall of the Empire. From the fifth to the tenth century A.D. the economy of western Europe was developing in more or less the same direction. Industry, commerce, trade and town life declined; farmers reverted to archaic methods of agriculture; rival communities retired more and more into themselves, becoming closed and shuttered. All this led to the disintegration of the state, the fragmentation of political power, and to the development of the feudal system. Yet two attempts at recentralization were made, under the first Merovingians, and particularly at the beginning of the ninth century with the Empire of Charlemagne. Both were attempts running counter to social and economic development, and because of this they were short-lived. Even so, they did last for a certain time, and had some permanent consequences. They seem to have sprung directly from institutions inherited from Rome, particularly through the influence of a class of educated clerks, men of vision who had little connection with the socio-economic structures of their time which were the vestiges of an advanced and centralized Empire.

## IDEOLOGIES AND VALUES

The word 'ideology', coined by Destutt de Tracy in 1796, was used by Marx in a different sense which has become current today. Ideologies are systems of ideas, of opinions and beliefs. Marxists believe that ideologies are the product of social class. Ideologies and social class are only two complementary aspects of the same reality. Marx wrote in *The Poverty of Philosophy* in 1847: 'Those men who establish social relationships in accordance with their material productivity also develop principles, ideas and intellectual categories in accordance with their social relationships.' He frequently used the term 'ideology', and it served as a title for the three volumes of his *German Ideology*. In this work ideologies are systems of ideas and images attempting to justify the situations of different classes. Later Marx widened this definition and absorbed into the ideological superstructures all the products of culture: law, morality, language and everything that reasoning and consciousness bring forth. He does not alter the fundamental idea that ideologies mirror the class structure and tend to camouflage it.

This theory to some extent describes the situation existing at the time Marx was writing. Ideologies, like political parties at that time, corresponded above all to social classes. Conflicts between the Conservative and the Liberal ideologies since the French Revolution clearly reflected the conflict between the landed artistocracy, and the bourgeoisie with their industrial, commercial, banking and intellectual interests. Later the Socialist ideology expressed the needs, desires and aspirations of a new social class, the proletariat which developed with industrialization. In these struggles, even non-political ideologies were openly used by one class against another. The famous Marxist saying, 'Religion is the opium of the people', should be reset in its historical context. During the Second Republic F. de Falloux was basically following the same principle when he organized religious teaching in order to preserve the social order and protect it from Socialism.

Even at the time, the Marxist theory exaggerated the dependence of ideology on social class. That ideologies, and particularly political ideologies, largely reflect the class situation is unquestionable, but many factors other than class play a part in their development. Certain ideologies, concerning centralization and bureaucracy for example, express conflicts between the leaders and the mass, the rulers and the governed, within the same class. Nationalistic ideologies sometimes express needs common to all classes of a country oppressed by another country. Decentralizing ideologies often correspond to the aspirations of the provinces to free themselves from the domination of the capital. To reduce religion to the role of 'opium of the people', even if it is true that this is part of its role, is to ignore the existence of religious aspiration independent of the class struggle. Literary, artistic and philosophical doctrines also have their own reality, outside the class situation which they sometimes cloak.

That ideologies and beliefs reflect social forces does not mean that thinkers, philosophers, the makers of systems, in fact the ideologists themselves, do not greatly influence their formation. Even without Marx, there would have been a Socialist ideology with an important part to play, but it would not have had exactly the same content, and perhaps would have lacked the same penetrating power and wide appeal. The combination of social factors with individual creation does not differ fundamentally in matters of ideology and art from their combination in fashion and invention generally. The creator of ideas, forms and technique works under the pressure of a social need; on the other hand, the fate of his work depends on the welcome given to it by society: between the two occurs the mysterious alchemy of individual creation. Montesquieu, Adam Smith and Karl Marx are 'échos sonores' like Victor Hugo, echoing the pre-occupations of their own time. They are in some respects the instruments and organs of social forces. The doctrines they elaborate and the systems they construct do not spring from their minds by spontaneous generation; they translate the needs of society, and the elements of their systems come from society.

The makers of doctrines are not simply recording instruments. Society provides them with the stones, and from these they erect the buildings. Their job is to be the architect. The influence of their personal genius, and particularly their ability to synthesize, is very important. Many ideologies have suffered through never having found a first-rate thinker who could combine their separate elements and make from them a powerful construction, a system with all the pieces strongly interlocking. Fascism or Christian Democracy lack a Karl Marx, and this has hindered their development. The revival of Conservative ideologies in France between 1900 and 1940 was very dependent on the intellectual power of men such as Maurras. Vigorous expression is just as important as the ability to synthesize, and many ideologies have suffered from having no literary genius to express them in gripping terms.

Ideologies have two leading roles in the development of political conflicts. On the one hand they co-ordinate and systematize individual oppositions, and thus set them within the context of a larger conflict. On the other, ideologies give such disputes the appearance of a conflict of values, and this in turn causes deeper and more absolute commitment. In France and elsewhere opinion polls show that five main factors help in deciding the choice and attitudes of citizens. The first is standard of living, salaried or non-salaried employment and social status in general; the second is age group, and to a lesser degree, sex; the third is standard of education; the fourth religion; and the fifth sympathy for a particular political party. The last three are ideological, since parties are based on political ideologies, linked more or less to religious doctrines, and the standard of education partly determines the degree of understanding of both.

By integrating all individual behaviour into an overall view of politics, ideologies can influence this behaviour. The influence is stronger when the ideology is more complex, precise and systematized, and when the citizen is better acquainted with it and his adherence is more complete. The concept of political awareness throws some light on the part played by ideologies. Each particular political attitude is both the response to a concrete situation arising in social life and the manifestation of an overall view of power, of its relations with the citizens and of the conflicts in which it is the prize; an overall view, that is, which in fact constitutes political awareness.

The more developed political awareness is, the greater is its influence, and the less each attitude is ruled by the facts of the particular situation. Political awareness is moulded by many factors, such as education, environment, experience, and so on. Ideology generally holds pride of place among these, and its primary function is to develop political awareness among citizens.

Another function of ideology is to propound a system of values. All societies are based on definitions of Good and Evil, of Justice and Injustice, that is on value-systems. These definitions themselves are beliefs, for Good and Evil, Justice and Injustice do not depend on experience, but on faith and voluntary allegiance. Thus they are by their very nature ideological. Indeed, all ideologies are in some measure value-systems, even those which pride themselves on their objectivity. All phenomena and all social activity are not the subject of value-judgements, but many are. In some spheres evaluation is broader and deeper than in others, particularly in the sphere of religion, family, sex and, of course, politics. In their passage from the level of useful or harmful, agreeable and disagreeable, to that of just and unjust, good and evil, political conflicts gather force. They become much more difficult to resolve and so ideologies tend to aggravate conflicts.

They can also moderate them. Indeed, if each class or social category manufactures its own ideology in the political struggle, government similarly develops its own, and this is biased towards the settling of conflicts and towards integration. The notion of legitimacy, so important in reducing dissent, is also based solely on a system of beliefs, on an ideology. All the members of a single society share certain collective images, certain value-judgements, which constitute a unified ideology, interacting with the partial and conflicting ideologies of different groups struggling with one another. The notion of culture illuminates this aspect of the problem.

### CULTURE

Sociologists give the name culture to the combination of techniques, institutions, behaviour, ways of life, customs, collective images, beliefs and values which characterize a given society. Each of these elements could be traced comparatively in the different societies, and this study would prove to be a description of developed and underdeveloped countries, capitalist and Socialist systems, authoritarian and autocratic régimes and so on. In reality, these general types combine to form particular wholes. Each concrete combination with its time and place constitutes a culture. Lying behind this concept there are two fundamental notions: history and nation. On the one hand, each culture is the product of history, bringing the weight of the past into the present; on the other, with the exception of underdeveloped countries, nations today are the most strongly defined cultural units.

All peoples follow by and large the same historical pattern. In this sense, the sociologist can describe the development from feudalism to capitalism, the different successive stages of capitalism, and so on. In the same way the biologist can describe the different stages of man's life, the child, the adolescent, the young adult and the mature man. However, the personality of each individual, his uniqueness, depends on the particular context in which this general development takes place. Similarly, what constitutes nations or civilizations is the unique historical development of a people or group of peoples. This uniqueness is primarily the result of particular events, each of which imparts a stimulus which is then prolonged through its effect on the common sociological development. It results also from the fact that a particular feature developed earlier or later than elsewhere, and more or less completely, because of natural circumstances and the particular reactions of the population.

The order of appearance of different general factors in development and their respective progress varies from country to country, and from culture to culture. Thus the same general social and economic development takes in each case a particular form, and this particularity is itself an influence on the sequence of development. For example, the change from the closed feudal economy to more open economic systems is a general phenomenon consequent upon sociological factors common to all European countries. The effect of particular situations and circumstances was to produce in France an absolute and centralized monarchy; in northern Italy, the Netherlands and Germany, principalities and urban republics; and in Great Britain the development of parliamentary rights. These different institutions have in turn caused succeeding developments to take different directions, just as they were themselves the product of previous national differences.

On the whole, cultural and national frontiers more or less coincide, except in the technically subdeveloped societies studied by ethnologists, where tribes, clans and ethnic groups form the fundamental cultural framework. Even in these cases culture tends to become nation-wide. Some modern nations do not themselves have just one culture, but are the topographical centre of several; in Switzerland, for example, the Germanic and French cultures co-exist; but the very co-existence of several cultures defines a new cultural whole. Lastly, several neighbouring nations often belong to the same cultural whole which we call a 'civilization'. Thus we talk of European civilization, western civilization, Latin-American civilization, Asiatic civilization and so on. The differences between national cultures within the same multi-national civilization are still quite great, however, and though modern cultures tend to transcend national boundaries, at the present time they are still firmly centred within the individual nation. In practice, therefore, as factors in political tension, nation and culture need not be distinguished.

Nations, of course, are not simply cultures, but exceedingly complex phenomena involving many factors, and according to the emphasis we give to one or another of these factors we will reach very different conceptions of what a nation is. Some writers define a nation by the soil, the geographical surroundings and their influence on the inhabitants; the theories of natural frontiers and climate derive from this approach. Others, like Fichte, define nations by their language, the basic instrument of communication which gives a group of men its profound cohesion. Still others take race as their criterion. Against these 'materialistic' conceptions we must set the opposing 'intellectualist' conceptions. One such conception defines the nation in terms of some doctrine or ideology which it supports and propagates in the world. Thus, many Moslems speak of 'the Arab nation', a community embracing all Moslems, the 'ouma' of the Prophet. Many French Liberals tend to define France as 'la patrie des droits de l'homme'; if she ceased to defend and promote these rights, she would no longer be France and would be untrue to herself. Still others define nation as the product of the will to live together, as a sharing of destiny.

The definition in terms of culture is the broadest and most accurate. It does not exclude the others, but embraces and amends them. Culture is essentially characterized by the proportions and forms assumed in a given society by each part of

the social reality, and these proportions and forms are determined by history. This definition fits 'nation' exactly and also
covers the diverse components enumerated above. Thus a
nation is essentially the product of history. Just as a man is
determined by his past, as psychoanalysis has shown, and is at
each moment the sum of what he has been, and even more of
what he thinks he has been, so a nation is determined by its
history, and just as much by its imagined history as by its
actual history, by events as they really took place. Just as man
reconstructs his past at each moment, chooses certain events,
forgets others, exaggerates the real importance of some events
and minimizes that of others, so peoples manufacture for
themselves an artificial history which profoundly influences
their behaviour and their institutions. The countries which
struggled for independence in the nineteenth and twentieth
centuries began by reviving their history and often by inventing
it. In so doing, they were building the very foundations of the
idea of their nation.

A nation, however, is much more than a cultural framework.
It is also a community in its own right, the all-embracing society
experienced and imagined by its members. As such it constitutes
a system of generally approved values which sets itself against
the value-systems of the opposing subsidiary ideologies. Thus
some men describe political life in terms of an opposition
between 'national awareness' and 'partisan awareness'. In
reality, this opposition is none other than that of integration
versus strife, the two faces of the political Janus. The nation,
the national scheme of values, and the general agreement which
develop round these, are factors in political integration. Often
they also constitute disguises used by the opponent in the
struggle to conceal his particular objectives behind so-called
general interests. In the propaganda battle, 'others' are always
'partisan'; 'we' are always 'concerned for the nation'.

In this way the concept of the nation exerts two kinds of
influence on political conflicts, as a system of values and as a
cultural framework. As a value-system it tends to restrain
conflicts by the existence of a national consensus (its integrating
function) and at the same time to express them by concealing

party or class interests behind an ideology (its camouflaging function). From the latter point of view, it is often used today to conceal class conflicts. To the Marxist slogan 'Workers of the world, Unite!' nationalism replies with the Conservative slogan 'Oppressors and oppressed of the same country, Unite!' On the other hand, the concept of nation originally allowed the concept of a community composed of all the citizens to be set against the aristocracy or the monarchy as sources of sovereign power. The first meaning of nation was revolutionary. Throughout the nineteenth century in Europe nationalism was a Left-wing ideology, before being used later by the Conservatives who had paid little attention to it until then. In 1793 'nation' was the rallying call of the partisans of the Revolution: today it is used rather by the descendants of the Coblentz 'émigrés'.

Nationalistic ideology has not only changed its direction, it has also lost much of its importance. The nation plays an essential role in political conflicts only when its very existence is threatened. In wartime, or when war is contemplated, this is the case. It is also the case for countries gaining, or who have recently gained, their national independence, and nationalism in such circumstances regains its revolutionary significance. In these exceptional circumstances national opinion tends to suspend internal conflicts and, following a pattern common to all social groups, to concentrate on the conflict with other nations. Faced with an oppressor or a foe all communities tend to strengthen their bonds and to intensify their outward aggressiveness. This process is used, of course, in internal political conflict: to raise the bogy of the enemy, real or imaginary, is a classic camouflaging device.

As a cultural framework the nation retains an influence in political controversies under all circumstances. A few examples will suffice to illustrate the point. The first is of 'liberalization' in popular democracies. In a general way, 'liberalization' would seem to be the result of economic development and of the rise in standard of living diminishing tensions according to the pattern described above. Therefore, the more industrialized the country and the more modern its production apparatus, the greater should be the 'liberalization'. By and large this is true, and there is a clear contrast between the more liberal Communism of developed countries such as the U.S.S.R. and the People's Democracies of Europe and the more rigid Communism of underdeveloped countries like China and Albania. But in detail the parallel between the degree of development and the degree of 'liberalization' is far from being absolute, as can be seen especially in Poland and Yugoslavia. In these two countries 'liberalization' is more developed than in the Soviet Union, yet both are less advanced economically and industrially. The deviation in the pattern seems to be explained by national factors. Poland and Yugoslavia have an age-old tradition of fighting for freedom, which has no doubt developed in their peoples the desire for liberty. Further, their political personnel were largely formed in western universities, particularly in France, and there, they were moulded by liberal thought. The development of party systems in Europe in the nineteenth and twentieth centuries provides another example of the influence of national cultures on political controversies. As we shall see later, specific factors have embroidered arabesques differing according to each country on a piece of cloth which was common to them all.

None the less, national cultures exercise no more than a minor role in comparison with social and economic factors. They work not as the motor but as the accelerator or the brake. In Poland or Yugoslavia, for example, national factors accelerate 'liberalization' by comparison with the rate of economic development, so that the first is in advance of the second. In Germany, national factors acted as a brake on the development towards a western democracy in the nineteenth and at the beginning of the twentieth century, although with its level of capitalism it should have reached democracy long before the Second World War. National factors in France accelerated this movement towards a liberal democracy in the nineteenth century. In a more general way, national cultures determine the form of political combat, rather than the actual nature of the principles in conflict. So we come to a new set of problems.

Part II

# The Forms of Political Conflict

Like the very existence of the antagonisms in which it consists, the forms that political conflict takes also depend on biological, psychological, demographic, geographic, socio-economic and cultural factors.

An antagonism always occurs in a particular framework, where it is expressed in a particular way; and the factors which cause it also influence the framework and the mode of expression. In studying now the forms that political conflict assumes, rather than the origin of the antagonisms, we are changing, not the object of our study, but merely the angle of vision. Now we are focusing on cultural factors.

The forms of political combat depend basically on institutions, ideologies, value-systems and collective images. A distinction can be made between the overall cultural context, constituted by the combination of all these elements within the framework of a nation or a civilization, and other elements which more directly concern power and the struggles which take place around it, and which are more strictly political.

Antagonisms arise first of all within certain technical contexts which are called political régimes: western democracy, dictatorship, traditional monarchy, and so on. Within these contexts, fighting organizations, political armies, as it were, come face to face: such are, in particular, parties and pressure groups. These organizations make use of various means of action in order to gain victory: money, numbers, collective organization, propaganda. Their struggle follows certain types of strategy, among which camouflage always ranks high. Political régimes, parties, pressure groups, tactics and strategy are the forms that political combat takes. By displacing our angle of vision, we are focusing more clearly on politics. Up to this point, in our description of the factors which caused antagonism, we have been dealing really with the relation between politics and the other aspects of life in society. Now we are about to discuss politics itself, and the institutions which directly concern it.

# 1. The Context of Conflict

It is the culture of a society, that is to say the whole complex of institutions, habits, traditions, mentalities, beliefs, collective images and value-systems within which political conflict occurs, that primarily constitutes the framework for that conflict. Each nation, each country, each civilization gives to the class struggle, to individual conflicts and resistance to power their individual character. Politics cannot be separated from this overall cultural context without being impoverished.

Secondly, the framework consists of those special institutions which are known as political régimes. In any complex society, there is organized power: political régimes are the different types of power organization. They are the product both of formal and official institutions established by constitution, law and legal documents in general, and also of *de facto* institutions, of habit, custom, usage and established practice.

## THE DIFFERENT POLITICAL RÉGIMES

Any classification of political régimes is made, explicitly or implicitly, with reference to a value-system. Both Aristotle and Plato, in their classifications, tended to lay emphasis on the qualities of mixed régimes. Montesquieu did likewise, but his concept of 'mixed' was different. Western typologies, which contrast democracies with dictatorships, aim to justify the former and devalue the latter, for in western languages today the word 'dictatorship' is a pejorative word, whereas the term 'democracy' is commendatory. The Communist contrast between capitalist and Socialist régimes has similar implications, since, in the vocabulary of Marxism, 'capitalist' is bad and 'Socialist' is good. Our aim is to penetrate farther than these subjective classifications, and to seek a more objective typology which will highlight the similarity and differences between régimes existing today, particularly as frameworks for political combat. An historical approach will best serve our purposes here, for all contemporary classifications are based to a greater or lesser degree on those of antiquity.

Until the end of the nineteenth century, the classification of political régimes was dominated by a typology, inherited from the Greeks, in which the main types were monarchy, oligarchy and democracy. Monarchy or government of one; oligarchy or government by a few; democracy or government by all: these simple definitions were both a logical classification and a concrete description of the régimes which existed in Hellenic antiquity. The first precise formulation of this distinction is found in Herodotus, and probably dates from the middle of the fifth century B.C., but it seems to be the fruit of a previous tradition. Already, however, distinctions were being made between the correct or pure form of each régime, and its 'deviations'. Aristotle was later to draw up a well-known table in which the corrupted forms, tyranny, oligarchy and democracy, were contrasted with the pure forms of monarchy, aristocracy and 'timocracy' or democracy based on limited franchise. Plato had already expressed similar concepts, with in addition the idea of the different types succeeding each other, in unending rotation.

The trilogy 'monarchy, aristocracy, democracy' was to dominate political thought until Montesquieu, and later. Each important political theorist complicated the detail, without altering the basic idea. Bodin applied it separately to forms of state and forms of government, which enabled him to make some strange but often interesting combinations. In a monarchic state, for example, where sovereignty lay with the king, there might be democratic government if all citizens alike had access to public function, or aristocratic government if only the noble and the wealthy had access to it. The Roman principality had a monarchic government in a democratic state, since sovereignty lay with the people. This variation on a type is fairly similar to Bonapartism and some modern dictatorships. Bodin's typology is interesting, and has the merit of revealing how there can be contradiction between the value-systems which underlie the state (what Bodin calls sovereignty), and the technical apparatus of power.

Montesquieu appears at first sight to depart from the traditional typology, since he wrote: 'There are three kinds of government: the republican, the monarchic and the despotic.' But within the republic he immediately makes a distinction between democracy and aristocracy, which recalls the age-old distinction made by Herodotus, and the idea of pure and corrupt forms (despotism being the corrupt form of monarchy). His comparative study of democracy and aristocracy is fruitful, and was to be justified in the nineteenth and even the twentieth centuries. It was, and still can be, difficult to distinguish between democracy and aristocracy because of the important part played, in régimes based on universal suffrage, by both limited franchise and oligarchies. Similarly, Montesquieu well realized, as modern sociologists do, that there was a fundamental difference between monarchy and dictatorship.

Contemporary jurists still base their thinking on Montesquieu, though not so much on his conception of the three forms of government as on his theory of the separation of powers. They classify political régimes according to the internal relationship between the different 'powers', that is, the various organs of state. This leads to a new tripartite division: confusion of powers, separation of powers, and parliamentary régimes (collaboration between powers).

Confusion of powers may operate to the benefit either of one man or of an assembly. The first case covers both absolute monarchy and dictatorship, the difference between them depending on the means of investiture: the king inherits power, the dictator obtains it by force. The second case is that of an assembly régime, known also as the National Convention régime (because the French Convention of 1792–5 is supposed to have been a supreme embodiment of it). This category is illusory, however; it is rather like false windows in decadent architecture, which are only put there for the sake of symmetry. The Convention was more dictated to (by the Commune or the Committees of Public Safety) than dictating. Examples of assembly régimes are too short-lived, too rare and too unstable to form a general category equal in importance to the other categories.

Within régimes where there is separation of powers and in parliamentary régimes, there is a similar general subdivision into monarchies and republics. The royalist form of separation of powers is the limited monarchy, in which a parliament with legislative and financial competence limits the royal prerogatives. Its republican form is the presidential régime, the outstanding example of which is the American system. The connection between the two is not artificial: the presidential régime was invented by colonists in the United States in imitation of the government of eighteenth-century Britain, that is, limited monarchy. The parliamentary régime is characterized by the fact that the head of the state and the head of the government are distinct, the former fulfilling a purely honorific role without any real power, and the second being alone in charge of the executive, within a ministerial cabinet which is responsible, with him, to parliament. This complex system is the last stage in a type of evolution which has made it possible to pass from absolute monarchy to democracy without changing the outward forms of a traditional system, but emptying them in practice of any substance.

Schematically, the evolution of European monarchies occurred in three phases, as in Great Britain: absolute monarchy, limited monarchy, parliamentary monarchy. The emergence of a parliament independent of the king – or more accurately the extension of the powers of this parliament, which grew out of the assemblies of feudal vassals – brought about the change from the first to the second phase. The development of democratic ideas forced the monarch to take increasing account of the will of parliament. The ministers, who at first were just the king's secretaries, putting his policies into effect, had gradually to gain the confidence of parliament in order to act; this brings us to the intermediary stage of 'Orleanist parliamentarism' (so called because it corresponded in France to the monarchy of Louis-Philippe, ex-Duke of Orleans), in which the minister had to have the confidence both of the monarch and of the parliamentary representatives. This phase was short-lived, and in the following one the confidence of the representatives alone was necessary. All governmental power was concentrated in the ministerial cabinet, and the king's role became purely ceremonial. In 1875, France was to transpose this parliamentary system into a republican context, and has since been imitated by many states. There is very little real difference between parliamentary republics and parliamentary monarchies, since the head of state, whether president or king, has in practice no power. In this way the opposition between monarchy and republic, which rent Europe in the nineteenth century, has been emptied of all substance and meaning.

These juridical classifications do not represent with much accuracy the differences to be found between political régimes existing today, and they are gradually being abandoned in favour of another typology which is based on the distinction between pluralist or democratic régimes, and monolithic or autocratic régimes. In democratic or pluralist régimes, the political struggle takes place freely, in broad daylight, for all to see. First, there are several political parties, whence the term 'pluralist' régimes; there may be more than two, but there are always at least two. The struggle is public and open; there is freedom of speech, and freedom of the Press and of the other media of information: pluralist régimes are also liberal, that is régimes where public liberties are safeguarded, and all may freely express their opinions, orally, in writing, by joining organizations or taking part in public demonstrations. Pressure groups, which attempt to influence the government indirectly, sometimes act more secretly, for all political life has its shady areas; but they are reduced to a minimum in pluralist régimes.

In monolithic or autocratic régimes, on the contrary, there is officially no struggle for power, except in the guise of conflicting individual attempts to gain the favour of the prince. But the prince himself cannot be challenged, any more than the régime itself. His authority is not subject to action by the citizens, whereas in pluralist democracies even the supreme power is competed for at regular intervals, every four or five years, in the general elections; those who hold it only do so precariously, like tenants whose rights cease when their lease expires, and who have to get it renewed or quit. Nevertheless, the most absolute monarch can scarcely escape the influence of his immediate collaborators, his counsellors and favourites, or the great institutions of state, so that a long list of functions which give a share in the supreme power become the object of bitter struggle. Sometimes the prince becomes the tool of the men or institutions which surround him: the Pharaoh, of the priests of Ammon; the Merovingian king, of his majordomo.

Within each of these categories – democratic or pluralist régimes, autocratic or monolithic régimes – subdivisions can be established. In the latter category the distinction can be made between hereditary monarchies and dictatorships resulting from conquest. Similarly, one can distinguish between moderate autocracies, which allow some measure of challenge, and totalitarian autocracies, which destroy all opposition and force the struggle to become clandestine. In pluralist democracies, the best classification takes into account both the juridical forms of the régime and the nature of the opposing political parties within it.

We have already pointed out how important the distinction between bi-partism and multi-partism is for aggravating or attenuating antagonisms. It is just as important from the point of view of the structure of parliamentary régimes, since it conditions the solution to the problem of the majority in the national assembly, a problem on which the whole edifice of government is based. In a two-party system, the majority belongs to one party, inevitably; it is therefore homogeneous, is not paralysed by internal disagreements, and is stable. In a multi-party system, no one party has the majority, which is formed by a coalition of several parties, and is therefore heterogeneous, divided, and unstable. But the number of parties is not the only factor to be considered. In a two-party régime the stability and homogeneity of the government depend essentially on the internal discipline of the majority party. If all the parliamentary representatives vote in the same way, as they do in Great Britain, the executive rests on a really coherent and lasting majority. If on the other hand voting is completely free, as it is in the United States, then the government finds it just as difficult to stay in power and to govern as it would in a multi-party régime. The only true bi-partism is the 'rigid' bi-partism of the British type, in which each party controls the way its M.P.s vote; 'flexible' bi-partism of the American type is a 'pseudo bi-partism' which in practice has the same results as a multi-party system.

Pluralist régimes can thus be classified according to three types: (1) *presidential régimes*, some of which have a pseudo bi-party system (United States), while others have multi-party systems (Latin America), but none have a true bi-party system; (2) *bi-party parliamentary régimes*, of the British type; (3) *multi-party parliamentary régimes*, of the continental European type. Juridically, the last two are very close to each other, and very different from the first. But in practice, in the way institutions work, the stability and authority of the government in a two-party parliamentary régime are much more similar to those of a presidential executive than to those of a multi-party parliamentary government. There is even greater similarity in the part the citizens play in choosing their leaders, which is a factor of capital importance in any political régime.

During parliamentary elections the citizen of Great Britain is aware not only that he is voting for a member of parliament, but also that, primarily, he is designating the leader responsible for British policy. Because of party discipline, he knows that by voting Conservative or Labour he is electing X, the Conservative leader, or Y, the Labour leader, as head of the government for the next five years. His situation is exactly that of the American citizen designating the presidential electors, who have committed themselves to choosing one of the two rival candidates for president. In Great Britain and the United States alike, despite the difference in juridical structures, all the citizens themselves in practice choose the real head of the government. In western European states, on the contrary, the multi-party structures prevent this direct choice; the head of government is designated by the different party headquarters, according to manoeuvres which appear esoteric to the ordinary citizen.

On this basis we can establish a new distinction between 'direct' democracies and 'indirect' democracies. In the former the electors themselves, in fact, choose the head of the government; in the latter the electors designate those who will freely make the choice. This distinction is tending to become basic in the West. The executive is the real centre of power in modern states, the legislative having only a supervisory, limiting and preventive role. Direct designation of the leader by all the citizens is therefore essential. It is much easier to establish reciprocal trust between the citizens and the government with such a system, whereas in an 'indirect' democracy the people feel that they are scarcely involved by the lobbying and committee intrigues which lead to the nomination of the head of government.

In a 'direct' democracy political competition is more real, more alive, and of more direct concern to the citizens; the importance of this phenomenon can readily be appreciated.

## POLITICAL RÉGIMES AND SOCIO-ECONOMIC STRUCTURES

The setting up of one or another political régime in any country does not depend on chance or human whims. Like all institutions, it is conditioned by many factors, particularly socio-economic ones. There are two main conflicting theories in this matter. Marxists see political régimes as a reflection of the system of production; in doing so they deprive political institutions, like other institutions, of any autonomy, and thus attribute to them only secondary importance. Western thinkers, who in the past went to the opposite extreme of exaggerating the independence of politics in relation to the economy, are beginning to moderate their original theses in this respect. They are more and more ready to admit that there is a close connection between political régimes and the level of technical development.

We have already described the general Marxist scheme of relationships between political régimes and systems of production. Marxism distinguishes first of all between types of state, of which there are four: the slave state of antiquity, the feudal state, the bourgeois state, and the Socialist state, each type corresponding to a mode of production and a system of ownership. Next, each type of state can be subdivided into several 'forms of state', that is, into political régimes. The slave state subdivides into eastern despotism, tyranny, republic and empire; the feudal state into seigniories and centralized monarchy; the bourgeois state into western democracy and fascism; the socialist state into Soviet-type régimes and peoples' democracies. Thus different political régimes can correspond to the same mode of production and ownership. But the diversity of régimes itself reflects differences within the same system of production.

Let us take, for example, the medieval system of production, based on primitive and extensive agricultural techniques, engendering opposition between lords and serfs. Roughly speaking, it had two successive forms. It developed first of all within the framework of a closed economy, in which each seigniory, turned in on itself, produced nearly everything that was needed for subsistence by the people living on its lands, exchange and commerce existing only in their simplest form. To this variety of the feudal production system there corresponds a very decentralized political régime, in which power is fragmented among feudal lords linked with each other in very relaxed hierarchies. With the development of communications and commerce, and the substitution of an exchange economy for a closed economy, the local autonomy of the lords gradually disappears, and the centralized state emerges in the form of an absolute monarchy.

In the same way the differences between the forms of the bourgeois state depend on differences in the capitalist production system. For example, when this system begins to predominate, but the great landowners still play an important part in the economy, the bourgeois state tends to take on the form of an Orleanist-type parliamentary monarchy, as in France under Louis-Philippe (1830–48). On the other hand, when the capitalist production system begins to be shaken by the strength of working-class movements, and evolution towards Socialism becomes threatening, the bourgeois state inclines to violence of the Fascist type. Thus parliamentary monarchy corresponds to the first phase of an expanding capitalist system, and Fascism is the form of state corresponding to the last phase of a capitalist system in decline. At its height, the capitalist system gives rise to the western democratic state, based on a system of political liberties, party pluralism, competitive elections and so on.

The same correspondence between varieties in the system of production, and forms of state, can be found in Socialism. Marxist theoreticians today recognize two forms of the Socialist state: the Soviet system, and the people's democracy. They both 'arose in different conditions, from the point of view of the disposition of class-forces' (*Les principes du marxisme-léninisme*, Moscow, 1960). Both are essentially based on the working class and on Socialist production. But Soviet dictatorship is based on the single party and liquidation of the bourgeoisie, while peoples' democracies maintain forms of party pluralism (much weakened by the domination of the Communist party and the tendency to form 'national fronts'), and are based on the collaboration of some middle-class elements and the maintenance of a large private sector in agriculture.

These Marxist theories overestimate the influence of production and ownership systems on political régimes. The existence and importance of this influence cannot be disputed. But political régimes are not simply a reflection or a by-product of ownership and production systems. The correspondence between the main types of state described by the Marxists – slave, feudal, bourgeois and Socialist – and the main types of production system is on the whole accurate. But the 'types of state' are badly defined from the political point of view; they are very broad categories, which in reality encompass very varied régimes, and it is sometimes difficult to connect the differences between these régimes with differences in their production systems. Let us take Fascist régimes for example. Can it be said that the system of production in Germany in 1933 was very different from that in Great Britain at the same period? A Marxist would reply that Germany had no colonies, unlike

Great Britain, where imperialism found other outlets than Fascism. This is not a convincing argument, however; neither the Scandinavian states nor the U.S.A. had colonies either, yet they did not become Fascist. Certainly German Fascism, like any Fascism, depended on economic factors, but the influence of the production system as such seems to have been fairly small.

The development of Stalinism in the U.S.S.R. is another good example. The Russians themselves do not try to explain it by the production system. Doubtless, it was a contributory factor: centralized planning tended naturally towards dictatorship. But planning was just as centralized at the time when Stalin died, when the need for liberalization made itself felt strongly; the relative economic decentralization which has since come about in Russia is not the cause of destalinization, but its consequence. To explain the tyranny of Stalin by attributing it to his personal vices and defects of character, as is officially done in the U.S.S.R., is not at all Marxist, and is inadequate. Stalinism is a form of state, a type of political régime, which developed in a Socialist production system, after a régime of a very different form (Leninism) and before one equally different in form (Krushchevism), and no change in the system of production accounts for these differences.

We have said that there are important differences between the three main forms of western political régime – the American presidential régime, the British two-party parliamentary régime, and the continental multi-party parliamentary régime. These differences, too, cannot be attributed to differences in the production and ownership systems. The fact that the public sector of production is much smaller in the U.S.A. than in Great Britain or in France seems to have no effect on the question. The differences in the political régimes of the main western states today are due to historical and cultural developments not directly connected with the system of production. Inversely, the transformation of the economic structures of France, Great Britain and other European nations in the last twenty-five years, bringing in its wake the replacement of the capitalist system of production by a mixed, half-capitalist, half-Socialist system, with a large public sector and fairly well developed overall planning, has not been followed by political changes of the same importance. The growth in the executive is obvious, but it has scarcely been greater than in the United States, where economic structures have remained more purely capitalist.

Nevertheless, the difference between the two main economic structures defined by ownership – capitalism and Socialism – does roughly correspond to the difference between the two main categories of political régime today, the pluralist régime and the monolithic régime. In a capitalist or semi-capitalist economy, political power and economic power are separate, the latter being shared by many private firms (and sometimes by private firms and public organisms), which constitute so many autonomous 'decision centres' more or less independent of the state. Private ownership of the means of production leads therefore to a pluralist economic structure, which is reflected in the political field. On the contrary, public ownership of all the means of production, and total planning, have the result of concentrating political power and economic power in the same hands: they lead to a monolithic system.

This description calls for many reservations. The separation of political power and economic power is in part an illusion, for the latter has at its disposal powerful means of applying pressure on the former. A new feudal structure has sprung up on the foundations of large-scale capitalism, and like medieval feudalism, it is able victoriously to challenge the central power, or more simply, to unseat it to its own benefit. Western governments often resemble some child-king, a docile plaything in the hands of the great feudal lords. In a purely capitalist régime political power scarcely exists as such; it is little more than a reflection of the economic power; the distinction between the two is only a real one in mixed régimes. Furthermore, the concentration of economic power in the hands of a few large firms means that the picture of a multiplicity of autonomous 'decision centres' is deceptive. The connection between private ownership and political pluralism is not as clear as it is said to be. The case of Nazi dictatorship shows clearly that an ultra-totalitarian autocracy can be set up within a capitalist system. Fascism is, moreover, connected with the development of capitalism and its resistance to the establishment of a Socialist economy.

The connection between a Socialist economy and a monolithic régime is not better founded. No valid conclusions can be based on the too brief and too rare experiments in Socialism. We can analyse the evolution of capitalism over more than a century, in a fairly large number of western European and North American states, whereas the evolution of Socialist societies can only be analysed over a period of forty-seven years and in one state, the Soviet Union. In European people's democracies, where the experiment has lasted for less than twenty years, the problem of foreign domination falsifies the evolution of Socialism, except in Yugoslavia. In China, where the experiment is more recent still, the aftermath of a terrible civil war, and the level of underdevelopment, make any comparison impossible. The Socialist state régimes are still too infrequent and too new for political sociology to make any valid analyses of them. It is not impossible that their totalitarianism and the absence of pluralism are the result of their revolutionary state and so are only temporary. Such, moreover, is the view they themselves take, basing it on the theory of dictatorship of the proletariat, which is of its nature transitory.

At any rate, one can discern fairly clearly within the Socialist countries a tendency to economic decentralization, which is bringing them closer to the 'plurality of decision-centres' that is alleged to characterize capitalist régimes. Yugoslavia entered on this path several years ago. In the U.S.S.R., Krushchev's reforms are following the same direction. A very suggestive comparison could here be made with the historical evolution of political decentralization. In feudal times, the latter was maintained by the hereditary transmission of power to local chieftains; in our day, it is based on their election by the people. Today, private ownership provides a fairly effective system of economic decentralization, based on heredity. But we can already foresee the possibility of economic decentralization based on different and more democratic processes, such as nineteenth-century Socialists dreamt of.

The correlation between political régime and level of technico-economic development seems to be as strong as, if not stronger than, the correlation between political régime and system of ownership of the means of production. Pluralist democracy corresponds to a high degree of industrialization. To say that a free people is a rich people is to express brutally, but without exaggeration, a fundamental truth. It is in practice impossible to apply a pluralist system to nations where the greater part of the population is almost starving, uneducated and illiterate. Under a cloak of modern procedure, the old feudal autocratic régimes still function, and far from helping to destroy them, democratic processes only prolong their existence by camouflaging them. Pluralist democracy developed during the nineteenth and twentieth centuries among the rich western countries; its growth followed the development of industrialization and the rise in the collective standard of living.

The autocratic and monolithic nature of the Communist régimes is a consequence, not only of their concentration of political power with economic power, but also – and perhaps mainly – of the state of underdevelopment or partial development of all the countries where they have been established: Russia in 1917, the People's Democracies in 1945,[1] China and North Vietnam. Following this line of thought, the 'liberalization' which can be glimpsed in the U.S.S.R. would correspond to the economic evolution of Russia, which has now become one of the greatest industrial powers in the world. Development by the Socialist method, which gave preference to industrial capacity rather than to plenty, to plant rather than to consumption, slowed down the consequences of this evolution, but they are beginning to be seen. Like the industrial nations of the west, Russia is approaching a state of relative plenty, in which the whole population can more or less satisfy not only its primary needs (food, housing, clothing), but also its secondary needs (comfort, culture, leisure): a state, in other words, which fulfils the conditions for democracy.

[1] Except Czechoslovakia, as far as Bohemia is concerned: but Communism was introduced there by the Red Army, and its spread was facilitated by the crisis which began at Munich.

Certainly, there are many factors restraining this evolution: the influence of the political class, the 'administration men' who are bound to the dictatorship which gives them power and honour; the foreign menace, and competition with the capitalist states; the dangers of crisis at home if liberalization is too rapid; the risk of reaction in the satellite countries; the technical difficulties inherent in relaxing an authoritarian régime. All in all, the evolution seems irreversible, in the long run. But only the developed Communist countries (Russia and the European peoples' democracies) are affected; the underdeveloped Communist countries (China, Vietnam) will continue for much longer to be subject to the political dictatorship which corresponds to their economic level. It is possible that one day the basic distinction will be drawn, not between western-type régimes and eastern-type régimes, but between régimes in developed countries, and those in underdeveloped countries: in other words, the level of the economy, rather than its legal constitution, will be the deciding factor.

We have already said that the rate of development is as important as the level of development. By smashing the traditional social structures and provoking opposition and conflict, rapid development makes it even more difficult for pluralist democracy to function. In history, rashes of dictatorship correspond to eras of rapid change. Violence then serves either to accelerate the transformation and precipitate progress (revolutionary dictatorship) or to maintain the traditional order and slow down the change (reactionary dictatorship). In our day, Communism provides a good example of the first type, and Fascism of the second. These phenomena occur at different levels of development. In Germany, Hitlerism aimed at preventing a highly industrialized society from gradually becoming Socialist. In Spain and Portugal, dictatorship slows down the evolution of an aristocratic society towards liberal democracy. In China, Communism is a means of speeding up the first stages of industrialization and of emerging from underdevelopment. Naturally, dictatorships are more frequently found in archaic societies, where the effects of the level and of the rate of development work hand in hand, than in industrial societies, where they conflict. Moreover, social upheavals other than those which result from rapid technical progress can have the same results: speedy decadence, war, economic crisis.

Inversely, in undeveloped but stable countries one can find interesting examples of pluralist democracy. This was so in some Berber cities of North Africa, which had well-developed electoral systems, fairly rigorous separation of powers, and political assemblies, the 'djemaas'. Before the coming of the nation state many small societies had a similar type of structure; the ancient democracies are an outstanding example. They were agricultural communities of land-owning peasants, or fishing communities, where there was no marked inequality of income. Frugal habits, which had long been traditional, ensured economic balance by tempering needs which did not noticeably exceed the supply of goods available. A traditional oral culture maintained a high general intellectual level, though few could read and write. The Republics of Greece and Rome corresponded to situations of this type. The collapse of their intellectual and material equilibrium which followed on their political expansion and economic development brought about the downfall of democracy and the advent of dictatorship.

Other examples could be borrowed from even more archaic societies, like those studied by ethnologists. In such societies decisions are often made collectively by assemblies of tribal members. African tribal meetings are an application of the process of discussion which characterizes democracies; they may be compared to debates in the Greek Agora or the Roman Forum. This 'small-unit democracy' did not always disappear when the nation states were formed, but often persists, on the local level. The administration of rural or urban areas and parishes has nearly always depended on some degree of participation by the inhabitants, even within régimes which are autocratic at the national level.

The important part played by socio-economic factors (level of development and ownership régime) in determining political régimes should not cause us to forget that there are many other factors at work, too. We have already stressed the importance of history and of the whole cultural context in forming a nation's institutions. The British régime is inseparable from Great Britain, the American régime from the United States, the French régime from France. The particular combination of circumstances can also have an influence which should be taken into account. A particular event, an outstanding person or an exceptional situation can play a great part in the formation or the evolution of political régimes. In this respect, there is a basic notion which has been largely neglected by political sociology: that of the 'conjunctural régime'. In the normal course of things a country's political institutions are determined by its structures, and unimportant happenings, like ripples on the sea, cannot modify them much. But occasionally the conjuncture can exercise such strong pressure that it overrides the influence of structures, and then a nation has to bear for a while with a political régime which does not correspond to its structures. The French *coup d'état* of 13th May 1958, and the dangers of a military putsch from 1960 to 1962, are a good example of such exceptional situations. 'Conjunctural régimes' are transitory, but the very fact that they have existed modifies to some extent the structures of the country and its historical development.

# 2. Political Conflict: Organizations

In the major human communities, and particularly in modern states, political conflict is waged between relatively specialized organizations, which form political armies of a sort. These organizations are structured, articulated and hierarchical groups, adapted to the struggle for power. They represent the interests and objectives of different social forces (classes, local communities, ethnic groups, communities with special interests), and are the means of political action for these social forces. The organized character of political combat is an essential and more or less general feature of modern times, but during this last century the techniques of collective organization, the methods of organizing men, have been greatly improved.

Political organizations can be divided into two main categories: parties and pressure groups. The immediate objective of parties is to gain power or to participate in the exercise of power. They try to win seats in elections, to have M.P.s and ministers, and to take over government. Pressure groups do not envisage assuming power themselves or even participating in its exercise. They try to influence those who are in power, to exert 'pressure' on them – whence their name. Parties and pressure groups are not the only political organizations, and we shall later describe the underground movements which develop in régimes where the political struggle cannot take place in the open. Examples of 'leagues', 'fronts' and other semi-party organizations might be quoted also.

## THE STRUCTURE OF POLITICAL PARTIES

Political parties came into being at the same time as electoral and parliamentary procedures, and developed parallel to them.

They first appeared in the form of electoral committees, whose function was to provide the candidate with support from local notabilities and to collect the funds necessary for the campaign. Within assemblies parliamentary groups developed, as M.P.s with similar opinions united with a view to common action. This meeting of M.P.s at the top naturally brought about a tendency for their electoral committees to federate at the base, and in this way the first political parties came into being. In the United States the need to agree at national level about the choice of a candidate for the presidency, and then to pursue an electoral campaign on a huge scale, combined with the need at local level to nominate a vast number of candidates for the numerous elective posts, has given the parties their own particular form, but this is still closely related to elections.

Originally, political parties were formed from local committees within each electoral district, grouping together those with influence and reputation. The quality of their members was more important than their numbers. The qualities most in demand were prestige, which has a moral influence, and wealth, which helps to meet the costs of propaganda. The inner organization of these committees was poor, for with few members there was no need for a rigid structure; their autonomy was considerable, for the central party organization had little authority over the local members. The parties remained something of a federation of cómmittees and most of these were dominated by a single outstanding man, usually the M.P. himself. Parliamentary members, each backed up by their committee, retained a great deal of independence. Except in Great Britain, voting discipline did not exist, and this made battles in the assemblies rather like gladiatorial contests. This primitive structure has persisted in most European Conservative and Liberal parties, and in the American parties. Parties formed on this pattern are called 'cadre parties'.

At the beginning of the twentieth century the Socialists invented another political structure, that of mass parties. The basic problem was to ensure financial support for the electoral campaigns of Socialist candidates who were considered at the time as revolutionaries and so were refused support by the bankers, industrialists, merchants and landowners who financed the election of Conservative and Liberal candidates. Since they could not rely on a few large amounts contributed by a small number of people, they had the idea of soliciting a very small regular contribution from a very large number of people. This led to enlisting the maximum number of followers in the party organization. Instead of forming a group of a few thousands at the most, the party had to enrol hundreds of thousands, indeed millions. This system also made possible the political education of the vast working-class section of the population which had lacked it hitherto. Lastly, it ensured a more democratic recruitment of candidates, who, instead of being chosen from the narrow circle of a small committee, were nominated within local and national congresses by the body of members or by their representatives.

There seems to be a fairly close correlation between this new party structure and the development of the social classes on which mass parties are based. The traditional cadre parties corresponded to the conflict between aristocracy and bourgeoisie, classes which were small in number and perfectly represented by local notabilities. The narrowness of the parties reflected the limited area of the political field and the true nature of a so-called democracy from which the majority of the people were in practice excluded. On the other hand, the mass parties correspond to an extension of democracy, opening up to include almost the whole population. The population only exercises its rights completely if it is not limited to voting once every four or five years and if it participates permanently in the administration of the state. With the new party organization this becomes possible.

The permanent grouping of hundreds of thousands of men, and sometimes even of millions (from 1913 onwards, the German Social Democratic party numbered more than a million members), and the regular collection of subscriptions, the party's tax, required a much stricter administrative organization than that of cadre parties. From this there resulted the progressive development of a complex and hierarchical apparatus, and the formation of a group of 'internal leaders' which weakens the position of parliamentary members. The conflict between the two leaderships is sociologically interesting, for it expresses the conflict of two basic communities, that of the party members who elect the internal leaders and that of the electors who elect the parliamentary representatives. The party members, who are more committed than the electors, are more intransigent. However, the movement of Socialist parties towards social democracy and their integration into the parliamentary system have changed the facts of the problem. By accepting the value of parliamentary government, they were naturally led to give priority to those who stood for those values, that is, the parliamentary representatives. In Communist or Fascist parties, on the other hand, where these values are more in dispute, parliamentary representatives are subordinate to the internal leaders who enjoy greater prestige.

The mass structure has been subsequently adopted by other than Socialist parties. Christian Democratic parties have generally tried simply to transpose the Socialist organization, without always succeeding. They often have a mixed structure, half-way between that of the cadre party and that of the mass party, which corresponds to the mixed character of their social basis. Communist parties have modified two important points in the Socialist structure. In the first place, instead of grouping their members in sections or 'committees', they group them in cells according to a local framework based upon residence, place and type of work: in factories, workshops, shops, offices, schools and so on. Secondly, they have emphasized centralization and established a rigid discipline. Fascist parties have carried this tendency even further, and at the same time have increased the number of intermediate steps in the hierarchy between the base and the centre. Thus they present the pattern of a pyramid composed of interlocking groups. This structure, an exact copy of army structure, is accounted for by the para-military character of Fascism, where the party is designed not only to play a part in elections and parliament, but also to sabotage its opponents' meetings, destroy their headquarters and installations, beat up their members, start street fighting and so forth.

In underdeveloped countries mass parties generally assume a

different shape. In all mass parties the leaders form a group which is fairly clearly distinguished from the other members and the militants. This 'inner circle', in fact, somewhat resembles a cadre party buried in a mass organization. And yet in developed countries there is no rigid separation between these two groups. The 'inner circle' is very open and ordinary members of the party can enter it quite easily. The distinction is related more to technical needs (like the need for concentration of power, for reasons of efficiency) than to any sociological situation. In mass parties in underdeveloped countries, on the other hand, the social distance between members of the 'inner circle' and the mass of party members is very great. The former have the intellectual and technical level of modern societies, while the latter are still very far from this level and nearer to that of archaic societies. Thus party structure reflects the general structure of these countries at their present stage of development.

Secondly, the modern political organization is superimposed upon traditional types, which it does not completely suppress; rather it often transfigures them by drawing from them its own principal strength. Tribal and racial fraternities, feudal attachments, religious affiliations and the bonds of secret societies are often used as the bases of allegiance to a particular party, and the party emblem is sometimes thought to have the value of a charm or mascot. Phenomena of this kind are also found within parties in the most modern and industrialized nations, but they are less obvious, and their importance much smaller. In certain parties in underdeveloped countries – but not in all – they seem, on the contrary, to play an essential part, at least in the organization of people in the countryside; in towns the parties are much nearer the modern type.

It has been said that the authority of political leaders in underdeveloped countries depends more on personality than elsewhere. The individual authority of the leader would in this case be the essential factor in the cohesion of the party and the allegiance of its members, while programmes and ideologies would have little importance. This third distinctive element, the authority of the leader, seems more controversial than the others. There is no doubt that power is personalized in under-developed societies and that parties are essentially constituted round a single man. But in the last few decades the development of the most modern societies seems similarly to have tended towards the personalization of authority. That the nature and significance of leadership should be different in the two types of country seems probable, although these differences are difficult to define, but it is doubtful whether the personal character of power is greater in one rather than in the other. It is rather a question of a different kind of personalization.

A third party structure is found in the British Labour party and certain Scandinavian Socialist parties. At the beginning of the twentieth century, when the problem of financing workers' electoral campaigns had to be faced, it was solved in Great Britain by the direct action of the trade unions, who decided to pay part of their members' subscriptions into a political fund. The administration of the fund and the choice of candidates was to be undertaken by committees composed of representatives of trade unions, friendly societies, co-operative societies and various Socialist societies. On this basis a new type of party, known as the 'indirect' party, was established. Citizens do not, in fact, belong directly to the party, but only indirectly through other organizations: trade unions, friendly societies, co-operative societies and other similar associations. (Nevertheless, a system of direct membership was later developed in the British Labour party, parallel to the indirect system, so that today an indirect party and a classic mass party exist side by side. Local branches of the latter, like the trade unions, friendly societies, co-operatives and Socialist associations, all send representatives to the Labour committees, where the views of the whole party can thus be expressed.) Certain Catholic parties, notably the Belgian Christian party between the two wars, and the Austrian Christian Democratic party, adopted a similar corporately based structure.

## THE NUMBER OF PARTIES

The development of political parties is linked with that of modern western democracy. Previously there were no real

parties, except in an embryonic form (Armagnacs and Bour-
guignons, Guelphs and Ghibellines, the ultra-Catholic League
in sixteenth-century France, Jacobins, Girondins and so on).
Yet contemporary authoritarian régimes have transposed the
democratic organization of parties into their single-party
system which really corresponds to something different from,
and even contrary to, pluralist democracy. For the organization
of political combat there should by definition be several parties:
for a battle to take place two opponents are required at the very
least. The single party aims to end political struggles and replace
them by unanimity, but it still combats those who oppose the
régime: the system results simply in refusing its opponents the
right to form themselves into a party, and in reserving only for
the supporters of power the possibility of using this kind of fighting organization. The opposition continues its struggle through
other means. However, the single party can itself become the
framework of political combat if it is not absolutely monolithic.

The contrast between several parties and a single party
characterizes two systems of political combat, that of modern
western democracies and that of modern authoritarian régimes.
(Archaic-type authoritarian régimes know nothing of parties.)
Despite this, the contrast is less severe than one would think.
There is an intermediate system, 'the ruling party', where many
parties may flourish in one country, but one of them is so much
stronger than the others that they cannot oust it from power
nor hinder it much in its exercise of power. Yet their presence
allows open criticism of the state and the questioning of its
acts, in elections, parliament, the Press, public meetings and so
on. This notion of a 'ruling party' system remains somewhat
vague; in practice it swings between two poles: either the
opposition is powerful, the other parties have real strength and
threaten one day to end the government of the party in power,
as, for example, in India – this verges on pluralism – or the
opposition is very weak and the ruling party very powerful –
this approaches the single-party system. (The latter has been
the case in many African Republics in the last few years; most
have now become single-party systems purely and simply by
suppressing organized opposition.)

In pluralist régimes there is a fundamental distinction between bi-partism and multi-partism. We have already assessed its influence on the development of political differences and its importance in establishing a modern classification of political régimes. It must now be examined in its own right yet without its importance being exaggerated. The formation of stable alliances which enter the electoral campaign with ·definite programmes drawn up in common, and afterwards apply them in government, moves the multi-party system closer to bi-partism. Inversely, when each party has a flexible structure and there is no voting discipline in parliament, government majorities become incoherent and unreliable and bi-partism is more like multi-partism. This flexible bi-partism is much closer to multi-partism than the British type of rigid bi-partism. As we have seen, this problem is of prime importance for the classification of political régimes. There are thus intermediate categories between bi-partism and multi-partism.

The existence of one or other party system in a country is explained by three basic types of factor: socio-economic factors, historical and cultural factors, and a technical factor, the electoral system. The first were predominant in the development of European party systems in the nineteenth century. The original opposition between Conservative and Liberal parties reflected a class conflict between aristocracy and bourgeoisie, which Marxist analysis has aptly described. A tendency towards bi-partism thus clearly emerged. In the second half of the century industrial development and the growth of the proletariat brought into being a third political and social force, which is embodied in Socialist parties. The former bi-party system then tended to become a three-party system. The phenomenon can be seen in its pure state in Great Britain, Belgium, Australia and New Zealand. Elsewhere other factors intervene, but its trace is still clearly discernible.

However, the growth of Socialist parties offers the Liberals an alternative. Both have in common their opposition to monarchies and aristocracies and their attachment to political equality and freedom; but Liberals support free enterprise and private ownership of the means of production, which Socialists want to abolish. The former factors lead the two parties to unite against Conservatives; the latter tend on the contrary to bring Liberals closer to Conservatives and increase the distance between them and Socialists. In the first phase, when the old political systems are firmly entrenched, when domination by the aristocracy seems the worst possible and most likely danger, and weak Socialist parties offer little danger as yet in the eyes of the bourgeoisie, Liberal parties generally adopt the first tactic. As political democracy is established and becomes a recognized system, and as the counter-attack of the aristocratic system becomes a more remote possibility, the contrast between Conservatives and Liberals gradually loses significance. They naturally draw together then, in a common desire to defend property and the established order – the Liberal order to which Conservatives, having no alternative, now rally.

Then there arises a tendency to fuse Conservatives and Liberals into one party, in opposition to Socialists. Thus a twentieth-century bi-partism tends to replace nineteenth-century bi-partism. This development is seen clearly in Great Britain, New Zealand and Australia. In other countries, a Liberal party manages to survive, though greatly diminished, since much of its support has been transferred to the Conservatives. This is the case in Belgium, the Netherlands, northern Europe, and in France in the form of the Radical party. Often, the Liberal party strives to hold the balance between the two, sometimes forming an alliance with Socialists against Conservatives, and sometimes with Conservatives against Socialists, this last becoming progressively more frequent than the first.

Bi-partism and multi-partism do not depend only on socio-economic factors, but also upon cultural factors affecting the latter. In the Netherlands, for example, religious ideologies played a great part in elaborating the party system. From the beginning the Conservative body was split into two parties: Catholic Conservatives and Protestant Conservatives ('Anti-revolutionaries'). A split in the latter, giving rise to the 'Historical Christians', finally resulted in the Conservatives being divided into three distinct parties. In France political régimes and the conflicts they have aroused have brought about a similar division in the Right-wing camp. In the mid-nineteenth century Conservatives split into three parties: Legitimists, Orleanists and Bonapartists. The lack of Right-wing organization, which is characteristic of the French party system, derives in part from this fact. In other countries ethnic or regional divisions have played a similar role and tended to increase the number of parties.

Finally, a technical factor, which is of its nature really institutional, comes into play: the electoral system, to which a great deal of study has been devoted in the last few years. Its role has been summarized in three sociological laws which were defined in 1946: (a) the simple-majority single-ballot system leads to bi-partism; (b) proportional representation tends to multi-partism; (c) the simple-majority two-ballot system leads to multi-partism moderated by alliances. These laws have been much discussed, and often heatedly, but they have never been seriously contested. The criticisms lodged against them concern the exact consequences of the laws rather than their substance, which is self-evident. Certainly electoral reform cannot itself create new parties: parties are the expression of social forces, and cannot be created by a simple act of legislation. It is also certain that the relation between electoral and party systems is not mechanical and automatic: a particular electoral system does not necessarily create a particular party system; it only makes that system likely to arise. It is a force tending in a certain direction, which works in the context of other forces, some of them tending in the opposite direction. Similarly, it is certain that the relations between electoral and party systems are not one-way. If the single-ballot system tends towards bi-partism, bi-partism equally tends towards the adoption of the single-ballot system.

The precise role of the electoral system seems in the last resort to be that of either accelerator or brake. The description just given of the development of parties in Europe in the nineteenth and twentieth centuries shows this clearly. Economic growth and the social changes it effects, on the one hand; and on the other, the circumstances particular to each country (religious divisions, ideological conflicts, constitutional instability): these are the creative forces behind political parties.

The simple-majority single-ballot system has a dual effect on the working of these forces. In the first place, acting as a brake, it erects a barrier against the appearance of a new party (although not making the barrier insurmountable). In the second place, as an accelerator, it leads to the elimination of the weaker party, or the weakest parties where there are more than two. The braking effect can be seen at the end of the nineteenth century, when the electoral system retarded the growth of Socialism, and again since the First World War, when it hindered the growth of Communist and Fascist movements. Acceleration is even more evident in the case of the British Liberal party, which was practically eliminated in fifteen years (1920–35), although it retains a certain measure of support from those obliged by the electoral system to choose between Conservative and Labour.

Proportional representation has exactly the opposite effect. It does not slow down the development of new parties, but passively records it, sometimes amplifying it beyond its actual state, like a resonating drum or a seismograph. (In order to counter this effect, proportional representation is very rarely used in its purest form, but is usually adjusted by different majority measures: the local distribution of 'remainders', the need to win a certain percentage of votes in order to participate in the distribution of seats, and so on.) On the other hand, proportional representation slows down the elimination of old parties which are tending to disappear as a result of social and political change; the rescue of the Belgian Liberal party through proportional representation after 1900 is typical of this effect. Yet a distinction must be made between old movements firmly rooted in a section of the population and superficial movements corresponding to passing political moods. Proportional representation records both the appearance and disappearance of the latter equally clearly, as was seen with Belgian Rexism in 1937 and in France with the *Rassemblement du peuple français* in 1951 and Poujadism in 1956.

The effects of the simple-majority two-ballot system are on the whole similar to those of proportional representation, with some slight differences. It seems to slow down the appearance of new parties a little more, although its influence is not comparable to that of the single-ballot system, which is much more effective in this respect. Perhaps it also reduces the speed of elimination of old parties rather more, but it is difficult to reach precise conclusions about this. On the other hand, it seems to place some kind of obstacle in the way of swift changes of opinion, passing whims and political moods. (The instance of the *Union nationale républicaine* in France in 1958 would seem to contradict this, but the circumstances were very special.) Where it differs most from proportional representation is in the matter of electoral alliances: as a system favouring coalitions, the two-ballot system sometimes allows the formation within a multi-party context of a sort of bi-partism in which two rival alliances are in opposition. France under the Third Republic, and Germany from 1870 to 1914, illustrate this phenomenon.

The influence of the electoral system is therefore minor compared with that of socio-economic factors and even cultural factors. Yet the particular circumstances are very important here. The replacement of the simple-majority ballot in Great Britain by proportional representation would cause the appearance of a three-party system almost immediately and would facilitate possible splits within the Labour and the Conservative parties. The influence of the single-ballot system in maintaining a pre-established bi-partism is indisputable. It is much less certain that the adoption of this system could destroy an established multi-party system and, for example, reduce the number of French or Italian parties to two. Such a reform is inconceivable, moreover, for the single-ballot system produces erratic results when more than two parties confront each other. But in Federal Germany it would no doubt complete the already well advanced movement towards bi-partism; above all, it would prevent a counter-reaction by placing obstacles in the way of a possible split in the Christian Democratic party or a revival of the small parties.

### PRESSURE GROUPS

Political parties are organizations particular to a certain type of system, western democracy, at a certain period of history, the twentieth century. Pressure groups, on the other hand, are found in all systems at all times. The term is applied to a very large and indistinct category of organizations. They all have in common the fact that they play some part in political combat, but indirectly. Parties aim at gaining power and exercising it: they aim at winning municipal, departmental and state elections, at securing the election of mayors, senators and parliamentary representatives, at obtaining ministerial posts in the government, and at appointing the head of state. Pressure groups, on the contrary, do not participate directly in the winning of power and its exercise. They act on the party in power while remaining outside it; they exert pressure on it and aim at influencing those in power, but without pushing their own men into power, officially at least, for, in fact, some powerful groups do have their 'representatives' in assemblies and governments, albeit secretly or very discreetly.

The pressure-group category is less clearly defined than that of 'political party'. In fact, parties are organizations devoted exclusively to political action; parties are only parties, but most pressure groups are non-political organizations whose primary activity is not concerned with influencing the authorities in power. Thus a distinction can be made between 'exclusive' and 'partial' groups. A pressure group is exclusive if its only concern is to act in the political field, to intervene with public authorities. An example of an exclusive group is the *Association parlementaire pour la défense de l'enseignement*, or the well-known Washington lobbies, which are organizations that specialize in approaching Congressmen, Ministers and top civil servants. A group is partial if political pressure is only a part of its activities, if it has other objects and other means of action: a trade union, for example, sometimes makes representations to the government, but pursues wider aims. There are large numbers of partial groups: all societies, trade unions, co-operatives, and organizations of any kind can be brought to use political pressure at some point in their activities. The French Academy has sometimes acted politically in an attempt to decrease the tax burdens imposed on books and writers. Churches do not abstain from exerting pressure on public authorities, any more than do philosophical societies, intellectual groups, and other such associations.

The implications of this distinction are not to be exaggerated. Very few pressure groups are absolutely exclusive, that is, have as their sole aim participation in political activity. The majority more or less conceal this function behind others and thus present the appearance of partial groups. Moreover, purely political action is difficult to distinguish from other types of action. A strike set in motion by a trade union is sometimes political, sometimes economic, and often both at the same time. In short, establishing the precise part played by pressure activities in partial groups is more important than distinguishing between partial and exclusive groups. For certain groups, political pressure is episodic and exceptional. At the other extreme, alongside declared exclusive groups, there are groups which are almost exclusive, (for example, the *Association pour la défense de la libre entreprise*) despite the appearance they try to adopt of pursuing other activities. Between the two are found all kinds of intermediate organization.

From the point of view of structure, mass groups and cadre groups can be distinguished, just as we distinguished between mass and cadre parties. Workers' trade unions, peasant organizations, youth movements, war veterans' associations and so on come into the first category. In the second are groups appealing to small but influential social categories, for example co-operative organizations in industry, societies of highly placed civil servants, associations for higher education. In this category we also find groups in which there is a deliberate policy of appealing to notabilities, the academies, for instance, and certain intellectual groups.

There is a third category, which, unlike the mass and cadre groups, does not have a political party equivalent. This consists of purely technical organizations which do not correspond to any group or community except that of the people in the organization. One might hesitate to class them along with pressure groups, for though there is pressure, strictly speaking there is no group. First in this category are American lobbies, in so far as they are no longer the emanation of a particular group of interests, and have more or less become agencies specializing in pressure and selling their services, like a barrister in chambers or an advertising agency. Into this category also come propaganda bureaux such as the *Centre de propagande des Républicains nationaux* whose moving spirit in the thirties was Henri de Kérillis. Equally part of this category are campaign chests which collect the funds of employers' organizations and business circles and arrange for their distribution among the candidates. They usually cloak themselves in the guise of peaceful research organizations. The *Union des intérêts economiques* of Senator Billiet played this role under the Third Republic; an organization under the management of Senator Boutémy replaced it under the Fourth. A certain section of the Press may belong to this category, for some newspapers are only the mouthpieces or agents of particular groups: declared agents in the case of trade-union or co-operative papers; disguised and camouflaged agents in the case of papers supported by industrial groups, i.e. the 'industrial press' of which the French paper *Le Temps* was the best prewar example after it had been acquired by the *Comité des Forges* in 1929.

The activity of pressure groups is multiform. Sometimes they bring their influence to bear directly on the authorities by approaching the government, high civil servants and members of parliament, and sometimes indirectly by acting upon the public, whose own attitude influences the authorities. Press campaigns, spectacular strikes, road-blocks, demonstrations, etc., are used to this end. Their activity is sometimes open, public and declared, and sometimes circumspect, hidden and camouflaged. Sometimes it uses permissible, straightforward, lawful means and sometimes corrupt and violent procedures. In democratic systems it often acts alongside political parties. Some groups are outposts of political parties which use them to extend their influence. Through youth movements, women's groups, cultural, sport and co-operative societies under their control, parties can reach people who would reject the idea of direct membership. Inversely, some parties are only supplementary organizations of pressure groups: a particular Conservative party may be the political instrument of employers' organizations and closely controlled by them; the British Labour party is primarily the offshoot of the trade unions.

The notion of pressure groups has the advantage of being general, and allows a comparative study of political strife in democratic and authoritarian systems, in nations both modern and ancient. Certainly the above description deals mostly with pressure groups in modern western countries, but it is simple to transpose it to other countries. In particular, it is equally applicable to movements, associations and private groups, and other organizations existing within the state. The state is not the hierarchical and centralized organization depicted by classical lawyers. In the U.S.A. today it is depicted rather as a group of decision-centres overlapping with private organizations in such a way that the boundary between the two is scarcely discernible. But in the Soviet Union also there exists a multiplicity of centres of decision, though in another form. Administrative bodies, ministries, public enterprises and local collectives there play the part of pressure groups in relation to the central power, parliament, or other decision-centres. Political combat is made up not only of the battle for power, but also includes battles between the powers, because power is never totally unified.

# 3. Political Conflict: Weapons

Various types of weapon are used by the men and organizations who meet in political conflict. One or another will predominate according to the era, the type of society, the institutions, the culture and the conflicting classes or groups. But one kind of weapon is, in theory, ruled out: that is, weapons which imply the use of physical violence. The first aim of politics is to eliminate violence, to replace bloodshed by less brutal forms of struggle. Politics begins beyond the boundaries of war, civil or international. It is a form of combat, but it is also a restriction of combat. Later, when we examine more deeply this latter characteristic, we will see that it is never absolute: politics tends to eliminate violence, but never manages to do so entirely. In fact, weapons in the strict sense of the word, military arms, are never quite excluded from political strife. They must be studied first.

## PHYSICAL VIOLENCE

'The first man to be king was a successful soldier': this quip suggests that military weapons are the source of power, and that power depends primarily on them. In many human communities authority rests on physical violence. It is the strongest, at fisticuffs or with the knife, who is the leader among teddy-boys and criminal gangs, as well as in the playground. This element also enters into the domination of children by adults, of women by men. In the state, praetors, janissaries, gestapo, strong-arm men, soldiers and policemen are the buttresses of the rulers, whose palaces were originally fortresses designed to protect them, not against external enemies, but against their own people. Politics tends not so much to destroy the means of violence, military weapons, as to concentrate them in the hands of the government and to prevent their use by the citizens. The state is, in fact, characterized by this monopoly of constraint, which gives to the ruling class, party or faction a terrible power. An armed government amid an unarmed people means that the latter is at the mercy of the former. We will come back to this problem later. Suffice it to say here that a government monopoly leads to suppression of the use of violent weapons in political conflict, since only one of the sides has them.

Apart from their legitimate use by the state to maintain the authority of the government over the governed, military weapons are used in politics in three main cases. First, at a primitive stage of social development, when the state is still too weak to monopolize them for its own benefit. Then, armed factions can be seen fighting for power, and political organizations take the form of militia. Such phenomena can be seen in the ancient city-states, in Italian renaissance republics, and in some underdeveloped countries today. The Middle Ages offers other examples, in the feudal struggles. Similar situations can arise at a more advanced stage of political development if one of the parties is organized as a paramilitary formation, becomes powerful, and is not controlled by the state; then the opposing parties are forced to adopt the same methods and to take up arms, if they are not to be crushed. This kind of process occurred in Germany in the 1930s, alongside the growth of Hitlerism. In order to resist the Nazi militia, the Left-wing parties were obliged to form other militia (the Socialist Empire Banner, the Communist Red Front fighters).

Secondly, political conflict also takes on a military form when the opposition has no other means, when it has no other way of making itself heard, or when the means it is allowed to use are ineffective. Armed resistance to authority then usually develops in two stages: a phase of clandestine resistance, which we will describe later, and a phase of open rebellion, prepared for by the first phase. The two are not absolutely distinct. Open rebellion can manifest itself in two forms, as a brutal revolution, in which power is quickly taken over by the ex-opposition, or as a long civil war, in which clandestine resistance plays a great part. This second form is tending to replace the first because the state now has more highly developed means of constraint. In the past, when armies were relatively weak, it was fairly easy for the people to defeat them quickly. Today, the might of modern weapons, monopolized by the state, is such that popular revolt can destroy them only by protracted guerrilla warfare.

Political strife is settled by violence in a third situation, that is, when the military cease to serve the state and to be at the disposition of the rulers, and instead enter the struggle for power on their own account. In Rome in the third century A.D. the legions made and unmade emperors, giving the throne to one or another of their generals, frequently in exchange for his promise to hand out money and various advantages. A little later they would kill the emperor they had set up, and put another in his place. In Latin America, the Middle East, and elsewhere today, the military make and unmake governments. In the years 1958–62, France was not far from this type of situation. Sometimes different sections of the army will start to compete with each other in these struggles for power. In the Roman Empire there was sharp competition between praetorian guards and frontier garrisons, as well as between legions from the different provinces; these various factions would finally come face to face in bloody battle. In the Latin-American countries conflicts frequently occur between the army, the navy and the air force. In Algeria there was a clash in 1961 between professional soldiers and conscript regiments.

The fact that the army should thus set itself up as an independent political organization and cease to obey the government betrays profound disorganization in the state. Nevertheless, by its very nature, the army is always a danger to the state. Those with arms in their power are inclined to misuse them, paralleling the urge which makes anyone with authority tend to abuse it. Arms are the ultimate expression of power, the most decisive expression of it in the short term, the most immediately irresistible. Whoever holds a sword is naturally tempted to throw it on to the scales. Armed soldiers constitute a permanent danger to unarmed rulers and citizens. Efforts are made to lessen this danger, first by inculcating in army officers a sense of total obedience to the state, in all circumstances, whatever

be the form of the state and whoever be the rulers who represent it. Compulsory military service, which creates citizen-
soldiers, lessens the risks, too, by forming the army in the
image of the people. But the danger still persists. Rulers and
citizens must always be watchful of the armed forces. In
countries where there is a strong tradition of military *coups
d'état*, as in Latin America, the formation of popular militia is the
only way of preventing the military from dominating the state.

It is, however, rare for the army to seize power just on its
own account and to set up a purely technical dictatorship. Most
often it acts as the instrument of collective forces, and as such,
except for the difference in means used, its role then is identical
to that of political parties or pressure groups. Usually, the
military supports the privileged, minority classes, which need
guns, machine-guns and tanks in order to preserve their
domination over the exploited classes which threaten to over-
whelm them by sheer weight of numbers. In Latin America
military *coups* generally serve the interests of the great landowners or the upper middle class. Occasionally, however, the
army acts as a Left-wing political force. This was so in France
at the beginning of the nineteenth century, because the officers
whom the Revolution had produced were on the whole of
humble origin and were liberal in their opinions. Today, it is
the same in some developing countries where military colleges
provide for the gifted children of the working or lower middle
classes a means of rising in the social scale. The officer corps
tends therefore to represent these social groups in opposition
to the great feudal lords who hold political power. Military
plots and *coups d'état* tend to push aside the aristocracy in favour
of the lower middle or even the working class. Clear examples
of this can be seen in the case of Mustapha Kemal in Turkey, of
Nasser in Egypt, and in a certain number of military rebellions
in the Middle East and Latin America.

## MONEY

The 'money is all powerful' theme is a caricature of the political
reality; money has never been the only important factor. But

in many societies, and not only in capitalist societies, money does play an important part in power. Unlike military means, wealth cannot be used directly in political conflict: a regiment can itself seize power in the state; a banker cannot. In exceptional cases it is possible to buy a parliamentary seat: the 'rotten boroughs' of nineteenth-century England provide the type of this. A few senatorial seats were literally bought in this way in France during the Third and Fourth Republics. But such cases are rare. On the whole, wealth serves to obtain the means of gaining or keeping power. Money is used to buy weapons, consciences, newspapers, television broadcasts, propaganda, campaigns, politicians. In most cases, however, the wealthy seek not to exercise power themselves or to govern personally, but rather to put into power men they can trust and on whom they can bring pressure to bear.

The efficacity of money as a political weapon can be shown by the parallel development of the forms of wealth and the forms of authority. In agrarian societies, where exploitation of the land is the main source of wealth, political power is held by the landowning class. This produces aristocratic régimes, in which authority is linked to possession both of the land and of equestrian arms (cavalry), in which authority is both feudal and military. In industrial and commercial societies ownership of a factory, a store or a bank becomes the main foundation of wealth; then political power falls into the hands of the middle class. Needless to say, the change from an agrarian to a commercial or industrial society takes place gradually. In the latter type of society the role of wealth is more obvious, because money has a high place in the system of values. In the former its role is rather more hidden, because the aristocracy give pride of place to disinterested military values and affect to scorn riches. But this scorn is mainly directed against wealth that is acquired by commerce, trade and banking, and not against landed property, which is the main type of wealth in aristocratic societies. Aristocrats derive their political power from their great wealth as landowners rather than from their military function.

The advent of bourgeois societies in the nineteenth century

gave the people of the time the impression that henceforth power would be based on money, and that this was something new. The newly rich, gauche and parvenu, were replacing the old moneyed classes, who were more discreet and better bred. The aristocracy had based its power both on wealth and on arms, with the former mainly camouflaged by the latter, the mainspring of prestigious and heroic values. The middle classes, on the other hand, put forward a value-system based on wealth, and so openly admitted the source of their power, instead of disguising it. The aristocracy loved wealth, whether it came from land or from royal pensions, but they did not say so, at least in public. The middle classes shouted it from the roof-tops and were proud of the fact. Actually, one type of wealth was replacing another as the source of political power.

However, the development of the middle classes also parallels the development of liberal democratic ideas. Thus there appeared some contradiction between the officially stated political values and the value attached to money. The use of money as a political weapon was surely a breach of the legal equality of all citizens and an interference with the normal working of elections and parliament. It is noteworthy that efforts should have been made to disguise the part money played in political conflict: the financing of electoral campaigns and newspapers, for example, has always been done more or less secretly. In this respect nostalgia for aristocratic values, which were not entirely destroyed in Europe by the coming of capitalism, may have played a part; this could explain why the influence of money in politics is camouflaged less in the United States than in Europe, and why money has greater social prestige there. However, capitalist theories assert that in the last analysis the influence of money in politics is democratic. In a competitive régime, they say, everyone has the chance of acquiring wealth and of using it to influence politics. This is fundamentally what Guizot meant when he used the formula 'Get rich!' in reply to those who criticized the wealthy for monopolizing political power. A whole modern mythology has grown up round this idea, particularly in the United States, where there was very great social mobility in the nineteenth century, and Guizot's principle could be put into practice on a broad scale, in an emerging society where the weight of past achievement had not yet restricted the effective possibilities of competition.

This argument errs by omission. It does not take into account the accumulation of capital. Hereditary transmission of acquired wealth alters competition entirely, by taking away its democratic character. The power of money becomes to a large extent the power of birth, even if it is not the same originally. The further liberal societies develop, the more does getting rich depend on having capital, rather than on work. Even if one does not fully accept the Marxist theories of the absolute impoverishment of the proletariat, it is difficult to deny the existence of a relative impoverishment: the real share of the workers in the growth of the national income tends to diminish rather than to grow, while the owners of the means of production see their share increase; it is the latter who retain the power of money. The estrangement which results from this is political as well as economic: the transfer of the added value also deprives the worker of part of his influence over power, of some of his political arms.

### THE INFORMATION MEDIA

There is one area in which technical progress has particularly important political consequences, and that is the mass media of information. The invention of printing was one of the decisive factors in the Renaissance, the Reformation, and the growth of liberal ideas which culminated in the French Revolution. The development of newspapers in the nineteenth century contributed much to the growth of democracy. It was the Press which was first called the 'fourth power', to stress its political importance. Today, the spoken Press (radio) and the visual Press (television and illustrated weeklies) have as much influence as the written Press, and they, too, are part of the 'fourth power'. The name 'mass media' is now generally given to these modern techniques of spreading news and ideas. They are a very powerful political weapon.

In autocratic régimes the mass media are generally a state monopoly and are used to spread the official propaganda which, alongside the police, is the principal foundation of power. The aim of this propaganda is to obtain unanimous support for the government from all the citizens. It is directed, at least to all appearances, towards the unity of the whole nation, and not towards class war between the social categories which compose the nation. It is not a weapon in the armoury of political warfare; at least, the state claims that it is not. (In fact, the state is usually ruled by one class or one social group, which uses propaganda to destroy the influence of the other classes or groups.) It is a means of social integration or pseudo-integration, and will be studied as such in the next chapter.

In democratic régimes, on the contrary, the state does not have a monopoly of the mass media. At least some of them are organized as private enterprises on a capitalist basis, i.e. with income balancing expenditure. Pluralism in the mass media is part of the pluralism of the régime, along with pluralism of political parties. Moreover, party pluralism would be illusory and merely formal were it not accompanied by pluralism of the mass media. Nevertheless, there are very few democratic countries where (as in the U.S.A.) the state has control of no medium. Television is nearly everywhere organized as a public service, in part at least. The same is true, though rather less frequently, of radio, and less frequently still of the cinema. Only the written Press is entirely independent of governments, though the latter do have means of applying pressure to it.

The degree of state control reflects the date when the medium was invented: the oldest (the written Press) being more independent than the more modern (radio, followed by television). This fact is disquieting, both because it indicates how government is tending more and more to restrict the liberty of the citizen and because the most modern media are gradually becoming the most influential. Television is of capital importance in electoral campaigns, both in underdeveloped countries, where education is far from widespread, and in highly developed countries where every home has its set. However, state control of the mass media is not always harmful.

Here as elsewhere, free enterprise should not be confused with true liberty.

The main advantage of free enterprise in this field is that it ensures expression of a variety of opinions. If one wants to hear the conflicting arguments, one can do so simply by buying several newspapers or switching to a private radio or television station. By reading the *Telegraph*, the *Guardian* and the *Sun* every day the Englishman can learn all the arguments put forward from various sides, and through them can form his own opinion. All these and other newspapers, just like those in authoritarian régimes, try to impose their point of view, by similar means. But their very co-existence prevents them from fulfilling this aim. Pluralism makes them set a limit to untruth, whereas when no one can contradict, and the truth cannot be known, it is easy to lie. It is much more difficult when other voices can be raised to rectify matters. It is very difficult to hide the truth in an information system based on free enterprise and competition. We should not, however, exaggerate the variety that results from such a system: just as in the U.S.S.R. it is impossible to find a newspaper that defends capitalism, so in the U.S.A. it is impossible to find one that defends Communism.

Free enterprise is not freedom, first of all because it is based on money. In law anyone can found a newspaper; but in fact one would need about three thousand million old francs to start a daily paper in Paris. One can write what one likes in an existing paper, provided the board of directors, which owns the paper, does not object. The mass media are free where the state is concerned, but not from the financial point of view. The power to dispense information resides with the economic powers. Doubtless, large popular parties or powerful trade unions can find the capital needed to found a newspaper or even to set up a radio station, but experience shows that they have the greatest difficulty in supporting these enterprises.

For today the domination of news by money is not so much a matter of ownership as of the conditions of exploitation of the enterprise. The mass media of information are made available to the public for nothing (radio, television) or sold below their cost (newspapers). Every copy of a daily paper is worth at least twice the price it is sold at; sometimes the difference is much greater. It is advertising that makes up the deficit, just as it finances private radio and television programmes. The masters of modern news services are the advertisers, which in reality means the advertising agencies. These capitalist firms, whose clients are themselves capitalist firms, are obviously not inclined to favour anti-capitalist ideas; they incline rather to guide the manna of advertisement towards conservatism.

But this phenomenon is relatively unimportant in comparison with the basic fact that the mass media are becoming little more than supporting programmes for advertisements. Radio programmes, television shows, editorials, newspaper articles and news bulletins are all being used to attract as large a public as possible for the advertising, which forms the foundation of capitalist information. Making money is the aim of news services, just as it is the aim of other private enterprises. To make money one needs as much publicity as possible. To obtain maximum publicity the maximum number of readers, listeners and viewers is necessary. The editorial sugar which surrounds the advertising pill must therefore be made palatable to as large a number of people as possible. This leads to a whole series of consequences.

Every day the newspaper kiosk, or the radio or television station, must attract as large a crowd as possible. A sensational event sends the number of readers, listeners and viewers soaring, and increases profits. The problem then is to find a sensational event every day, with the result that news items of no real interest are exaggerated, provided there is something picturesque about them. If necessary, quite anodine matters will be blown up and given large front-page headlines, which boost sales. This sociological law of the system leads first of all to exaggeration of sex crimes, famous love affairs and various scandals. Politically, it leads to problems being dramatized in order to arouse interest in them; the hatred or enthusiasm of nations is artificially stimulated so that more copies of a newspaper may be sold.

The 'personalization of power' which has been talked about

so much in the last few years is in part a result of this process. The public at large is not very interested in abstract ideas and doctrines, which do not adapt very well to headlines and illustration. All is changed, if these ideas are made incarnate in one man, who is turned into a hero. The theatre and the cinema have shown that 'stars', created by the modern media, are good box-office. In politics the same system can pay. So the Press, the illustrated weeklies, the radio and television start creating political heroes, mainly prefabricated and mythical, who will attract the public all the more because it has a feeling of familiarity with them. These 'heroes' naturally make use of their fabricated popularity in politics.

Further, the basic rule for getting as wide an audience as possible is not to offend anyone's opinions. So Press, radio and television try for all they are worth to avoid controversial, important or dangerous topics. To express an opinion about such topics would be likely to offend part of the public and drive it away. If it is absolutely necessary to mention them because they are highly topical, it must be done with many precautions, by trying to satisfy everyone, that is, by avoiding the heart of the matter, treating it from an angle, distracting attention. Citizens are therefore treated as if they were somewhat backward children, unable to face up to difficulties. In this way, instead of being prepared to meet their responsibilities, people are on the contrary diverted from them.

However, if public opinion seems ready to grow excited one way or another, then it pays to fall in step and to exaggerate that side of the matter, to howl with the wolves, and louder than them. A capitalist news service tends to be a soporific when things are normal, instead of keeping people awake; it stimulates them when they are already excited, instead of tranquillizing them. Examples of this second attitude can be seen, among others, in the American anti-Communist hysteria of 1953, at the time of Macarthyism; in the ardent belligerence of autumn 1961; and in the rush to build private fall-out shelters. Capitalist news services do exactly the opposite of what should be done by an information system which seeks the general interest.

Furthermore, it pays better to defend traditional values, established systems and existing institutions, so offending no one, than to express critical and reformist attitudes. People are naturally conservative, they are naturally afraid of anything new. If the theme of progress has often to be dealt with because it is fashionable, it will be treated in an abstract, distant manner, vague enough not to disturb anyone whose situation it could threaten. It will be admitted that everything evolves, but there will be no details about what must change. Existing abuses will never be attacked, if such attacks shock average opinion, or if they clash with the advertisers' interests. Courting average opinion leads to conservatism.

Finally, although modern techniques make it possible for the elements of a real culture to be universally diffused, the capitalist information system leads to what could be called the 'cretinization' of the public. It tends to confine people in an infantile world at a very low intellectual level. A typical example of this process is the development of romantic myths, destined to provide sensational news during the 'silly season', like sea-serpents in the heroic age. Kings, queens, princes, princesses and other such pseudo-great provide good topics, with the pomp of their clothes and their palaces, and the vague memories of history they evoke. The public revels in romances, and is enthralled by these half-legendary tales, like overgrown children with a fairy story. So Margaret, Farah Dibah, Soraya and Paola are sentenced, like Tintin, to endlessly storm-tossed lives, which fill the pockets of the Press, radio and T.V. entrepreneurs.

Many other techniques of 'cretinization' of the public could be quoted. The cinema and sport offer many examples of it. By these various means the public is plunged into an unreal, artificial, phantasmagoric and puerile atmosphere, and so distracted from real problems. The victim of capitalist information media is ill prepared to fulfil his civic duties. The Communists say that this is a conscious process, that the capitalists deliberately use love stories, royal romances and sporting and cinema adventures in order to make the masses forget that they are being exploited and to paralyse their will to rebel. Objectively, the news services in liberal régimes tend to produce this result.

Subjectively, it does not seem to be the result of a conscious process, deliberately willed, but of the process of pleasing the customer.

Variety in the media of information, which is the only real justification for the system, tends to destroy itself. On the one hand, technical advance makes it necessary to use means which are increasingly complex, and so increasingly costly, and which can therefore only be afforded by giant enterprises. On the other hand, advertising tends in particular to use the information media which reach great numbers of consumers; it does not pay to disperse it over a crowd of secondary newspapers or unimportant radio and television stations. There is therefore a tendency for news services to be concentrated. The little nineteenth- or early twentieth-century newspapers, which were centres of real independence and diversity, can no longer survive. Newspapers are becoming fewer in number, and bigger in size. The Press is being concentrated in a few hands. In recent years this phenomenon has been particularly marked in Great Britain, where it has received considerable attention. It is, however, a general phenomenon. In France, for example, the local Press is monopolized nearly everywhere by one or two papers. In radio and television, moreover, concentration is necessary because of the small number of wavelengths available to each country. Thus pluralism and diversity are gradually disappearing to the benefit of a few very large firms who wield within the state an enormous and essentially non-democratic power.

The picture we have just outlined is perhaps too pessimistic. It describes the natural tendencies of information media in a free enterprise system. They are restrained or counterbalanced by various elements, which could be developed. One remedy is to have a capitalist and a Socialist information system coexisting within the state, mutually correcting each other. In practice, in many western countries, the Press is organized on a capitalist basis, while radio and television are controlled by the state or by a public body. Being free of the slavery of advertising and the primacy of money-making, radio and T.V. can do educational work and compensate for the 'cretinization' effects of the capitalist information media. Pluralism will prevent them from putting out authoritarian propaganda, as a free Press exists side by side with them. Original kinds of pluralism can even be introduced into state-controlled radio and television, giving the citizens the chance to hear the different conflicting arguments. Capitalist pluralism is largely an illusion: few people buy several newspapers; most people only read one, and so have only a partial view of things. On the contrary real pluralism is achieved on radio and television, in a truly democratic spirit, by panels of journalists or personalities of different opinions. The allocation during election campaigns of equal amounts of broadcasting time to the different parties achieves a similar authentic pluralism.

Co-existence of the two systems usually give good results. In some countries, for example Great Britain and Canada, radio and television do remarkable work in educating the citizens, reinforcing the democratic institutions. But abuses are possible. Governments may tend to use radio and television for their own propaganda as happens in authoritarian states. A good example of this is the development of French broadcasting in the last few years. Its general level is still higher than that of private radio and television of the American type, but socially and politically it can be criticized in every way.

Occasionally one finds in capitalist countries some original kind of institution which aims to give really independent information, unfettered by either the state or capitalist needs. Some ensure the personal freedom of the journalist, like the 'conscience clause' which allows him to refuse to write what he does not believe, and even to leave the newspaper with a sizeable indemnity. In practice it is not always easy to invoke this clause, and advancement within the profession presupposes that it is not invoked. Some journalists manage, too, to make a name for themselves, and to create a public demand for it; they are then in a situation strong enough to allow them to write more or less what they want. Walter Lippman in the U.S.A. is a typical example of this. There are others, though they are not common in any country.

Of much greater importance is the situation of some independent newspapers like *The Times*, *Le Monde* and the *New York Times*. Their independence is of varied origin. Sometimes it derives from ancestral reputation, as in the case of *The Times*. With *Le Monde* it results from the 1944 provisional constitution. All newspapers which had appeared during the occupation were seized, and management of them put into the hands of groups of uncommitted journalists. One by one, the new papers fell back into the clutches of financial groups, with the exception of *Le Monde*, which never had a deficit; on the contrary, the regular profits it made allowed the ex-proprietors to be indemnified. Thus the freedom of the team set up in 1944, and enlarged since then, never met any obstacles; a tradition was created and a spirit developed, helped by the personality of a high-principled and respected editor.

The independence of papers like *The Times* and *Le Monde* now seems well established, and the quality of their readers puts them in a special situation with regard to advertising. Other papers need very high circulation figures if the business is to pay, which leads to more and more concentration. These 'top people's papers', on the contrary, can impose high advertising tariffs in comparison with their medium circulation figures, because of the quality of their readers. Everyone of any importance, the whole *élite* of the nation, reads *The Times* in Great Britain, *Le Monde* in France. A certain type of advertising needs to reach precisely this category of people, and can therefore not do without these newspapers. But their independence is not shared by the mass-circulation papers: is the liberty of the Press, then, restricted to a few? It is possible that in developed countries the general rise in the level of culture will gradually close the gap between the information of the masses and the information of the few, with the former progressively falling into line with the latter. There are signs that point towards this possibility: the standard of mass information does seem to be rising slowly. However, even from the most optimistic point of view, this would be a very long-term development.

It can be speeded up by establishing other centres of resistance. Organizing radio and television as public services independent of the state, directed by administrative boards composed of representatives of journalists, of the listening and viewing public and of outstanding people of independent opinion, seems very effective in this respect. The B.B.C. is organized in this way, and both its independence and its cultural level are remarkable. For a long time there has been talk of adopting a similar constitution for the French R.T.F., and some detailed plans have been worked out, but neither governments nor parliamentarians have yet agreed to put them into effect. Some people wonder whether that is not the sole way of organizing a really independent information service, even in the sphere of the Press. One day, perhaps, the French 1944 constitution will appear as a precursor.

### NUMBERS AND COLLECTIVE ORGANIZATION

For thousands of years, the struggle for power took place within a limited circle which excluded the mass of the population. Their low standard of living kept them at a poor level of intellectual development, which in turn prevented them from becoming aware of their strength, and from organizing their forces accordingly; moreover, strict surveillance by the powerful and their men-at-arms prevented any effort to do so. Sometimes, at very exceptional moments, when the degree of enslavement, poverty and oppression became too marked, the masses would break into the political arena like large clumsy animals, destroying all as they went, but incapable of rebuilding. So at different times there were slaves' revolts, peasants' risings, urban riots. Atrocious repression, equal in intensity to the fear the privileged class had felt, would for a long time to come kill any renewed desire to revolt. After the defeat of Spartacus, the first hero of a popular revolt to be remembered by history, sixty thousand slaves were massacred in Lucania, and six thousand were crucified along the Appian Way.

Numbers became an effective political weapon when a rise in the general standard of living made it possible for the masses to emerge from their long night and to enter the struggle for power. The theories that the bourgeoisie had developed in order to wage its own war on the aristocracy helped this evolution. In order to combat the hereditary transmission of power and privilege, which it found hampering, the bourgeoisie proclaimed the legal equality of all men and the sovereignty of the people; logically, this principle led to universal suffrage, that is, to arbitration by numbers. Nineteenth-century Liberals attempted by various means (limited franchise, inegalitarian suffrage) to slow down this development or to limit its consequences. Using the power money has over the information and propaganda media in a capitalist régime, they tried to influence the people and make the weapon of numbers ineffective.

The power of propaganda in political conflict cannot be denied. Support from the popular Press and television often decides the result of elections. A campaign run on lines similar to those of commercial sales drives has more chance of success than one run on classical lines. In 1960 the Liberal party was victorious in Quebec Province because of such methods, which are used on a large scale in the U.S.A. and are beginning to be widely used in Europe. But these methods are expensive. The political power of propaganda amounts finally to the political power of money, in western democracies. (Elsewhere propaganda is a state monopoly and is used to achieve political integration; we will come back to this aspect of the problem.) Legal regulations – limitation of expenditure, or reimbursement by the state – are hardly effective. Through propaganda the power of money tends to defeat the power of numbers.

The latter may regain momentum through the techniques of mass organization. The perfecting of processes of social organization by which vast numbers of people can be grouped, educated politically, their energies harnessed, their activity channelled and given direction, has created some highly effective political instruments. The techniques developed at the end of the nineteenth century and used by mass parties and workers' unions, served as models. They are still being used. The Communist parties have perfected them: one of the factors in their great power is undoubtedly the superiority of their organizational system. There is no doubt that these techniques present certain dangers, that they make it possible to 'manipulate' members of the organization to some extent, and that they contribute to bureaucratic phenomena. But the fact remains that without them numbers would be outweighed by money in the western democracies.

CONCENTRATION OR DISPERSION OF WEAPONS

The foregoing analyses show that political weapons are sometimes concentrated, and sometimes dispersed. Two types of society can be defined by this distinction. In one type all political weapons, or at least all the essential ones, are in the hands of a single class or a single social group. In the other type the fundamental weapons are spread among several classes or several social categories. In feudal and monarchic societies, for example, the basic weapons of the age (military means and landed property) were concentrated in the hands of the aristocracy. During the monarchy of Louis-Philippe or under the Second Empire in France, and in the U.S.A. before 1939, the middle classes in their turn controlled the main weapons of power, that is money and military formations, which were widely used to put down workers' revolts (e.g. the Lyons silk-workers, the 'June Days' of 1848). In the Stalinist state the ruling group had control over all the means of mass organization and the whole structure of collective grouping, which are essential political weapons in a Socialist state. Those are a few examples of monopoly situations.

On the contrary, in some ancient city-states at a particular moment in their development, in Italian and Flemish renaissance republics, in England under Cromwell, and in France under the absolute monarchy, the aristocracy controlled part of the wealth, and the bourgeoisie controlled another, sometimes greater part of it, while military weapons were mainly in the hands of the former, but passed sometimes to the latter; this was a pluralist situation. Present-day western societies offer another example. On the one hand, capitalists hold wealth, which they use for propaganda; they thus control important factors in political power. On the other hand, wage-earners have developed large mass organizations (people's parties and trade unions), which are also able to use forms of propaganda, and which constitute other important factors in political power. Some means of propaganda and information are in the hands of intellectuals and university people. Political weapons are over-all fairly widely dispersed.

In the West this form of pluralism tends to be considered as an essential means of ensuring the freedom of the citizen and of achieving democracy. This dispersion (or concentration) of political weapons is, moreover, largely confused with plurality (or unity) of 'decision centres', which is a mistake. The plurality or unity of decision centres has to do with the organization of the state, the structure of political power: plurality is achieved by the separation of powers, dear to Locke, Montesquieu and some other thinkers; by territorial decentralization; by the independence of public services and undertakings; by establishing independent administrative bodies, and so on. The dispersion or concentration of political weapons concerns the struggle for power and the situation of the various classes or social groups in this struggle. The two things are often connected: plurality of decision centres sometimes reflects the dispersion of political weapons, which leads to power being shared between the different classes or social groups. But despite everything they are independent of each other. Plurality of decision centres can exist, for example, in a Socialist régime, as in Yugoslavia, by decentralization in particular, quite independently of the dispersion of political weapons.

Pluralist theories about this dispersion cannot be accepted without reservation. First, in liberal democracies pluralism of this kind is still very inegalitarian. Certainly money is no longer the only political weapon; the mass parties, the trade unions and other mass organizations are effective, too, often highly so. But they do not counterbalance the influence of wealth. In western societies to-day money is still the strongest political weapon. This means that on the whole people with money influence the making of fundamental decisions. The other factors in political power may carry the day in some secondary decision, and affect yet another, but only in exceptional cases can they decide a fundamental issue. However, there is greater or less inequality depending on the country: it is very marked in the U.S.A. and less so in France. To some extent it is diminishing.

Furthermore, dispersion of political arms does not always bring about a strengthening of democracy. It can also lead to dictatorship. A social class which has hitherto been dominant, and which now sees some political weapons being stolen from it by another class, may have recourse to violence in order to avoid losing power completely or having to share it. The rising class may use the same technique, to accelerate the elimination of the old dominant class. In history the main epidemics of dictatorship usually coincide with situations in which political weapons were evenly dispersed among rival social groups. This was true of the ancient city-states, of Europe during the Renaissance and the eighteenth century, and again during the nineteenth century when the rise of the bourgeoisies divided power between them and the hitherto dominant aristocracies. Similarly, when the rule of wealth appeared to be seriously threatened within 'western pluralism', Fascism sprang up. The development of democracy is favoured, not so much by the balance of rival social forces with political weapons dispersed among them, but rather by the weakening of antagonisms.

# 4. Political Strategy

In political conflict, as in all complex battles, each side acts according to a preconceived plan, worked out in more or less detail, which takes account not only of its own moves but of the enemy's counter-moves and how to meet them. This plan of campaign constitutes a strategy, and the different elements of which it is composed (moves against the enemy and counter-attacks) are tactics. Analysis of political strategy has not yet made much progress, except in international relations and trade-union struggles. In other fields study has been mainly restricted to the conflict surrounding particular decisions. In the last few years there has been an attempt to apply mathematical methods in this analysis, using the theories of 'battle games' and the techniques of operational calculus. The findings of this research are interesting and valid, in a limited field. Here we shall consider another point of view, the overall strategies of political conflict; but at this level only a few brief outlines can be given.

## RIGHT AND LEFT, REFORMISM AND REVOLUTION

The form which political conflict takes varies according to the system. In the two-party system it takes the form of a duel, whereas in the multi-party system there are several opponents, all able to combine in various ways. The distinction between Right and Left allows us to compare the two situations and establish a fairly precise classification of political strategies in pluralist democracies. Reduced to its simplest terms and its basic elements, political conflict is the opposition between those who are more or less satisfied with the existing social order and who wish to preserve it and those whom this order does not suit and who wish to change it. The former constitute the 'Right' and the latter the 'Left' in the widest sense of these terms, deliberately bereft of any precise historical reference. We are not concerned here with the reasons for the satisfaction of one group and the dissatisfaction of another, and the ways in which these find expression. We simply state the proposition that in all social groups and communities there are the satisfied and the dissatisfied: however, this premiss is not an arbitrary assumption but a fact of experience. Right and Left are thus defined by their aims: to preserve the existing order, or to replace it. However, there are different means of attempting to achieve these ends, and each constitutes a particular type of strategy.

In Left-wing parties the distinction between different strategies has been established for some time. The existing order can be overthrown brutally and completely by a single '*coup*', and a whole new order substituted just as brutally: this is the revolutionary method. Or the old order can be destroyed progressively, piece by piece, each being replaced at every stage by an element of the new order: this is reformism. In Socialist parties there were at the beginning of the twentieth century many violent disputes between reformists and revolutionaries, and they died down only when Socialist parties ceased as a whole to be entirely revolutionary. Inversely, when Communist parties were on the whole revolutionary this problem did not exist; but it is beginning to arise in western European Communism, which exists in societies where revolution seems neither possible nor desirable; and the question will probably assume greater importance in the next few years.

The discussion between reformists and revolutionaries is often distorted by emotional considerations, since revolution is the long-standing dream of French Socialists and of most Communists, in whose eyes reformism is equivalent to betrayal of their aims. Speaking rationally, supporters of revolution declare that reformism is an illusion, because the old order can never be destroyed piece by piece. They state that only minor elements can be changed by this method, for as soon as the essential is under attack the supporters of the old régime react with violence, and since these supporters hold the key positions in the régime they win in the end. Without taking sides in this debate we may note that two strategies can be used to change the existing order, reformism òr revolution, and that some parties follow the former and others the latter.

Two parallel attitudes correspond on the Right wing to those called reformism and revolution on the Left. The distinction between them is less well known, has not been clearly formulated so frequently and has given rise to less discussion. But it has been of great practical importance, perhaps even more than the Left-wing distinction, because in practice it has prompted the actions of many Conservative parties. To maintain the existing order, one can cling to it in its entirety and refuse to change anything, opposing all reform and all amendment, however small; alternatively, realizing that some change is inevitable, one can agree to give way over a few details in order to preserve the essential; to prevent, so to speak, the fire from spreading. The first attitude' corresponds on the Right wing to the revolutionary theory of the Left and is the line taken by extreme Conservatives and Fascists; the second corresponds to the reformist theory of the Left and is characteristic of moderate Conservatives: the best example is Disraeli's policy in England in the nineteenth century.

This analysis leads us to express the twofold opposition of Right and Left in four types of basic political strategy, defined both by their ends and their means: extreme Right, moderate Right; reformist Left and revolutionary Left. Oppositions and alliances between these basic tendencies differ according to the country and the time. Thus we can distinguish two main categories of situation: the British type of situation and the French type. In Great Britain the moderates and extremists of each side usually unite to form a single organization, one on the Right, another on the Left: Conservative and Liberal parties in the nineteenth century, Conservative and Labour parties in the twentieth century. Thus political combat is dominated by the 'Right versus Left' strategy, which in France is called a division into 'two blocks'. Contrary to what might be expected, political differences are reduced by this tendency rather than increased.

Within each fraction the extremists have had, willingly or

unwillingly, to accept domination by the moderates. In inter-party competition, electoral victory belongs, as we have already said, to the party which attracts the marginal voters of the centre, who tip the scales towards the side for which they vote. To win, each party must appear to be moderate, and thus re-formists prevail over revolutionaries on the Left, and gradual-ists prevail over ultra-Conservatives on the right. The perma-nent, stable and organic links which bind extremists and moderates together on each side lead the former to moderate their extremism, so to speak, through contact with the latter, whereas isolation would tend to increase their extremism. The fact that they are associated in governmental and parliamentary responsibility, at least indirectly, within the framework of a large party, has the same effect. Strangely enough, the coagula-tion of political tendencies into two opposing 'blocks', one on the Right, the other on the Left, has the result of driving both towards the centre.

In France the political tradition is totally different, in spite of what some critics have said. The idea that French political life has been dominated since 1789 by a Right-Left conflict does not correspond completely to the facts. The real Right (i.e. extremists and moderates taken together) has very rarely been in power: between 1814 and 1830 with breaks; in 1871, 1919 and 1940 for short periods. The Left, similarly defined, has held power for an even shorter time in all: in 1793–4, February to May 1848, 1936–7, 1944–7. Most of the time the government has been in the hands of centre party coalitions, uniting reform-ist Left and moderate Right, while the extremists – ultra-Con-servatives and revolutionary Left – were reduced to the role of opposition or occasional support. The real battle lies between the two centres, fighting for control within the coalition. The pendulum does not really swing between Right and Left, but only between centre Right and centre Left; the political battle is ruled by a centre-party strategy.

The coalition of moderate Conservatives and Left-wing reformists has a natural basis. They both share an area of agree-ment in that they accept reform. For Conservatives it is an un-satisfactory expedient which must be practised as little as possible, while for the moderate Left it is a positive good to be developed. Final objectives and ulterior motives are another matter, but in the field of practical politics collaboration is possible to a certain extent: they can 'go part of the way together'. This being so, it is none the less true that because each side within the centre-party alliance is trying to gain the strongest position, it is led to rely to some extent on its corresponding extremist party. The ties between reformist and revolutionary Left are never entirely severed, because the former seeks the support of the latter in its attempt to dominate the centre coalition: the pre-1914 'Bloc des Gauches' offers quite a good example of this situation. In the same way, the moderate Right stays in contact with the ultra-Conservatives for the same reason: broad-based coalitions and the government of National Union under the Third French Republic illustrate this process.

Thus reduced to the role of occasional support, deprived of all real influence over the government, isolated within separate organizations, extremist parties are naturally inclined to become more extremist. Their members have a feeling of estrangement which neither the Leftist Labour member nor the Right-wing Conservative feels in Great Britain. The pragmatic day-to-day and down-to-earth aspect of centre-party politics, which are unrelated to particular principles – because the principles of both halves of the centre differ – arouses distrust and loathing in the extremists. This tends towards a dissociation between idealist policies, pure but inapplicable, and concrete policies, involving disregard for principle even more than compromise of principle. The two extremes have only one means of opposing this: to unite against the centre-party alliance, since the support demanded of them in order to tip the balance of the alliance in one direction rather than the other involves them in compromise without giving them any real political influence. However, coalition between the revolutionary Left and Right-wing ultra-Conservatives can only be negative: it can prevent the centre from governing but cannot replace it. If on joining forces the extremists are stronger than the centre parties, government becomes impossible: such was the situation in the Weimar Republic during its last years.

## CAMOUFLAGE

Reformism and revolution, centralism and extremism are strategies that can be adopted only in a pluralist democracy. By contrast, there is one strategic device which is used in all political régimes, even the monolithic and autocratic: this is camouflage. It consists in concealing the aims and real motives of political action behind pseudo-aims and pseudo-motives which are more popular and which therefore benefit from wider support in public opinion. Although it has naturally been much developed in democracies, where public opinion plays an important part, camouflage also exists in autocracies, which cannot manage without some public support. It is used by individuals, parties and pressure groups alike in their attempts to gain or influence power. It is also used by authority to secure the obedience of citizens, as we shall see in the next chapter.

Camouflage assumes many different forms. The most common is to disguise a less avowable objective behind one that is more avowable in relation to the scheme of values of the society in question. In the West this technique is used on a grand scale to protect capitalist interests. Instead of saying that private ownership of the means of production assures them substantial profits, owners allege that it is necessary to ensure the individual freedom of the citizens. They talk less of private enterprise than of 'free enterprise', less of property than of liberty (economic liberty is what they mean). Liberal parties play on the double meaning of the word 'liberty', making its political prestige reflect upon its economic aspects. When the state imposes price limits on shopkeepers they do not admit that their resistance is aimed at retaining a large profit margin; they protest in the name of freedom against government intervention in the economy. They accuse the state of 'controlling', of 'interfering', and of 'planning', all terms that a large section of the population dislikes.

Another method of camouflage is to appeal to values. We have seen the importance of the conceptions of Good and Evil, Justice and Injustice; in short, the importance of value-systems in politics. Value-judgements are made both within the structure of the whole society, according to a set of values common to all members – national values in the context of the state – and within the framework of various conflicting classes or categories, according to value-systems particular to each one and expressed in different ideologies. Values can be used as camouflage in various ways. First, each class or each party may try to conceal what is particular to itself and to identify itself with the national set of values, hiding its own aims behind the values common to society as a whole. Each of them accuses the opponent of being partisan and affirms that he himself is concerned for the nation; the nation is identified with oneself; other people represent sectional interests.

Each partisan set of values and each particular ideology can also be used as camouflage, internal or external. There is always a gap between the values we declare and those that we really practise. The image that a party, class or group presents of itself is an idealized image, like that of a product glamorized by publicity; idealization is a means of attracting the client or the party member, of fighting the rival or opponent who also practises the same kind of idealization. Internally, the degree of loyalty to the set of values varies. The picture of agitators using great ideas to appeal to the crowd is only partially true, though it is the strategy of certain politicians. In parties with a strong ideology, on the other hand, loyalty is usually more complete at the top than at the bottom; religions in which the clergy have less faith than the laity have little hold. Value-systems are also methods of self-justification, corresponding to self-camouflage; every ideology tends to give to its faithful an enhanced image of themselves which they can contemplate with satisfaction. Camouflage is often partly unconscious.

Another technique of camouflage is to persuade the mass of the population that their interests are involved, when, in fact, the question only concerns the particular interests of a minority. The French settlers who would have been ruined by the independence of Algeria (and who, in fact, were ruined) justified the continuation of the war by the argument that Algeria was a very important customer for metropolitan France and that its loss would severely compromise the whole of the French

P.—F

economy. Another common device used for camouflage takes the form of the 'bogy'. An enemy is invented, or the importance of a real enemy is exaggerated, and the necessity to defend oneself against him justifies measures really taken in the interests of the ruling classes. The attention of the traveller is distracted by crying 'Wolf' and his luggage is stolen while he is thinking only of how he can protect himself against the animal.

In this connection the bogy of Communism plays a very great part in most western countries. In fact, 'Sovietization' presents very little danger, but public opinion, with a very vivid memory of the establishment of People's Democracies in eastern Europe between 1945 and 1948, does not realize this. Although it is an illusion, the 'Red peril' is still feared by many people and can therefore be invoked to distract attention from other phenomena: economic exploitation, attempts to set up a dictatorship and so on. A strategic device employed by all governments for centuries past is to evoke the external enemy in order to weaken the opposition and force it to rally to the government's support. Taken to extremes, this device may lead to the actual waging of war in order to avoid excessively violent internal struggles. The war between Algeria and Morocco in October 1963 illustrates this age-old process.

The question arises whether camouflage is used more or less according to the level of technical development of societies. There is a theory that it would reach its maximum in an intermediate phase between under- and overdevelopment. In primitive societies the mass of the population, undernourished, illiterate and oppressed, is in practice excluded from the political struggle, which is carried on within a closed circle, between professionals or potentates. Camouflage is useless, because it would be immediately obvious to everyone. 'Don't teach your grandmother to suck eggs', says the proverb. In this case, all the participants in political combat are 'grandmothers'. They are also not unlike those augurs of antiquity, unable to look at one another without laughing because they all knew that they were lying. On the other hand, in a highly evolved society, where the mass of the population has the benefit of a widespread culture, where the development of the social sciences has revealed the techniques of camouflage, it becomes similarly ineffective, since the whole population is as expert as the small political *élite* of primitive societies. Each party and each group spends its time destroying the opponent's camouflage. To sum up, by this theory camouflage would be a characteristic of 'the intermediate phase' which began in western societies with the French Revolution, and which is gradually disappearing. During this period the mass participates in political conflict; it cannot be excluded, but it is insufficiently aware of the problems and so embarrassing features can be camouflaged.

These theories cannot be accepted without reservation. In primitive societies the small *élite* group is not so expert that camouflage is useless. In highly developed societies human credulity is still great enough to leave room for camouflage, especially since people do not learn enough about their opponent's point of view, which could open their eyes; and since the mass media of information tend to use other methods of camouflage, of the soothing, insipid and sweetening type; and finally since camouflage is not only a process of conscious lying, but in part a way of hiding from oneself a truth which one does not want to face. In politics many people deliberately blind themselves and refuse to have their eyes opened. It is likely that camouflage will tend gradually to become more rare and more refined. That it will disappear entirely from political conflict is more doubtful.

# 5. The Area of Conflict

The political battle obviously enjoys a wider field of action in democratic régimes, where it can take place openly, than in autocratic régimes, where it has to remain hidden. Moreover, in democracies, and in democracies alone, it is possible to distinguish between the struggle *within* the régime and the struggle *about* the régime. To these main areas of the struggle, which we are going to examine now, others should be added. The distinction between political parties and pressure groups corresponds to the distinction between direct conflict to obtain or to share power and indirect conflict to try to influence power without it changing hands. In a democracy direct conflict is possible at every level. In an autocracy it is only possible at the lower levels: supreme power can only be fought for indirectly, via a process of intrigues which tend to give influence over the man in power, but without replacing him. Curiously enough, this situation is to some extent inverted in a democracy, as far as the lower rungs of power are concerned. They tend to be entrusted to an administrative body of professional civil servants, who have such guarantees of permanency that it is scarcely possible for the political authority to dismiss them, and the direct struggle to obtain posts is therefore limited. Their permanence limits the influence of changes in political teams at the top. In autocracies, on the contrary, the sovereign appoints to and dismisses from all subordinate posts as he pleases, so that these posts become the object of much broader direct competition. Someone who has the full confidence of the supreme head meets no obstacles; changes of favourite can thus have more far-reaching effects than electoral upheavals.

Finally, it should be noted that in a democracy the struggle for power has a cyclic character; in an autocracy it does not. The consequence of general elections is to transform the whole state into the prize of battle, at fixed and determined intervals. The whole government apparatus of coercion, its whole system of constraint, are thus given up by the vanquished into the hands of the victor until the latter, vanquished in his turn, hands it over to a new victor. General elections are therefore naturally the time when the decisive battle takes place. Political conflict thus follows a regular rhythm, passing through a phase of intense activity every four or five years, and decreasing in intensity during the intervening years. Autocratic régimes do not experience this systolic and diastolic movement, the cyclical ebb and flow. There the web of intrigue is woven and unwoven continually, and outbursts of feverish activity are due only to the circumstances of the moment.

## OPEN CONFLICT AND HIDDEN CONFLICT

Outside general elections, political conflict in a democracy retains the same open and ordered character. In parliamentary debates, in Press polemics, in meetings and discussions, at the meetings of parties, unions and various organizations, it takes place for all to see. Not that this public character is absolute: even in democracies, part of the political battle takes place in the dark, discreetly, secretly. For example it is difficult, if not impossible, to find out how elections are financed, or the effect private interventions have on the government or the administration. But these shady areas are limited, whereas in an autocracy everything is in the shadow. Debate, polemic, discussion and public meetings are usually forbidden. Officially, public opinion is unanimous in its admiration and love for and its fidelity towards the government. The nation is united, and knows no factions. There are political struggles, but they are hidden under a mask.

Democracies appear to be more divided than autocracies, but, in fact, it is simply that one can see the divisions more easily, because expression of them is allowed, and indeed encouraged. In monolithic régimes the divisions are perhaps deeper and more serious, like suppressed psychological conflicts which poison the personality and lead to neuroses. The

open political divisions in democracies are paralleled in autocracies either by camouflaged divisions or by clandestine
conflict. Camouflaging of opposition can take very varied
forms. Even the very institutions of the state can come to
represent certain groups or classes. Any administration, any
organization, any corporate body tends to defend its own point
of view against the others. These technical rivalries can turn
into political struggles, if a particular institution identifies itself
more or less with a particular social force, and another institution identifies with another force. In authoritarian régimes the
one and only trade union can be seen opposing the one and
only party, so that these two instruments of unanimity become
instruments of diversity. Universities, the army, the administrative bodies can also become means of opposition.

Political conflict can hide, too, behind the non-political
opposition which is allowed in some spheres. In the U.S.S.R.
the quarrel between ancients and moderns in literature, painting
and music is, in fact, a quarrel between Stalinists and the partisans of 'liberalization'. Non-political organizations can thus
become political in reality. Students' associations, youth
movements, even sporting societies like the pre-1914 Czech
sokols have filled this function in many authoritarian countries.
The further removed their official object is from politics, the
less they are watched by the authorities. There are three categories which are closer to politics, and so are more dangerous:
the churches and philosophical associations, economic and
social-type organizations, and literary institutions. (The human
problems that literature studies are inseparable from social and
political problems: characteristic examples can be seen in the
role of the Petöfi circle in Hungary before 1956, and that of
philosophic societies in France before 1789.)

These camouflaged struggles, in which political objectives
are masked by non-political objectives, should not be confused
with the camouflage technique used in open conflict in democracies, which consists in hiding one political aim behind
another political aim which is broader in scope, more avowable,
nobler than the first, and therefore more suited to winning the
approval of the public. Any class, any group, any social category

which is fighting, in fact, for its own interests, claims in some measure that it is fighting for the common interest of the whole society: for the country, for justice, for truth. It thus strengthens its position by causing doubt among its opponents. This sort of camouflage presupposes that the political battle is being waged openly, and that power is admitted to be the prize. On the contrary, the other kind of camouflage which we have described hides political aims behind non-political aims, because it is forbidden to fight for political aims.

But in democracies Conservative parties often succeed in giving 'politics' a pejorative sense; this, too, leads to political aims being masked by non-political appearances. Many organizations which are connected with a party – youth groups, women's associations, artistic, literary and sports clubs, etc. – hide in this way behind a non-political exterior. Many pressure groups which are, in fact, pursuing political objectives, pretend to have only economic, social, professional, philosophic or artistic aims. There is therefore no strict distinction between the two sorts of camouflage. The fact remains, however, that in a democracy both are possible, because opposition can openly admit to being political. In an autocracy only one sort is possible, the dissimulation of political aims beneath non-political appearances, because open political conflict is not allowed.

This sort of camouflage can only be used in relatively liberal autocracies. In absolutist and totalitarian régimes camouflaged opposition is only superficial. It represents a variety of clans and factions within the ruling groups, rather than opposition to the government. The real fight for power can only take place in secret, through clandestine organizations. Good examples of this are the resistance of German democrats under Hitler, and the resistance to German armies in European countries occupied by them between 1940 and 1945. They can be compared to the clandestine nationalist movements which started the revolt of colonies against colonial powers in recent years, and to the secret societies which likewise prompted the struggle for independence in Europe in the nineteenth and the early twentieth centuries.

In all authoritarian régimes there is a natural tendency for clandestine struggles of this type to spring into existence. They only mature if two conditions are fulfilled. First, a large part of the population must consider the régime intolerable. The support of the masses is indispensable to clandestine activity; without it, secret organizations can achieve nothing, beyond a few individual acts of violence of no importance. Further, there must be a reasonable chance of overthrowing the régime. If the régime seems to be unshakably established, only a few intransigants will have the courage to engage in clandestine activity. The masses will only support them if they see a chance of succeeding. That was why clandestine movements during the 1939–45 war, and nationalist organizations in the colonies after 1945, were able to develop. That was why, on the contrary, anti-Nazi movements in Hitler Germany before 1944 had so little influence; why O.A.S. terrorism failed in France in 1962; why Quebecan nationalist organizations achieved so little in Canada in 1963. In the last two cases the clandestine struggle took place in democratic régimes, where opposition had other means of expressing itself. In such circumstances only very small minority groups, whose tiny following deprives them of any hope of playing an electoral or parliamentary role, are involved. Alternatively, those involved may be prohibited parties or groups to whom all legal means of action is denied – a breach of democracy.

Clandestine movements are different from all other kinds of movement in their means of action and their structure. To secret meetings, whispered rumours, hidden propaganda, spreading anonymously printed tracts and brochures, they add violence: infiltration of the machinery of government, plots, assassination and terrorism. Their clandestine nature forces them all to adopt the same type of organization, which is found everywhere: in the church of the catacombs, in eastern secret societies, among the nineteenth-century carbonari, in the pre-1914 Serb Black Hand, in the 1930 Croat Oustachis, in European resistance movements during the last war, in Algerian nationalist organizations fighting for independence, in the French O.A.S. of 1961. What characterizes this type of organization is that it is broken up into basic groups that are as small as possible (three to five men, usually), and that there is rigid separation between these basic groups. At every level only the leader of each group is in contact with the level above. In this way, leakages are reduced to a minimum: if one member of the organization is arrested and tortured, he can only denounce very few people; this is true also if the police introduce spies into the movement.

## CONFLICT WITHIN THE RÉGIME AND ABOUT THE RÉGIME

Even in a democracy open political conflict is limited in scope. In this respect there is a basic distinction to be made between conflict *within* the régime and conflict *about* or *concerning* the régime. In Great Britain, Scandinavia and Holland all parties accept the existing régime based on liberal parliamentary democracy; none of them questions it: conflict is all *within* the régime. In France and Italy, on the other hand, small groups of Fascists on the extreme Right, and a large Communist party on the extreme Left, do not accept the parliamentary structure and pluralist democracy: the struggle is also *about* the régime. In the first-mentioned countries political warfare consists in each party trying to gain power in order to exercise it to the benefit of the social classes and categories it represents, while still maintaining the existing institutions and rules. These are therefore accepted by an almost unanimous consensus of opinion. In France and Italy some parties consider that the interests of the classes and categories they represent cannot be satisfied within the framework of the established régime. They wish therefore to replace it by another.

Conflict about the régime takes two very different forms, according to whether the end alone is involved or both the end and the means. It always presupposes that some of the citizens do not accept the existing institutions and want to set others in their place. The aims of conflict about the régime are always revolutionary. But in order to achieve the desired revolution one may either repudiate the rules of the existing régime and use violence in the struggle against it, illegally, or on the contrary one may use its rules to gain power, which will then be used to build a new order. In recent years the Communist parties in France and Italy have more or less adopted the second attitude. They renounced the use of unlawful means and violence in their attempt to gain power and accepted the rules of liberal democracy. But if they had succeeded in gaining power in this way within the framework of the existing régime they would have used it to utterly destroy this régime.

In autocracies this distinction is irrelevant. Conflict about the régime is simply not tolerated. No one may openly question the existing institutions, which can only be opposed by illegal and violent means. In a democracy the situation is different. The very essence of democracy, and its greatness, is that it allows its enemies to express their opinions: it therefore allows conflict about the régime. Does it, thereby, leave itself defenceless? Does giving freedom to the enemies of freedom mean that they will be allowed to destroy freedom? Is democracy condemned, by its very principles, not to defend itself against those who would abolish it? On one point at least, the answer is simple: democracy only allows its enemies to express themselves if they do so within the framework of democratic methods. Respect is not due to other people's opinions if force is used to impose these opinions. Violence must be used in the defence of liberty against those who try to destroy it by violence, even in a democracy.

But if those who oppose the régime agree to abide by the rules of democracy, if they fight within the framework of existing institutions, then, by the principles of democracy, they must be allowed freedom of expression: in this form, conflict about the régime is possible. But it is possible only up to a certain point, and this point depends not on theories, but on proportional strength. If a Communist party acting within the legal framework only gains five to ten per cent of votes in elections, there is no problem: democracy can work perfectly well despite this opposition to the régime. If it gains twenty to thirty per cent of votes, but this proportion is counterbalanced elsewhere, then some precautions must be taken: Communists should be kept from holding posts of authority, and not allowed to participate in government, except in ministries where they can do no harm. On these conditions the régime can work without too much difficulty, as can be seen from the example of France and Italy since 1945.

But if, in a liberal democracy, a Communist party polled near the fifty per cent of votes which is needed for an absolute majority and total power, the situation would be very different. Then, to allow the Communist party to act within the framework of the régime would be to condemn the régime to a speedy death. But to prohibit it would also be the death of democracy: suppressing a powerful Communist party presupposes preventing it from re-forming via the trade unions, parallel organizations, and other Left-wing parties; in a word, it presupposes the development of a vast system of repression and prohibition, directed against half the population of the country. Only a dictatorship can effect this result. If a Communist party won nearly fifty per cent of votes in a liberal democracy, it would mean quite simply that the conditions necessary to liberal democracy no longer existed in that country, and that the only remaining choice lay between a Right-wing dictatorship and a Left-wing dictatorship.

Having made this point, we must distinguish between the appearance and the reality of conflict about the régime, and take into account the time-lag between the development of events and changes in one's picture of them. As they grow older revolutionary parties tend to become part of the existing order, the more so since this order develops more or less in the way such parties wish: they change from being opponents of the régime to being opponents within the régime. But they try to hide this transformation from their militants as long as possible, because in general revolution has more prestige than reformism, and this is particularly true in France. Their opponents facilitate this camouflage because it allows them to create a bogy which is likely to rally Conservative votes. The Socialists, who were revolutionary in 1900, began to form part of the régime in 1920. But neither they nor their opponents would admit it until after 1945.

The Communist party is developing the same way, in both

France and Italy. Most of its supporters no longer desire the coming of a Peoples' Democracy. They are integrated into the western pluralist system, and do not want it to be suppressed. At the militant level this development is less advanced, but it has gained speed visibly in the last few years. Many care keenly about public liberties and diversity of opinion, that is, in a word, about liberal democracy. They are seeking a path of pluralist Socialism, which would suppress capitalism without destroying political liberalism. They realize that a revolution is no longer possible in highly developed countries, though they do not yet admit it in public, and dare not always admit it to themselves. The change that has taken place is none the less real and profound. As always, developments in vocabulary and principles affirmed are lagging behind developments in practice and attitudes: people want to appear revolutionary long after they have ceased to be so. In France and Italy today the Communist parties are still, to all appearances, opposed *to* the democratic régimes, but, in fact, their opposition is changing more and more into opposition *within* the régime.

The distinction between conflict about the régime and conflict within the régime is connected with the concept of legitimacy. The conflict stays within the framework of the régime if all the citizens consider the régime to be legitimate, if there is a consensus of opinion about it. The conflict is *about* the régime if this consensus is broken, if only some classes or groups or parties consider the existing régime to be legitimate, while other classes or groups or parties think a different régime would be legitimate. In a general way, the term legitimate means conforming to a value-system. A régime is said to be legitimate if it conforms to the image of power that a political ideology presents. Legitimacy is based therefore on beliefs. Every ideology has its own kind of legitimacy: there is monarchic legitimacy, democratic legitimacy, Communist legitimacy, etc. Legitimacy is not something abstract, to be defined in relation to some ideal type of government having the value of an absolute, but rather something concrete, which can only be defined in relation to the particular conceptions of the ideal type of government that have existed in history.

In general, at a given period and in a given country, there is a certain amount of agreement about the form of government, the processes by which power is transmitted and exercised, and the rules of political opposition. In this sense the régime which corresponds to the generally held idea of legitimacy is called legitimate. Thus monarchy was legitimate in the seventeenth century in France, democracy is legitimate in France today, a Liberal government is legitimate in the U.S.A., and a Socialist system is legitimate in the U.S.S.R. If the governed think their government is legitimate, they will be naturally moved to obey it. Then political opposition occurs within the framework of the régime, which itself is set above the fray, with regard to the means at least, if not to the end.

Ferrero thus calls legitimacy the 'invisible guardian of the community', which maintains the social order and the state by providing a foundation for civic obedience. As we shall see, this sacralization of power is often a piece of camouflage. But it has the effect of lessening governmental violence towards citizens. If a government is legitimate, the citizens will obey it naturally, as it were, so that constraint and threats need only be used in a minor way, towards a few recalcitrants, or in exceptional circumstances. But if on the contrary the citizens are faced with an illegitimate government, they will naturally tend to refuse obedience, and will only be swayed by constraint and force. Violence and threats then become the only foundation of power, which despite appearances is much more fragile in such circumstances. Illegitimacy therefore leads governments to be very authoritarian and harsh; this is why dictatorships tend to violence.

It is rare for a government to be thought illegitimate by all its citizens. Most frequently, if there is no consensus of opinion, one finds a variety of opposing conceptions of legitimacy, one of which is embodied in the government. Then political strife bears on the régime itself. In a situation of this kind no government can be considered legitimate by all the citizens. A government which some think legitimate will be thought illegitimate by others, and vice versa. Any government is based on force as far as a significant section of the population is concerned. That, for example, was the situation in France in the nineteenth century, when the country was more or less equally divided between monarchic legitimacy and democratic legitimacy.

Such a situation is revolutionary. It means there is a crisis in the social structures, which are being questioned by a significant section of the population. The new political ideology, which clashes with the traditionally legitimate system, expresses the desire of new classes or new social forces to play a greater part in the state. At the same time, the breakdown of the consensus of opinion aggravates the potentially revolutionary situation, by setting alongside the crisis in structure a moral and intellectual crisis and a crisis of beliefs. It makes the old political system more vulnerable by 'desacralizing' it in the eyes of part of the population, that is, by stripping it of the value that the consensus of opinion had so far conferred upon it.

# Part III

# From Conflict to Integration

The two faces of Janus – conflict and integration – are inseparable. First, they are not always clearly to be distinguished; political systems, for example, are concerned with both, as are the parties which battle for a better social order and a more real integration. To define the rules of combat and delimit its area involves both organizing the expression of differences and helping to diminish them. The struggle within the régime is at one and the same time a form of combat and a form of integration, since it expresses agreement on the fundamental principles of the society and the institutions which apply them. When legitimacy is contested it becomes a weapon of war; when it is the object of a consensus of opinion it is a means of integration. Many of the notions analysed thus far in the context of political conflict can also be analysed in the context of integration.

In the second place, nearly all political ideologies consider that conflict brings about integration, that the development of antagonisms leads to their suppression and to the advent of an authentic social order. Every party conceives politics as conflict when in opposition: once in power it sees it as integration. In the West we tend to believe that integration has already been achieved or will soon be so, that it is dependent only on techniques of public relations, or psychoanalytic cures; that only a few anti-social and therefore abnormal people resist it. In the East a long period of transition is still thought to be necessary, even after the proletariat has come to power, to establish at long last a just society. The contrast lies in the speed of transition from conflict to integration, not in the transition itself.

This transition seems indisputable, but the optimism professed about it, in both East and West, is much more questionable. The cessation of all conflict brought about by the coming of an affluent society or of 'the higher phase of Communism' is probably no more than a pipe-dream. Certain conflicts are disappearing, or rather diminishing; others persist, and are even growing worse, notably the conflict between citizens and authority which technical progress has made much more dangerous. New conflicts spring up, transposing the old into new contexts; at the time when the proletariat is disappearing from western societies the rift between wealthy nations and proletarian nations is growing.

# 1. The Theory of Integration

Lalande's 'Vocabulary of Philosophy' defines integration as 'the establishment of a closer interdependence between the parts of a living being or between members of a society'. Integration is therefore the process unifying a society, tending to transform it into a harmonious City, based on an order recognized as such by its members. By political integration, we mean the part played in this process by organized power, the government and the state. Integration has two aspects, one negative and the other positive. The unification of a society requires first of all the suppression of the conflicts which divide it and the end of the struggles by which it is rent. But a society without conflict is not really integrated if the individuals composing it are simply juxtaposed, like a crowd in which each individual is isolated from his neighbours, having no real link between him and them. Integration presupposes not only the suppression of conflict but also the development of solidarity. In practice these two aspects are sometimes confused.

## THE LIMITATION OF CONFLICT

Political antagonisms by their very nature tend to find expression in violence, because they are concerned with fundamental questions. When some men struggle to rise above their wretched condition and leave behind them a world of privation and poverty, when others fight to avoid a similar world, to defend their privileges against the onslaught of the oppressed and exploited, it is natural for all possible methods of ensuring victory to be used, including physical violence: riots, revolts, revolutions, civil wars, acts of violence, repression, executions, armed seizure of power; the way of politics is strewn with corpses. The tendency to resolve conflict by bloodshed is ever-present.

Yet politics can also be defined as a constant effort to eliminate physical violence and to give social and individual conflicts outlets that are less harsh, brutal and violent. Politics is
civil war continued by other means: that is to say, it is the
negation of civil war, since war, whether civil or international,
is, in fact, defined by its means: there is no such thing as a 'cold'
war, for war is the use of physical violence to settle conflicts.
Politics is the use of non-violent means, or more exactly, less
violent means. When class and racial struggles, local rivalries
and individual disputes are settled by arms and bloodshed we
are, so to speak, outside the realm of politics. Politics tries to
replace fists, knives, pikes and guns with other weapons.

The elimination of violent methods can be divided into three
stages. At a primitive stage authority is not strong enough to
prevent determined opponents from confronting each other
with physical force. It can only restrict its use by restraining and
regulating it. Into this first category come systems of legalized
private vengeance, single combat and the Truce of God: i.e.
the medieval proscription of fighting from Thursday to Sunday.
Fisticuffs and sword-fighting are not abolished, but only limited
by regulations which reduce their consequences. At the second
stage these brutal and barbarous rites are replaced by more
civilized kinds of violence: pillage or massacre become strikes;
forced labour or imprisonment become the lock-out. Finally,
at the last stage, politics completely eliminates physical violence,
replacing it by other modes of fighting: electoral battles, parliamentary debates, committee discussions.

Thus democratic procedure is a more moderate, more gentle
and less brutal means of expressing political controversies than
physical violence. To reproach democracy with giving open
expression to controversies, disputes and conflicts is to mis-
understand one of its fundamental aims. It tries to substitute
discussion for battle, dialogue for weapons, arguments for
blows and electoral majorities for bigger muscles or better guns.
Majority rule is more civilized and less brutal than the rule of
might. It may be questioned whether numbers should settle
every problem, and indeed the view that they should do so is
not entirely satisfactory, although it is based on the idea that all

men are equal. In concrete terms, the choice is between the rule of numbers and the rule of brute force and military strength. To replace the second by the first is a great step forward.

The limiting of conflict by the exclusion of violence is not strictly speaking integration. Limitation of the ways in which conflict finds expression, making the opponents face one another in newspaper polemics, in electoral campaigns and in parliamentary debates instead of letting them fight it out in civil war, still allows them to clash and confront each other. This is still the area of political combat and yet it is a step nearer to the realm of integration. To change the methods of warfare is to change its nature, too. Violence renders the struggle insoluble; it fosters hatred and a spirit of vengeance which makes the initial conflict worse. Its first motives tend to disappear only to be replaced by a desire for revenge. Groups which through the ages have lost their reasons for fighting each other find new reasons in the memories of past conflict and old wounds. There is a desire to return blows received, even if no other reason for giving them any longer exists. Further, and this is perhaps more important, for violence to be excluded from conflict it is necessary for both sides to accept the restriction. There must be agreement about the rules of non-violent competition; otherwise there will be a return to violence, *'ultima ratio'*. Any limitation in fighting is at least a first step towards compromise, the first sign of co-operation, and the first move towards integration.

Violence can never be completely suppressed. Politics strives to eliminate violence, but does not completely succeed in doing so. Violence is always with us, even in the most civilized, the best organized and the most democratic of states. There is a residue of violence which is employed by a few isolated individuals, a few small minority groups, and some fanatical elements, which resort to fists, bludgeons and even revolvers and bombs. There is also latent violence: classes, groups and individuals use lawful non-violent processes only so long as they provide adequate expression of their views; if they cease to do so, violence erupts.

Finally, the state itself is based on violence: ultimately it rests upon police, army, prisons, and hangmen. Their significance varies, of course, with the extent to which these means of physical constraint are really used in the general interest and for the common good. Authority uses violence to prevent greater violence. Legal violence is, in fact, one way of restraining violence. But practice does not always correspond to theory. When they describe the state as a collection of means of constraint used by the ruling classes to secure the exploitation of the lower classes Marxists are expressing part at least of the truth. In this sense, politics is not the suppression of violence, but the centralization, monopolization and organization of the instruments of violence, which are wrested from individuals and groups and entrusted to the hands of authority alone.

This centralization, monopolization and organization nevertheless diminishes the use of violence. Lenin recognized this when he said: 'The state is an organization for class domination, for the oppression of one class by another: it is the creation of an 'order' which legalizes and strengthens this oppression by '*moderating* [1] the class conflict' (*State and Revolution*). Engels had already used this same expression 'moderating the conflict'. From the Marxist standpoint, the growth of the state and organized power reinforces the oppression of one class by another by institutionalizing and legalizing it, making it official. Control of this instrument of coercion, the state, strengthens the power of the ruling class. However, its domination thus assumes less brutal, less violent, more moderate forms. The definition of politics as the control of the means of combat, the attempt to suppress physical violence, is therefore generally applicable. What is involved is the transposing of violence, rather than its suppression in the full sense of the term; physical violence is replaced by legal, constitutional violence, violence perpetrated with clean hands.

ESTABLISHING AGREEMENT

The elimination of violence presupposes a preliminary agreement concerning the rules of combat. The process of integration

[1] Our italics.

only begins, however, when compromise on questions of content and not solely of form is considered. At this stage what is involved is not ordering the pattern of political competition but putting an end to it by reconciling the competing interests. Achieving a compromise is an essential function of politics. In democratic systems institutions are organized, in fact, for this purpose. Their procedure does not serve the sole purpose of giving expression to conflicts by non-violent means, but is also designed with the idea of putting an end to conflict by reaching compromise solutions. The apparatus of discussion, committee and debate allows each opponent to express his argument. It also ensures an overall understanding of all sides of the problem, enabling those concerned to understand the diversity and complexity of the conflicting interests. Each contender can make his strength felt by his speeches and his votes, but agreement and coalitions often prove necessary and these require concessions from both sides.

It is often said that compromise is hindered in democracies by the publicity given to the attitudes and positions taken up. In international relations it is traditional to boast of the superiority of secret negotiations over 'street-corner politics'. Autocracies, which keep their political conflicts under cover, would thus have an advantage, although the formal organization of their institutions is less well designed for compromise. This view is not totally false, but it is exaggerated. In modern states, where the mass of the population has a high level of political understanding, where the information media disclose and discuss the nature and implications of a given problem, the need for compromise is usually well understood. The alleged secrecy of autocratic institutions seems to offer no great advantage when one considers that their whole structure tends towards solutions unilaterally defined and imposed from above, by the party or class controlling the state.

Two important techniques of compromise can be distinguished: negotiation and arbitration. Opponents can try to reconcile their points of view themselves by debate and dialogue. This is the usual procedure in diplomatic relations and the form generally adopted for democratic discussion. The conflicting parties gather round a table and, at the cost of mutual concessions, attempt to define the terms of an agreement which will take their respective interests into account. But opponents can also appeal to a neutral third party to decide between them. This recourse to arbitration is used fairly regularly in international relations and in social conflicts. It has sometimes taken an interesting form in politics. In the seventh century B.C., when Greece was rent by great internal conflicts which caused many of them to fall victim to tyranny, some of her city states appealed to men of wisdom to give them new constitutions and codes, based on new compromises enabling their citizens to continue to live together. Often, a stranger would be called in to lead them for a short time because he seemed more neutral and impartial.

Democracy on the whole has recourse to the first technique of compromise, for the organization of its procedure is such that opponents continuously confront each other. Autocracy, on the other hand, is alleged by some to have more frequent recourse to arbitration. Independent of parties, and over and above classes, factions and individuals, the state is said to hold the position of arbiter and to draw up compromises based on objective and impartial analysis of the facts and not on negotiation between opponents as were those of lawgivers like Solon. The state is also considered as arbiter by western democratic doctrine, but autocratic theorists criticize this view. For them the democratic state is by its very nature in the hands of a faction, party or class, which uses it in its own interests against other factions, parties or classes. Only the autocratic state can act as arbiter, since it is independent of all social categories. This theory confuses appearance with reality. The autocratic state pretends to be above parties and classes, but this is never really true. It is always in the hands of one class or party to some extent, like the democratic state, and usually more completely, since it cannot be overthrown by the opposition. It will be seen that no form of state is entirely dissociated from political conflict, the autocratic state least of all.

Political compromises are limited by their very nature. The principle of compromise is 'to cut the cake in two' and to give each side half. The ideal and perfect compromise would weigh in the balance the advantages and sacrifices of each member of the community; thus it would be based on justice in its elementary form of equity, symbolized by the scales. Thus each individual, group or class could be satisfied, and their reasons for fighting would disappear. The more just they appear, the easier compromises are to achieve; the notion of justice has therefore an important part to play in the process of integration.

The definition of justice depends on the ideology and the scheme of values of the particular society. It nearly always centres on the distribution of wealth and social advantages, and this preoccupation reflects the age-old and universal condition of penury in which the needs to be satisfied are greater than both wealth and social advantages. The change from aristocratic societies to bourgeois societies has replaced the principle 'to each according to his birth' by 'to each according to his ability', although birth in the form of inheritance is still important. Socialism wants to give 'to each according to his labour', but for reasons of efficiency this has not proved altogether possible. For Marxists the transition from Socialism to Communism will be expressed by the replacement of the principle 'to each according to his labour' by 'to each according to his needs'. This supposes an end to hardship and the coming of a society of abundance in which there will be sufficient goods to satisfy all needs. This aspect of the problem will be dealt with later.

There is a great gap between theory and practice. In fact, compromise expresses relative strength as well as, and perhaps more than, justice. If two opponents carried exactly the same weight, if they both negotiated with the same ability, the compromise between them would be perfectly equitable. This balance is rarely found in reality. Certainly if the inequality is too great, if one opponent can easily crush the other, there is no compromise, which can only be achieved when the disproportion between the opposing forces is not too great, when to continue the struggle offers more disadvantage than advantage for both sides. Usually some disproportion remains, and this makes compromise inegalitarian. The notion of justice can temper only slightly the demands of the strongest; it cannot modify them greatly. Thus compromise expresses the situation of the opposing forces at the moment when they agree to accept it.

Finally, there is no absolute contrast between conflict and compromise. Compromise is not the end of fighting, but a truce or armistice, which a change in the balance of forces may replace by yet another compromise. This process is well illustrated by the political life of democracies, but it is less evident in autocratic régimes where compromise is more secret. But it takes place there, too, when the disproportion of strength is not too great, and the conflict not too deep-seated. Change in the distribution of forces is often slow and therefore many compromises are long-lived. Habit, familiarity and general social inertia work towards the same end.

For political conflict to be not only postponed, but completely suppressed, the causes at the very root of the trouble must be destroyed, that is, the differences between the individuals and groups who constitute the total society. One can question the possibility of totally eliminating all factors of dissent, and we will consider this problem later; but it is undeniably possible for certain factors to diminish, and societies seem to be naturally developing in this way. If the extent of conflicts is limited, compromise becomes naturally less difficult and more enduring, and the armistice tends to turn into peace. There is never a clear dividing line between them: a long armistice strongly resembles a state of peace, the permanence of which can never be guaranteed.

### GROWTH OF SOLIDARITY

Supposing that it could exist, a society without struggles, conflict or differences would still not be fully integrated if all its members remained isolated from one another, with no common bonds, like the men one sees each Sunday evening on American highways, driving along shut up in their cars, obeying traffic lights and signals, unprotesting, strictly respecting speed limits and regulations, completely devoid of aggression and any competitive spirit, and so close that they sometimes bump into one another like huge beetles, yet so remote from each other, so solitary, in spite of all appearances. There can be no social integration without the development of solidarity.

Solidarity is primarily the product of the structure of communal life, in which each individual needs the others and their exchanges form a network. Durkheim saw the source of this first type of solidarity in the division of labour. It is scarcely developed in closed and primitive economies, but as exchange becomes more specialized so solidarity increases. The naïve poem adorning old manuals of civic education, 'Without the baker, would you have bread?' expresses this in its simplest form. In a capitalist economy solidarity is purely materialistic. It is not felt psychologically, because individual activity is directed only by men's private interests. When he makes bread, objectively the baker is performing a service for his fellow citizens; subjectively he is above all concerned with earning money, and his fellow citizens know this. Advertising on the theme of the services which firms give to the community is designed only to attract consumers to their products; profit, not 'service' is the motive of their activity.

Socialist theorists think that relationships based on exchange ought to be radically transformed so that they express a true solidarity. For them the notion of social service must replace that of personal interest. Experience has shown that this is a difficult change to make. In the Soviet economy it was found necessary to devise a system of personal incentives if productivity was to be raised. Yet this personal interest is only one element among others in the activity of citizens and is not the fundamental element. Its importance perhaps derives from the persistence of the capitalist mentality which is gradually being reduced by change. The fundamental aim of Socialism is still to eliminate motives of personal interest and to replace them by altruistic motives. Egoism, too, is a form of alienation.

Durkheim thought that similarity was the second source of solidarity. All societies are based on resemblances: language, religion, customs, myths, value-systems and more generally, culture, are held in common. The similarity is all the more noticeable because one can see the difference between oneself and members of another group: the image of the foreigner is very important in the development of solidarity. Physical contact, proximity, the very fact of meeting together are all essential factors. Equally important is the position of the community in relation to others. Isolation, by clearly defining the boundaries and making them seem natural, strengthens the common accord. The existence of an external danger or a foreign threat is also important, whether the enemy and the danger are real or imaginary. Toynbee has stressed the influence of adversity, of the 'challenge' and the response to difficulties in developing bonds in the community.

Solidarity is based less on the resemblance or physical proximity of members of a community than on their collective image of this resemblance and proximity. In this respect the picture of their past held by members of a community, the picture of themselves and of their future as a group are very important. We have mentioned the essential part played by history, true or legendary, in forming nations: it plays a similar role in other human communities. 'National stereotypes', the simplified profile of the average citizen in which members of a society can recognize themselves to some extent – for the French Jacques Bonhomme (Jack Goodfellow), for the Americans Uncle Sam; these play a part not to be overlooked. The picture of the grand collective project to be realized together is probably an even more powerful factor in integration. 'Without vision, the people perish', says the Bible. Every society needs a Promised Land.

Finally, the growth of solidarity is probably based on a deep instinct in man. To explain certain animal societies, a biologist has spoken of the 'interattraction' impelling their members to live together. This exists also in human societies. Psychologists, describing the anguish of solitude, adopt the words of Genesis: 'It is not good for man to live alone.' The desire for communion in the group, in which each individual achieves complete self-fulfilment, probably constitutes the essential motive for collective life. Over and beyond the present City, imperfect, unjust and superficial, there persists the vision of a City of Harmony whose members will at last be wrested from their egoism, their self-contained life, their isolated existence; in which each will be bound to the others, not by legal contracts, not by processes of exchange and of division of labour, not by bonds of debit and credit, but by mutual understanding, by altruism, by love. In their separate ways Marx and Teilhard de Chardin both think that this is not a fanciful dream, that mankind is developing along a path which will bring it one day to the gates of that perfect City.

# 2. The Technique of Integration

Many of the elements which contribute to social integration do not depend on the government. 'Interattraction' is a natural phenomenon; similarity and proximity are not created by the state; the economy grows more diverse, division of labour increases, and exchange multiplies without reference to the state, in part at least. Integration may be the supreme end of politics, but the means of achieving it are not all political. However, the state can foster it in four main ways: by defining rules and procedure; by organizing collective services and managing society as a whole; by providing for the education of the citizens; and, finally, by using constraint towards recalcitrants.

## RULES AND PROCEDURE

The first means by which the state within the nation, or organized power in any collectivity, fulfils its function of social integration is the establishment and the application of rules and procedures which as a body constitute law. Doubtless there is law based on custom and usage (mercantile custom, village customs, etc.) and law based on agreement (contracts between individuals). The first, which is essential in primitive societies, plays only a minor role in modern societies, while the second is still very important, although state regulations are constantly lessening its influence. Both the one and the other, however, can only be effective in so far as they are recognized and sanctioned by the government. Custom can only be invoked before a tribunal or the administration if the law, the child of power, has decided that one may do so. Similarly, contracts only have the effect that the legislators grant them. In the last analysis, it is the government which defines law: the law is made up of the totality of rules and procedures that the state sets up, recognizes, and sanctions.

The first aim of rules and procedures is to control the expression of antagonisms by excluding violence. In conflict between individuals the limitation of private vengeance is the first and most elementary form of law. At this stage, violence is only contained or limited. At the next, all private taking of revenge is suppressed and reparation is guaranteed by the state, which at the same time punishes those who cause damage to persons and property and so transgress the laws of the state. In class conflicts and collective political struggles the law also lays down the means of non-violent combat such as elections, parliamentary debates, competitive administrative examinations.

Rules and procedures also help to settle conflict by compromise. In the early stages the state simply validates and makes enforceable compromises agreed to by private individuals; that is, it lends its secular arm to put them into effect. This system is still widespread in modern societies, where it more or less corresponds to law based on agreement. Contracts between individuals, agreements between groups, between local communities or public services are all means which ensure the settlement of a large number of the conflicts which can arise. The state intervenes in the compromise itself, by forbidding the insertion of certain clauses or enforcing the insertion of other clauses: what are known as 'law and order' clauses are tending to proliferate in comparison to those which are open to free negotiation between the parties. These governmental interventions are usually intended either to protect the weaker party against domination by the stronger or to prevent private agreements from going against the general interest.

In the second stage of development the state facilitates the working out of difficult compromises. The most typical example is that of compulsory conciliation or arbitration procedures. Their use in international relations reflects the embryonic state of supranational communities, which have no highly organized political power which could resolve conflicts and work out compromises on its own. In such cases this kind of procedure forms the maximum intervention of power, and represents progress in the integration of society. When they are used to settle labour disputes within a nation they represent, on the contrary, a retrograde movement of integration caused by the intense class warfare of the nineteenth and twentieth centuries. The state, unable to enforce in this sphere the authoritarian solutions which it formerly imposed almost everywhere else, has had to resign itself to coming to terms with violence, replacing bloody conflict by less brutal expressions of violence like strikes and lock-outs, and attempting to limit use of the latter by making preliminary attempts at conciliation and arbitration compulsory.

Authoritarian compromises are the last stage in this evolution. In these, the state, or the established power, itself ensures settlement of the conflicting interests by laying down the terms of the compromise and putting it into effect. The line between these authoritarian compromises and negotiated compromises is not very clear. Direct or indirect negotiation between opponents plays a large part in the democratic processes of elaborating laws and governmental decisions. Parliamentary debates, for example, allow each party to express its point of view, to 'let off steam', to measure its strength and to come to arrangements with the other parties. Committees, memoranda, consultations, and 'round table discussions' operate in the same way. In modern societies, public debate, in the Press or on radio and television, is itself a means of reaching compromise before decisions are made by the state.

While negotiated compromises are only applicable to the people who made them, state-imposed compromises are of general import, and are applicable to all similar situations, both present and future. In them, interests are settled not by analysis of a concrete case, but on principles which are applicable to all similar cases, and which express not only the value-system prevalent in the society when these rules of law are drawn up, and therefore the society's idea of justice, but also the respective power of the different classes or groups of which it is composed. The rules of law are therefore inegalitarian, like private compromises; and, like the latter, they can only have lasting effect if they are in some way agreed to by all the parties concerned. Analysis of international treaties throws some light on this contradictory aspect of law. A treaty which lasts is never simply a *diktat* on the part of the victor, which the vanquished at heart rejects but has to bow to because of his weakness. If a treaty is to last, it must be accepted by the vanquished party: that is, it must be in his interest to keep it rather than to reject it. The same is true of all the rules of law: though the stronger group imposes them on the weaker, they can only be preserved if their existence is preferable to their non-existence, if they are based on authentic compromise, and if they also, at least in part, reflect the idea of justice common to the society.

Rules and procedures are inseparable from a certain degree of formalism which plays an important part in the process of social integration. Legal formalism was originally based on religion and magic. Because certain gestures are performed and certain words pronounced, the promise is hallowed in everyone's eyes. The same is true today of the legal force of an oath, of the importance attached to the written word beyond its value as proof, and of ceremonies of investiture. But formalism has come to be based on more empirical grounds. Social life is impossible without the rules of the game, and the rules of any game imply some measure of formalism. Legal proceedings must reach an end, and the decisions arrived at must be beyond challenge. Judgements must carry authority, even if they were ill judged. The arbiter's decision must be put into effect, even if it is questionable. Otherwise, social life is impossible. The fact that in Great Britain, because of the uneven spread of voters throughout the constituencies, the Labour party can obtain more votes in the country as a whole than the Conservative party, but fewer seats in Parliament, and that it can be kept in opposition although it represents the majority, as happened in 1951, is contrary to the principles of democracy. But those are the rules of the game, and they must be respected, if the foundations of the British political régime are not to be destroyed.

In its own right, formalism is a factor in integration in other ways. Courtesy is not only the result of a lack of brutality; it is also a means of preventing brutality from recurring, as it accustoms people to repressing their individual violence. In the same way, legal forms help in containing social violence.

The law is rarely what it ought to be: it represents the relation between forces rather than justice, and it disguises violence more than it suppresses it. But by proclaiming what it is not it progresses a little beyond what it is. Lastly, politeness and formalism are also sign systems, by which the members of the same society can recognize each other, and become more clearly aware of their belonging: solidarity is thereby strengthened.

## COLLECTIVE ORGANIZATION

Classical Liberalism restricts the integrating function of the state to the juridical activity of elaborating rules and procedure. Doubtless, it admits the need for communal services such as communications, postal services, educational and information media, hygiene and health services and currency, but it considers that private initiative and free enterprise guarantee the greatest efficiency in the running of such services, with the exception of justice, the police, the army and diplomacy. Only in these small and residual spheres is it necessary for social organization to be undertaken by the political authorities.

This theory corresponds to the situation of societies which are technically not very developed, separated into inward-looking basic groups; societies in which production takes place within a framework of small units, and in which the role of the central government is in effect fairly limited. In closed agrarian economies, where each community tends to live entirely off its own land, collective services do not exist. With the first phase of capitalism, however, the economy becomes open, trade and exchange develop, and collective services multiply. But they are usually a product of private initiative, and they are of little importance in the life of the community. Individualism and mistrust of the state are the attitudes which reflect this type of social structure. They can be found today among artisans, small shopkeepers, and traditionalist farmers, who cannot look beyond themselves and their circle of acquaintances. When this archaic type of capitalism finds itself gradually stifled by the development of modern capitalism, these groups of people show aggressive, poujadist-type reactions.

The structure of contemporary industrial societies is quite different. Collective services are many and important. The economy needs them for management of resources, land-use planning and large-scale operations of the Tennessee Valley type, roads, tele-communications, technical research in fundamental spheres, overall forecasting and so on. The social services like education, social insurance, welfare and public health of necessity become more extensive. The external defence system becomes highly complex, very large and very expensive: modern armies are some of the largest human organizations, and the most costly to equip. Some of these services can be guaranteed by the interplay of private activities and competition, but in relation to the whole this part is steadily growing smaller. No one would dispute this fact today. American economists have themselves shown that in a purely capitalist economy the collective sector is underdeveloped, and that this delay is slowing down overall expansion. Only the state can adequately provide communal services, and so its social organization function becomes very important.

Moreover, this function extends beyond the sphere of communal services, which only affect particular sectors of social life. Technical development makes power into the general organizer of the community, co-ordinating the activity of all the individual sectors within the framework of a general plan. In modern countries, economic planning is only one aspect of social organization. To be more accurate, the economy is but one element of the overall plan. Planning decisions about investment and priorities in development involve every aspect of national life. Education, culture, art, scientific progress, town and country planning, style of life – and also military power, technical aid to underdeveloped countries, that is, the foundations of diplomacy – are for a large part determined by the direction of the plan. Governmental organization of society extends to the whole range of collective activity.

The very structure of the state is affected by the extension of its communal organization function. The growth of the executive in relation to the legislative is a direct result of this extension. The legislator has more importance in societies where integration is not very advanced, where private enterprise provides for the main collective activities, and where the prime function of government is to limit conflicts between individuals and groups, to assist in working out compromises which will end such conflict, to lay down general compromises, and to manage communal services of an administrative nature such as the police, the army, and finance. In a planned society, where the state co-ordinates all collective activities, this organizing function cannot be fulfilled by legislative means, but only by the government, which becomes the centre of initiative and of political decision-making. The weakening power of legislatives and the development of executives, trends which are found in the way all democracies are evolving today, are the political results of the transformation of socio-economic structures brought about by technical progress.

## THE EDUCATION OF THE NATION

Integration does not only depend on the structures of a society, but also on the psychology of its members. Doubtless the latter partly reflects the former: but only partly. Education can foster integration in various ways. First, it makes the citizens aware of the need to diminish the antagonisms which divide them, and of the importance of the material links which unite them. Secondly, it develops in them a sense of the community.

Political power, the state, makes wide use of education to foster integration. Sometimes it does this to achieve a false integration which serves to disguise the domination of the ruling groups and classes; we will examine this aspect of the problem later. But even in this case the process is not entirely one of camouflage and falsehood. Education nearly always contributes to real integration, besides serving as camouflage, the proportions of each element varying according to the régime and the age. In all societies education is the basic means of integrating the rising generations into society, and the established political power never takes complete control of it. Even in the most totalitarian régimes the family exercises considerable influence in the early years of childhood; and afterwards the family milieu and the close circle of acquaintances or friends and comrades give a very important education by 'osmosis'. But the political power always has some share in the process of education, and this share is mainly directed towards social integration.

In modern nations education achieves integration in two ways. First, by direct teaching about the bonds which tie the individual to the community, that is, by the teaching of civic duties. Some civilizations stress the moral aspect of these bonds, and teach the civic duties of the individual towards the collectivity. Others stress what could be called their trade-value, showing the advantages gained from community life. These two aspects are complementary and are taught together most of the time. Furthermore, since civic education is always based to a large extent on history, the picture that the members of a community have of its past is an important element in social integration. Inevitably, civic education is always more or less nationalistic, since its very function is to foster attachment to the community, which, in the modern world, is the nation. It is therefore liable to encourage hostility towards other nations; to combat this, efforts have been made in the last few years to restrict the inculcation of nationalism, particularly in the teaching of history.

Education tends to social integration in a second way, that is, by vocational instruction adapting the individual for the task he will perform in the collectivity. If this is properly done, social integration will obviously be deeper than if the society is encumbered with a host of failures and maladjusted members. For centuries this adaptation took two forms: the *élites* received an education which corresponded to their functions; the masses were left without technical instruction and so prevented both from realizing the extent to which they were being oppressed, and from rebelling against their condition; at the same time they received a religious education which preached resignation. In industrial societies, where everyone has to be given advanced instruction, adapting the individual to his future social function is more difficult. It is not possible without some anticipation of the way the society will develop in the next few years, and so forms part of the task of overall planning which only the state can undertake. The role of the authority in education is therefore tending to grow larger.

Education, moreover, is not only a matter for children; in the guise of information, which is difficult to distinguish from propaganda, it concerns adults also. In democracies information and propaganda are used by individuals and groups (political parties, newspapers, private firms, pressure groups) in competition with the state. They are therefore both weapons in the armoury of political warfare, and instruments of integration. Their use as weapons obviously hinders the development of integration. Government propaganda is less influential if the government does not have a monopoly of the information media, if its voice is not the only one to reach the citizens. It sounds more loudly than the others, however. Solemn government pronouncements are always highlighted by the newspapers, because they are important news. In a liberal democracy with private television channels de Gaulle and Khrushchev could appear on T.V. as often as they liked, because they fascinate the public. In a system that creates 'stars', rulers are stars. One can distinguish, too, between propaganda for the benefit of the government and propaganda for the benefit of the nation. Democracy restricts the first more than the second, which is directed towards social integration. In democracies the role of the state in this sphere is much more limited than it is in authoritarian régimes; but it is still considerable.

## SOCIAL CONSTRAINT

The ultimate means which government has at its disposal for integrating society is recourse to the police, the army, prisons, the public executioner. The fact that established power monopolizes violence to its own benefit, and withdraws military weapons from individuals and factions, represents a first stage in integration, since it prevents citizens and groups from using violence themselves in their political conflicts. Threatening to use force, if the opposing parties are unwilling to accept a compromise, helps a great deal in concluding the compromise. For in that case each opponent no longer thinks only of what he is gaining or losing in relation to the other, but of what he would lose if the sword of power were to strike him down. If litigants are dissatisfied with their judge, they nevertheless have to bow before enforcement by the military arm. General compromises, such as those which result from codes and rules, would be difficult to put into effect, however just they were, if the citizens could refuse to accept them; but the law can be enforced, because the law is supported by force. In its negative aspect of limitation and suppression of conflict, social integration owes much to governmental constraint, the frequency of whose use corresponds to the depth and bitterness of the antagonisms, to the acuity of the struggle between classes, groups and individuals, and therefore to a low degree of integration.

Some thinkers also argue that constraint is a factor in positive integration, that is, in the development of solidarity. At first sight, this is a strange argument. If violence has to be used against individuals to keep them in the community, does it not mean that their community sense is weak? But some moralists think that violence withdraws men from their wicked passions, frees them from evil, makes them aware of their interests, and so makes them more sociable. When Joseph de Maistre said that the principle foundation of a society was its hangman he was thinking that terror alone can prevent an individual from being dominated by his evil tendencies and make him live an authentic social life. These old theories, which derive more or less from the pseudo-Christianity of the Inquisition, have been taken up today by the Fascists, who, like H. de Montherlant, think that 'the morals of the populace are formed by kicks in the behind'. Many apparently moderate Conservatives think the same, but dare not say so.

The Right wing is not alone in demanding that the government use violence to foster sociability. The Jacobin theory of the Terror, a necessary means of ensuring the triumph of 'virtue' – that is, civic feeling – leads to the same conclusions. But the reasoning which leads up to the conclusions is different. For the Right wing, man is born wicked. His nature is antisocial: 'man preys on man', and is opposed to the development of any real community life. Power uses force towards the citizens as a trainer uses it towards animals, in order to train them and replace their original evil nature by a good one. Thus, in the past, the rod was used in education to turn children towards the good. On the contrary, for the Jacobins, who were disciples of Rousseau, 'man is born good, but is corrupted by society'. For them the purpose of violence is not psychological – the modification of human nature – but sociological: destruction of the institutions and social habits which corrupted man in order to liberate him.

A Marxist would say: to put an end to his alienation. The theory of proletarian dictatorship is an accurate continuation of the Jacobin theory of the terror. Man is born good, but capitalism corrupts him. In order to destroy the system of oppression, exploitation and alienation developed by capitalism, violence must be used. Violence against the state, in the first place, as long as it is in the hands of the exploiting classes: this means revolution. Next, when the working class has taken power, the force of the state is directed against the exploiters and used to destroy every trace of exploitation: this stage is the dictatorship of the proletariat. The word dictatorship implies a harsh, pitiless, violent form of government, because the old exploiters are still powerful, and capitalist institutions and customs are deeply rooted in society, and cannot be extirpated by gentle means. When they have been removed, and all traces of exploitation abolished, then men can live in a society of fraternal solidarity, as befits their true nature, which capitalism had alienated. In this society violence ceases to be used, and it becomes useless to resort to force: authority itself tends to disappear.

There is another difference between Right- and Left-wing attitudes towards the use of violence for fostering sociability. For Conservatives it is a permanent process. Men will always be evil, and however strict and complete their training may have been, it is never definitive. Like a wild beast which may at any moment devour the trainer from whose hand it eats, human beings are liable, from one moment to the next, to relapse into their evil passions. Culture, courtesy and civilization are fragile structures which can only be kept standing by constant and unceasing vigilance. Power must always be armed, ready to strike. At the first suspicious movement it must strike, and harshly, to avoid the onrush of the masses which, relapsed into savagery, would blindly destroy the foundations of the social order from which they themselves benefit. Thus, as Maurras said: 'When the rod is spared, it is not the rod and the authority behind it which are spared; it is the whole mass of the people, the nation, and the human race who are the first to suffer.'

For Jacobins and Marxists, on the contrary, the use of violence by the state to develop solidarity is simply a temporary measure. The egoism and wickedness of man are caused only by the social structures, which set up inequality and exploitation and give some men the power to dominate others and 'alienate' them. Once these structures are totally destroyed men will return to their natural sociability, and violence will disappear for ever. Then the state as an instrument of constraint will wither away. All that will remain will be a technical structure which provides for the planning and organization of society in much the same way as automatic traffic signals control the circulation of motor vehicles in towns. There will be no more police, guards, soldiers, prisons or hangmen. Human nature alone, free at last to show its real goodness, will suffice to unconstrainedly sustain and expand social integration. Authority, according to this theory, only uses violence to cut the Gordian knot; once men are freed of their bonds they will live without violence.

The position of contemporary neo-Liberals falls between these two. Like Jacobins and Marxists, they do not think that the use of force is the permanent basis of states; they consider that men are naturally good and sociable, that violence is on the whole of no avail for integrating them into the community, and indeed is harmful. Like Fascists and Conservatives, they do not think that power can ever abandon constraint; on the contrary, they think it must be used sometimes to foster sociability. But this recourse to violence is in their view secondary, marginal, and as it were residual. Violence is used against a few individuals who are incapable of fitting into the community; these asocial people are also abnormal, that is, sick. Their violence is medical rather than criminal, they need hospital treatment rather than a prison sentence. These ideas, which are very widespread among some western sociologists, are very dangerous. To say that those who are asocial, which is to say atypical, are abnormal or ill is to condemn all eccentrics and all small minorities. The suggestion that aseptisized, white-coated violence be used against them, rather than the police and executioners, is very disturbing.

Looking beyond these theories, one is led to wonder whether technical progress is not transforming social constraint. The replacement of jailers by nurses is part of this change. More generally, the development of collective organization is leading to a bureaucratic type of constraint, which arises from a mechanical type of solidarity like that of cogs in a wheel. Each part of the machine is by force subject to the whole, and cannot escape. When automatic traffic signals replace policemen social constraint is transformed, not abolished. The relations between a citizen and the modern state are coming more and more to remind one of a Kafka novel, and while those who contemn technical progress give exaggerated descriptions of it, nevertheless what they have to say should not be ignored.

# 3. Integration or Pseudo-integration

In describing the methods of integration used by authority we did not consider whether it was real integration or only pseudo-integration, providing a screen behind which authority could hide the part it plays in political struggles on behalf of one of the contenders. Are rules and procedure, collective organization, education and propaganda, police and prisons really used by the state as means of promoting order, social harmony and justice, or do these officially stated aims conceal totally different and much less avowable aims? Conservative doctrine has always denied this, and revolutionary doctrine has always affirmed it, though revolutionary doctrines distinguish between the established power they are fighting and the future authority which they wish to put in its place. In changing from one to the other there would also be a change from false to authentic integration, they argue.

## ILLUSORY INTEGRATION

It is argued by some that the theory of the state as integrator, regulating the common good, and creating order and justice, is but an illusion. When the state affirms that it represents the general interest and that it works for the triumph of this general interest over individual interests, and when it declares itself to be the arbiter above the fray, a judge independent of parties, these affirmations are said to be nothing but falsehood and mystification. In fact, the state is in the hands of certain men and certain social categories, who use it fundamentally for their own interests; it is involved in the fray on the side of one of the warring parties and against the others. It maintains the domination of a privileged minority over the exploited mass. Rulers, officials, judges, policemen, soldiers and hangmen do not work to establish justice, order and solidarity for the common benefit, that is to achieve authentic social integration, but to maintain a situation favourable to them and those whom they represent, a situation which they call 'order', but which is, in fact, what Mounier nicely describes as 'established disorder'.

The natural attraction that material peace and physical order have for all men, and the fear that violence causes them, play a very large part in this illusion. The state always guarantees one kind of 'order': order in the streets, that is, absence of civil war and of armed conflict. It propagates the idea that this material order is a real, authentic order. The vision of order, justice, harmony and solidarity cherished by all men, the great hope of escaping solitude and living at last in a true community, in a truly integrated society, is a vision which is useful to the state. Men tend always to see things as they would like them to be.

The state is also helped in this respect by the natural attachment of each man to the overall society and of each citizen to the nation. We have already noted the ambivalence of national values: on the one hand, they express the sense of belonging to the community and truly general interests, while, on the other, they in varying degrees conceal internal divisions to the advantage of the established order. To stress the opposition between national feeling and 'party differences' by exaggerating the former and minimizing the latter, is to play on factors that are common to the whole nation in order to divert attention from the domination of some classes by others within the nation. In this process of camouflage the use of the 'enemy' can be very effective. All social groups confronted with threats, danger or aggression tend to tighten their bonds and reduce any internal differences. To magnify a real enemy, describing him as more dangerous than he is, or to invent a pseudo-enemy out of nothing, are classic devices used by all states. Sometimes the enemy is within the state and is identified as Christian, Jew, Red, Capitalist or Communist; sometimes it is an external enemy – England for France before the 'Entente Cordiale', Germany for France between 1871 and 1949, the U.S.S.R. for the West.

Furthermore, the modern state enjoys the inheritance of

primitive forms of power based on religion and magic. In archaic societies rulers are the interpreters of the forces of magic or the gods which rule men and the world: social order can come only from obedience to these higher commands. Authority is therefore obeyed because it expresses the divine will or the power of hidden forces. It does so in so far as it acts according to certain rites and forms, like the priest administering a sacrament. Whether the priest himself is good or bad is of no account: the divine force works because he pronounces the sacramental formulae. The authority of archaic rulers is of the same nature, while that of modern governors is not very different. The notions of legitimacy and especially of legality lead to state decisions being recognized as valid according to their form, not their content, because the rulers have been invested and not because they are able or just. For commands to be translated into law, justice and social order, it is enough for the giver of them to wear the purple and bear the sceptre, to have been consecrated in Rheims or to have won the plaudits of the people.

By thinking in the abstract and not the concrete, jurists, often unconsciously, lend themselves to this mystification. They say that the law is the expression of the general will, while, in fact, it is the will of an assembly elected in particular circumstances, which may end by falsifying the expression of public opinion. They argue that judges dispense justice, while, in fact, they express their own conception of justice, which in turn reflects their social status, their education and their emotions. Law is one of the state's most powerful means of dissimulation. Even idealistic jurists who distinguish between law and justice, who distinguish between positive law established by the government and natural law based on true equity, are a party to this process. For positive law borrows some of its prestige from natural law by bearing the same name, written with a capital letter, Law.

## AMBIVALENCE OF THE STATE

Some Conservative theorists do not deny that the privileged minority uses the government to maintain its privileges and wealth in the face of a mass of people condemned to poverty and privation. In their view to distribute the wealth of the rich would not change the situation of the poor, whereas the wealth of the minority allows it to foster the development of art, culture, knowledge and civilization and thus the progress of humanity as a whole. In protecting their particular interests the privileged classes who hold power are said to benefit the general interest indirectly because their privileges are useful to the mass. Others claim that power falls naturally into the hands of the fittest, of the *élite'* in the course of the struggle for life, and that society is therefore governed in the best possible way, even if the way be inegalitarian. All these theories admit that political integration is in part illusory but they also affirm that the illusion is not total.

Even Marxist theories, which denounce the illusory nature of integration with such vigour, recognize that it has some limited existence. The state is a product of the class struggle and arises at a certain moment in the development of that struggle. Political power reflects a change in the methods of oppression of the ruling class. Violent, brutal and savage domination is replaced by rule that is in appearance more gentle, more organized and more legal, but also more efficient. The means by which the state acts – rules and procedures, collective organization, education and propaganda, social con-straint – do not serve to create a true order, to develop authentic integration, but only to consolidate the domination of one class over the others in the guise of order and integration. The legislative, administrative and police apparatus of the state is mainly designed to protect the privileges of the ruling class through exploitation of the classes they rule. Thus in the first place the state was in the hands of great landlords who used it to subdue their slaves and then their serfs. Next it fell into the hands of the middle-class owners of industrial and commercial undertakings who use it to oppress the working class.

Yet Marxism admits that the state is not in the exclusive control of one class when, in exceptional and temporary cir-cumstances, a balance is established between several classes. Where a class in decline and formerly dominant still retains

enough strength to resist complete elimination, and a rising
class, formerly dominated, has not enough strength as yet to
expel its rival, for a short time the state holds the balance between the two. Such was the case under the absolute monarchy
of the seventeenth and eighteenth centuries; under the Bona-
partes of the First and Second Empires in France; under
Bismarck in Germany and Kerensky in Russia. The state in
such situations acts to some extent as arbiter, standing slightly
aloof from the fray. It does not act in the exclusive interests of
one class, but attempts to achieve certain compromises between
the classes in balance, and thus it works towards integration.
This integration is only partial; the state does not take into
consideration the interests of all classes in society, but only
those of the rival classes in balance. The absolute monarchy
of the seventeenth and eighteenth centuries and the First
Empire took into account the interests of the aristocracy and
the bourgeoisie, but not of the peasantry and the working class.

Nevertheless Marxists do not entirely reject the idea that the
state works for true social integration. Within the capitalist
system it is the instrument of the bourgeoisie who maintain
their dominance through its means. For the proletariat revolution entails seizing this apparatus of the state, wresting it from
the hands of the bourgeoisie and turning it against them, by
using it for the establishment of Socialism. In this second stage
the state is still an instrument of coercion in the hands of the
dominant class, in this case the workers, who use it in their
own interests, that is, to destroy the remains of the bourgeois
order and the after-effects of exploitation of their class. But in
so doing the working class is acting in the general interests of
mankind, for it is abolishing all exploitation, all domination and
all oppression. At one and the same time it is destroying the
bases of the differences which created the class struggle and is
allowing the construction of a fully integrated society in which
the state will wither away and in which there will be no more
need of political power or coercion. In following its class
interests the proletariat is working for the benefit of the whole
of mankind. Thus, when the proletariat controls the state in
the post-revolutionary stage in which Socialism is being built

up, the state is working for integration in its fullest sense. With its help, and through the dictatorship of the proletariat exercised through its machinery, a human community can be erected which is founded on justice, harmony and co-operation and is therefore a fully integrated community.

This theory has been criticized as being itself based on illusion. Every party tends to consider that power is exercised in the general interest when it is itself in power, and in sectional interests when power is in the hands of its rivals. So much is true, but the fact that views are relative does not prevent some views from being closer to the truth than others. A philosophy of ends and means has contributed to spreading a confusion that favours the privileged classes and the 'established disorder'. Some means cannot be justified, whatever ends they are said to achieve.

None the less, all ends are not of equal value, and though the means may be, it is by the ends that power is judged. Dictatorship is bad in itself, but a dictatorship which tries to establish equality between men, to destroy the rule of the privileged, to free the people from exploitation and contempt is not as bad as a dictatorship maintaining the oppression of an oligarchy over a population sunk in misery and humiliation. Castro is better than Battista, not only because he uses less horrible means, but because he uses them for another end. Communism and Fascism cannot be weighed in the same balance. Confusion over ends and the application of moral judgement to means alone favour the 'established disorder', masking its true nature.

The real role of the state in integration cannot be separated out from the people who, in fact, control the state. No formal analysis which confuses the vehicle and its contents, the sword and the wielder, can adequately describe and explain the facts. Political integration is always in part an illusion. Power is never used exclusively in the service of the social order and the general interest. Inversely there is always some measure of integration even under the worst régimes: they build roads, control traffic, ensure the disposal of household refuse, maintain the fire service and so on. Between these two extremes there is considerable variation in the amount of real and pseudo-integration. It depends primarily on the people in power. When the state is in the hands of the privileged classes they use it basically in their own interests and only secondarily in the general interest: the amount of illusion is greater and that of integration smaller. When the state falls into the hands of those who have till then been dominated and exploited, in their efforts to suppress domination and exploitation they act in the general interest by acting in their own interests, and then the amount of illusion diminishes, while that of integration increases, at least until the former exploited become exploiters in their turn. Nevertheless, by destroying exploitation of themselves they are abolishing for ever certain forms of camouflage.

Marxists affirm that, through this process, total authentic integration without illusion will be achieved, since the working class cannot abolish exploitation of itself except by destroying for ever all forms of exploitation. Western thinkers question this pattern of development, but propose another which would lead in the same direction. They think that technical and economic development, by ending penury and bringing about plenty, will put an end to divisions, inequality and the exploitation of some classes by others, and that one day government will truly exercise its function of integration.

# 4. Integration and the Level of Development

Western thinkers and Marxists disagree about the paths along which modern societies will develop, but they are in agreement both as to the result to which these different paths will lead and as to the motive force behind the development. They consider that the natural movement of history tends to diminish conflicts and increase social integration, and that this movement results from technical development. According to western theorists, technical development has the direct effect of reducing poverty, which is the main cause of conflict: in an affluent society antagonisms have no basis and integration comes about naturally. Marxists, on the other hand, think that technical development has an indirect effect. For them the new methods of production which result from technical progress give rise to new systems of production; in particular, they tend to abolish private ownership, and consequently the class struggle which it causes, so that a classless society, that is, a society where there is no conflict, can be established.

Observation of the facts partly supports this optimism. It can scarcely be disputed that technical progress helps towards social integration, but not everyone would agree about the end to which this evolutionary process will lead. Some western thinkers accept the Marxist vision of a fully integrated future society from which all conflict will have disappeared and where perfect harmony will reign. One may doubt whether this perfect City is possible. However, analysis of the processes which, as described by the opposing theories, would lead to this Utopia, throws light on the influence that technical progress has on political integration. Even if one cannot accept the conclusions, it is therefore of interest to examine the arguments.

## THE GROWTH OF INTEGRATION

Technical progress contributes to social integration in three main ways: by lessening the tensions caused by penury, by making it possible for all men to reach a better understanding of other men and of the society they live in, and by fostering solidarity between all the members of a community. The disproportion between the needs of individuals and the goods available has always been considered as a fundamental factor in social and political strife. The cliché, 'too many men chasing too few goods', sums up the state of mankind from its beginnings until the twentieth century. Doubtless, conflicts could have been attenuated if strict justice had been applied in the distribution of goods, but though it was often described by theorists, this ideal was hardly ever put into practice.

With technical progress has come the dawn of a day which may see the advent of an affluent society, when the level of production would enable both the elementary needs (food, housing and clothing) and the secondary needs (comfort, leisure and culture) of all its citizens to be satisfied. Not that any country has yet reached this level of development, but a few are approaching it. It is true that human needs expand, and grow as fast as they are satisfied, but as secondary needs replace fundamental needs failure to satisfy them is less keenly felt and the conflicts caused by their lack of fulfilment are less bitter.

This development tends to diminish antagonisms in two ways. First, it makes social inequalities more bearable. When the cake is too small all eyes are naturally fixed on the way it is cut up, and violent dispute ensues if the pieces differ in size. But when the cake is large enough to more than satisfy nearly everyone the respective size of the pieces matters less. A hundred and thirty years ago, when the silk-workers of Lyons rebelled, the slogan 'Bread or death' which they put on their banners was true; the political struggle was literally a matter of life and death. Today, in western Europe and North America, it has become a struggle for comfort, leisure and culture, which makes it less savage.

Secondly, technical progress does away with the most brutal forms of man's oppression by man. Today the level of development a country has reached is measured by calculating the number of 'mechanical slaves' which each inhabitant has at his disposition, a 'mechanical slave' being an amount of energy, derived from technical means, equivalent to the energy one man could supply by physical labour. Mechanical slaves are thus replacing human slaves, who for a long time were in some ways a necessity. Some thinkers say that it was only the invention of the horse-collar in the tenth century which made it possible to abolish slavery and bondage. Until the invention of mechanical slaves the privileged minority could only enjoy a pleasant life by using human slaves. Today they only need machines, and the amount of blood, sweat and tears on which inequality is based is less than it was. Inequality itself is diminishing, for technical progress tends to produce societies without marked differences in class, and in a large measure to close the gap there used to be between rich and poor.

Technical progress does not only help integration in a negative way, by lessening antagonisms; it also contributes to positive integration by fostering contact, understanding and solidarity between men. By increasing communication and information, it puts an end to isolation and rigid barriers, and makes all the members aware of the society they live in. By raising the level of culture, it allows everyone to reach a better understanding of others and of the community. By intensifying the division of labour, it increases men's interdependence, a process which the encyclical 'Mater et Magistra' calls socialization. These positive effects, however, carry less conviction than the negative ones. Solidarity, comprehension, and human contact were perhaps deeper and more authentic in the framework of small traditional communities than they are in that of large modern communities, where they are often superficial and even factitious.

However, observation confirms that integration progresses throughout history as technical progress advances. In archaic societies with a closed economy few services are rendered to the collectivity by authority, whether authority be the distant state or the local feudal lord. It does, however, render some services: protection against invasion by neighbouring lords, foreign armies or bands of robbers; arbitration and justice; repression of crimes against persons and property; use of the communal mill or oven; currency control, and so on. But these services are expensive. Authority, in the last resort, takes more than it gives. Its representatives live off the country, and they live in luxury and opulence while the rest of the country is very poor. Power benefits them rather than the community; above all, it protects privilege, and maintains inequality, and so has to rely on violence and arms. Fortresses did not only serve to protect the inhabitants of the region against foreign invaders, but also, and more important, to protect the lords against the population. Kings' palaces were originally fortresses, well armed and well defended, to shelter the monarch against the hostile attacks of his people.

This situation still exists in many parts of the world today. In Latin America, Africa, and Asia, the greater part of the population still lives in a semi-closed economy. It receives few benefits from the state, and has to suffer many disadvantages because of it. The main function of the state is to maintain the domination of a privileged minority which exploits the masses. In an intermediate type of state public services expand: the government builds roads, railways, ports, canals, aerodromes, and provides electricity and telephone networks; it stimulates and regulates credit facilities, and undertakes basic investment like irrigation schemes, mining and hydroelectric dams. But these public works are mainly of use to the privileged minority of the population, the aristocracy and the middle class. The wonderful motorways to be found in some underdeveloped countries only benefit car-owners, the mounted cavalry of modern times, a small minority amid the vast foot-slogging masses.

In comparison with archaic societies, integration has progressed. More people benefit from power, and their circle is growing. Before, only a handful of aristocrats did so; now, the bourgeoisie, which is becoming the median class, does so, too, as do the few members of the peasant and working class who can make use of schools, the welfare services and social security. For the latter group the advantages offered by the state are outnumbered by its disadvantages, but they are increasing, however, and help to foster a sense of integration. This intermediate stage corresponds to the first phase of capitalism. Nineteenth-century Europe, Latin America today, North Africa, the Middle East, and non-Communist Asia can be grouped in this category.

In highly developed western societies political integration has advanced much farther. The rise in the general standard of living is lessening tension and widening the area of agreement. State-controlled communal services are increasing in number, and the role of government as collective organizer is expanding. Even if the economy is not wholly planned, the state is regulating it more and more, by foreseeing crises and modifying their effects, by correcting the distortions caused by private initiative, and so on. Communal services and collective organization are no longer solely a matter for a limited 'inner circle' within the total society; they are gradually extending to the very boundaries of the society. The first cause of this development is the rise in the standard of living: motorways, which only serve a privileged minority in Latin America, benefit nearly all the citizens in the U.S.A. and western Europe. The second cause is the development of social security and of public services whose aim is to correct the inequalities between men, by helping the weakest in particular.

Furthermore, the state is tending to be taken out of the hands of a particular class which uses it to maintain its own domination and privileges. Firstly, technical progress is making the division into classes more and more complex, so that power is never in the hands of a homogeneous social category, but rather of several. Next, the working classes are making authority realize their existence more and more, thanks to the development of universal suffrage, political parties, trade unions, and other mass organizations. The state can no longer be entirely controlled by minority classes, which now must at least come to terms with the majority classes. Finally, the evolution of society and of the state is fostering the development of a class of trained administrators who espouse the general interest, and really embody it, at least partly, as Hegel predicted. The Marxist notion that highly placed civil servants are in the service of the ruling class, from which they are for the most part recruited, was true for a long time, and still is so in part. But in some countries administrators are more and more becoming a class apart, which deliberately refuses to serve capitalist interests, but tends rather to assume the role of impartial arbitrator.

The famous argument Maurras used fifty years ago to show the superiority of monarchy: 'a régime where the private interest of the ruler merges with the national interest, since the nation is the patrimony of the king', could be applied to this emergent administrative class. The phenomenon is still not widespread, and there are dangers inherent in it, but it is important. As an example, consider the way French 'experts' acted as arbitrators in the miners' strike of 1962. No one has challenged the impartiality of their conclusions. It has been suggested that some highly placed administrators should be given the permanent task of 'pronouncing' on the distribution of the national income, as judges pronounce in legal matters. The ruling classes, seeing their influence threatened by this development, are highly critical of the power of these state administrators. They usually hide this feeling behind cries of 'technocracy', exaggerating a danger which is in other respects real. When administrators or state specialists take part in making a decision people speak of technocracy; but it is never mentioned when administrators or specialists from private firms are called in.

The influence of technical development on political integration cannot be disputed. It should not, however, be exaggerated. There are at least two other factors which combine with it, and either intensify or weaken its effect, depending on whether they work with it or against it. There is, first, the speed of development. We have already said that the distinction between stable societies and stationary societies is as important as the distinction between highly developed and underdeveloped societies. In stable societies – that is, where evolution is slow, and scarcely noticeable in one lifetime – the sense of integration is stronger. The social order, established several generations before, appears natural, however unjust it be; and because it seems natural it tends to be accepted. On the contrary, societies where there is rapid change show partial disintegration. The established order ceases to be felt as order from the day when it is no longer established and is visibly falling apart. Then, injustice ceases to be natural and bearable. Latent antagonisms emerge, and cause serious conflicts. The great class wars of the nineteenth and twentieth centuries reflect a change in the rate of evolution. Although their level of development was lower, the aristocratic societies of the seventeenth century were more highly integrated than the bourgeois societies of 1900.

Integration varies, too, according to the type of society. In archaic communities the merging of the individual with the community seems to have reached a stage which can never occur again. Primitive man is totally absorbed into the group, of which he is one element; he has no idea of a separate existence; he sees himself as a member of the community rather than as an individual. The sociologists of the Durkheim school have described the 'institutionalization' of power: according to them, authority, which first belonged to the whole group, to the collectivity as such, was gradually taken over by certain members of the group, who thus became leaders. The parallel process of 'individualization' of the citizens could be described also. Marxists connect it with the appearance of private ownership. Whether this be true or not, no later society seems to have been as highly integrated as primitive societies, which so far, along with some monastic communities and the first Israeli kibboutz, are the only societies to have practised nearly total Communism.

The development of integration is only seen in societies of the modern type, set up after the individualization of the citizens. Before that, progress in techniques seems to have had the opposite effect. It was probably the most important factor in the development of a sense of individuality which partly separated men from the community and caused conflict between individuals and between the group and its members. Even if one disagrees with the Marxist argument which explains the dissolution of an alleged primitive Communism by the emergence of private property, and explains this emergence by the development of the techniques of production, this development does seem to have been an essential factor in the process of individualization.

In modern societies, moreover, technical progress tends partly in the same direction: the development of capitalism corresponds to an increase in individualism. At the end of the nineteenth century and during the first half of the twentieth moralists and reformers were led to denounce the excesses of individualism. But from another point of view technical progress increases solidarity in the different ways we have described above. It would seem that the second movement is gradually gaining over the first. Since the Second World War technical progress has been accused, not of increasing individualism, but rather of crushing the individual under the collective organization. Thus there are contradictions in the development of integration brought about by technical progress. Those who scorn modern society depict it sometimes as a gigantic machine in which men are no more than cogs; and sometimes as a collection of comfortably isolated individuals lacking any real links with their fellow men. We should perhaps distinguish between social integration and political integration. Technical development favours the second kind, that is the integrating function of the state, rather than the first kind, the development of authentic solidarity between men. Power is indeed playing an increasing part in social integration, but it may be that this social integration is a pseudo-integration, less real, less vital than the social integration found in less-developed societies.

### THE MYTH OF TOTAL INTEGRATION

Few people would claim that total integration has been achieved in existing societies; observation of the facts would immediately belie such a claim. Some thinkers consider that it came near to being achieved in some societies in the past. Certain descriptions of the *ancien régime* or of the Middle Ages depict them as Earthly Paradises, rejuvenating the old myth of the Golden Age. But though these descriptions may be interesting as imaginative works or for their psychological content, they are not sociological. The only serious theories of total integration place it in the future, by extending forwards in time the lines of development which can be discerned today. In this field Marxist doctrines and some western ideas converge. Americans and Russians do not have the same conception of the society of the future, nor of the stages by which it will develop, but they both imagine it as a perfectly integrated society, from which conflicts will have disappeared, and where solidarity will reign. In both cases an important basis of total integration is considered to be the abundance of material goods which technical progress will make possible. Western theoreticians state this openly, while Marxist theorists admit it implicitly, since the principle 'to each according to his needs' on which the distribution of goods will be based in the 'higher phase of Communism' cannot be applied if this abundance is lacking. The differences between these two theories – and they are profound – bear on two main points: the process which will lead to the fully integrated society, and the nature of this society.

Western theorists think that integration will be a result of plenty, while Marxists think rather that plenty will result from integration. For the former, social conflicts are caused by the competition of too many men for too few goods, that is, by penury. If technical progress makes it possible for penury to be replaced by plenty and for everyone to satisfy nearly all his needs, not only of food, housing and clothing, but also of comfort, culture and leisure, then antagonism between men will disappear, political conflicts will cease, and an integrated, united society will be reached. For Marxists, real plenty is impossible in a capitalist régime, which is by nature Malthusian. The alienation of the worker diminishes the productivity of his labour. The private entrepreneur slows down the application of technical progress, preferring to go on using his old machines, which are paid for, until they are entirely worn out, rather than invest in costly new plant which would take a long time to pay off. Quite a few inventions and new methods are kept secret by agreement between the firms which dominate the market. In particular, once a certain technical level is reached research cannot be organized, and overall forecasting and planning pursued, within a framework of private enterprise, but only when there is state control of production. The greatest discoveries of the last decades, such as atomic science and rocketry, are the result of socialized research, not of capitalist research. In the U.S.A. nuclear studies were sponsored by the government for reasons of defence; they could not have been undertaken by the machinery of the private sector.

In Marxist theory, therefore, the abolition of the class war and the ending of political conflict are not a result of economic plenty, but the basic condition which will allow it to be attained. The facts would seem to contradict this idea. The most highly developed nations, those which are closest to achieving plenty in the world today, are capitalist, not Socialist. This argument however is not decisive, for to date Socialism has been applied to underdeveloped or semideveloped countries which, when they abandoned capitalism, were economically far behind North America and western Europe. The fact that this gap has not yet been closed does not prove anything: on the contrary, the fact that Socialist countries have a higher rate of growth seems to justify the Marxist theories. However, that argument, too, is inconclusive, as the rate of growth may drop naturally as the level of development rises.

According to western thinkers, plenty gives rise of itself to complete social integration. For Marxists, plenty is a necessary condition of integration, but not a sufficient condition. As long as men continue to act only in their own selfish interests, as long as their collective activity is directed towards a form of economic competition which gives some men dominion over others, as long as capitalist exploitation continues to lead to the alienation of the workers, true integration will be impossible. Here, the Marxist analysis goes deeper than the western one. It takes into account the contradiction which is found, in the evolution of modern societies, between a tendency to develop solidarity and a tendency towards the isolation of individuals, each sealed off in his own comfort and egoism.

Even if plenty were sufficient to destroy all antagonism, that is to achieve negative integration, it is doubtful whether it could also develop positive integration, based on authentic social communion and not simply on the technical solidarities produced by the division of labour and by collective organization. Only the substitution of altruism for egoism, of the common good for personal interest, as the fundamental motive of human actions, can bring about a fully integrated society. It is not certain that the suppression of capitalism would suffice to destroy egoism and the pursuit of private interest. It is not certain that ending alienation would suffice to make work once again that free creative activity, in which man finds self-fulfilment and joy, which Plato thought it was. It is not certain that this 'unalienated' work would automatically be directed towards the good of the collectivity. In a word, it is debatable whether Communism, in its highest phase, can attain that total integration of all men into the community which would allow the state, as an instrument of constraint, to wither away. It is quite certain, however, that these aims will never be achieved, even in a fully affluent society, if private interest continues to be the mainspring of man's activity: that is, if capitalism, which has this principle as one of its bases, continues to survive.

The Marxist theory of the withering away of the state has been taken up recently in the West in another form, that of 'depolitization'. In highly developed nations observers claim to have noted some attenuation of conflict in recent years, some lessening of antagonism. The weakening role of the parties, and their tendency to draw nearer together and resemble each other, have impressed some observers considerably. The gap between Conservatives and Liberals, which was very wide in the nineteenth century, has almost disappeared. The gap between Socialist and bourgeois parties, which was quite large before 1914, is today much narrower, and even the gap between Communists and non-Communists, which in 1945 was immeasurable, has now shrunk. The idea of revolution, which had dominated Left-wing parties in some countries for more than a century, is now no more than a vague dream: the revolutionary spirit is disappearing from among the working classes in developed nations. Many theorists see this phenomenon as a direct consequence of the rise in the standard of living and progress towards affluence. The partial depolitization of present-day societies, based on a similarly partial affluence, is thought to mark a stage in development, the end of which will be total depolitization, that is the complete withering away of the state, brought about by total affluence.

The success that the concept of depolitization has met with derives from its ambiguity. When the term is used to mean that political antagonisms are tending to assume less violent forms in developed societies, and in particular that revolutionary methods are being replaced by reformist methods, it expresses an indisputable fact, which is certainly connected with the rise in living standards; but it is linked, too, with other factors, in particular the complexity of modern societies which is incompatible with the use of rough and brutal methods. The idea that a revolution would cause a profound upheaval in the apparatus of production, which afterwards would take a long time to start functioning again, and therefore that a revolution would necessarily cause a prolonged drop in production and living standards, a long period of penance, is fairly widespread, and contains some truth. Whether one is dealing with biological organisms, with machines, or with societies, it is a fact that the higher they are in the scale of complexity the more fragile are their structures, which therefore need handling with greater care. Two earthworms can be made out of one, if it is cut into two, but this kind of treatment cannot be administered to the higher vertebrates. A cart can be mended with a few blows from a hammer, but a Boeing 707 cannot. Brutal revolutions can be effected in relatively undeveloped countries, but not in France or the U.S.A.

The expression 'depolitization' can be criticized, however, since the elimination of violence and its replacement by processes of discussion and compromise are the very essence of politics, which by its nature tends to replace physical combat, armed battles and civil wars by organized and moderate forms of conflict. So instead of 'depolitization' we should use the term 'politization', and should speak, not of the state withering, but of it being restored after the partial dissolution it underwent in the violent revolutionary struggles of the nineteenth century. Furthermore, if 'depolitization' is used to mean that conflict is disappearing, that antagonisms are coming to an end, and that politics is vanishing, then this concept does not represent the situation today in developed societies but is entirely false. The lack of interest in politics which some observers claim to find in western Europe and North America is simply a lack of interest in some forms of politics which have become archaic because of changes in the social structures. It corresponds to an increased interest in other forms of politics.

The decline of political parties in France and the indifference towards some traditional methods of representation coincides with the rise of the unions, peasant organizations and political clubs and with the development of new methods of representation. The decline of the parties is, however, not general in the west. In many ways interest in politics is increasing rather than diminishing; in this respect, too, one could speak of 'politization', not 'depolitization'. Technical politics is tending to eliminate heroic politics, retail politics is replacing wholesale politics, conflict about the régime is giving way to conflict within the régime, and concrete claims are becoming more important than general criticism of the system. Today, liberty and equality are being defended in committees rather than at the barricades, and by organized strikes rather than in romantic speeches. But the fight for liberty and equality still continues.

# 5. The Myth of the Golden Age

It seems clear that as technology develops political conflict decreases and social integration increases. It is less clear that the development which has thus begun can continue unhindered until finally all conflicts have disappeared and total integration has come about, as both the Marxist doctrine of the higher phase of Communism and the western theory of the affluent society claim that it will. Such an end to history and to conflict is imperilled by a number of facts. The penury which western thought denounces, like the capitalism denounced by Marxists, is not the only factor in social conflict. Were they to disappear, others which seem less easy to eradicate would survive.

Even if the Golden Age could, in fact, come to pass in a few highly developed societies, these would be rather like oases lost in the desert, islands against whose coasts beat angry seas. In the near future only a very few countries can hope to achieve affluence. For the remainder, it remains an inaccessible mirage, and indeed the difficulties of accumulating investment capital as well as demographic pressures make divisions more intense in these countries. There is increasingly a fundamental division between the rich nations and the proletarian nations. To think that the former could disregard the latter and protect themselves by a *cordon sanitaire* is to repeat the error committed by the bourgeoisie in the nineteenth century in their attitude to the working class.

## IRREDUCIBLE CONFLICTS

The concept of affluence is superficial, for in the first place as needs are satisfied they increase. The pursuit of affluence is rather like the race between Achilles and the tortoise. As old needs disappear, new ones appear to take their place. Objectively, no doubt, these are less vital and essential, but whether, subjectively, they are felt any less deeply is not at all sure. Secondly, and this is more important, the affluence in question concerns only economic matters. Now penury in other fields also creates social conflicts, which naturally tend to grow as economic conflicts disappear. The man with an empty stomach is concerned only with eating and struggling to stay alive, while the man who has eaten his fill does not think of food, but struggles to satisfy other desires.

Arther Koestler tells how, as a starving prisoner, he would dream of banquets, with the same intensity as he dreamed of women when an adolescent. In the eyes of Marxists and contemporary capitalists, affluent societies end the first privation but not the second. Some psychoanalysts think it more important than the first as a factor in the development of antagonism. The conflict between social imperatives and human desires, between the reality principle and the pleasure principle, seems to them more fundamental than disputes concerning the distribution of national revenue or freedom of speech. This conflict could indeed become more important once such freedom existed and economic affluence had pushed material demands into the background. The modern development of eroticism and of what American sociologists, with considerable exaggeration, call the 'sex revolution', could be studied in this light. Might this not be the demand for and the gradual realization, in a questionable form, of a kind of liberty, a struggle against privation, which is developing as other forms of liberty are established and other privations disappear?

Some scarcities cannot be eliminated, since they are in the nature of things. Every Frenchman cannot own a villa on the Riviera, because space is limited. Every Parisian may one day have a comfortable flat, but not all will be situated with equal convenience near the office, the factory and places of entertainment. All workers may one day be paid an adequate salary, but not all work will be equally interesting or bearable. Managerial posts will always be more pleasant than subordinate positions, but will always be more scarce. Competition for the best jobs will always be keen. The more talented will always have the advantage over the less talented, which in turn will inevitably cause bitterness and frustration.

Even in a socialist régime inequality will not be simply an individual matter. Classes will never completely disappear, because the children of the more talented parents who occupy the highest posts in society will always have more opportunities than the sons of the ungifted in lower positions. The son of the Permanent Under Secretary or of the manager of a public undertaking will be better placed in the competition than the son of a bailiff or a labourer, because of the education through osmosis conferred by his social status, of his parents' connections and of the material opportunities they give him. He will certainly be less privileged than the son of an important capitalist proprietor, but his privileges may seem more outrageous because they are more contrary to the accepted scale of values. In a world of equality a small inequality will perhaps be felt more than a major inequality in a world of inequality.

Another class division, the division between men and women, seems more difficult to eliminate. Under Socialism, as under capitalism, women are oppressed by comparison with men. To alter their position in law, to give them equal rights and end wage discrimination will not do away with the additional duties imposed on them by child-bearing and bringing up children. If the woman stays at home, she is economically dependent on the man; if she works like a man, she has family and household duties in addition to her professional work. The state of relations between the sexes in America, where man is at the mercy of woman, is no more satisfactory than the position in France, where woman is at the mercy of man, or the position in Italy, which maintains both in a state of permanent hypocrisy. Conflicts arising from this battle of the sexes, although not directly political, have considerable importance throughout the whole of social life.

It does not seem possible to abolish the conflict of generations either. As they become part of society young people always set themselves to some extent against the old, who naturally are not anxious to yield the positions which the young

P.—H

are eager to seize. The lengthening of the life span as a result of technical progress only adds to the conflict. On the one hand, the younger generation has to bear a heavy burden of providing pensions; on the other, the older generation is reduced to the position of an oppressed class. Ancient civilizations mitigated the natural tragedy of old age by surrounding the old with prestige and respect. In highly developed societies old age is twice as much to be feared because the effects of society are added to those of nature. In a capitalist system a man over forty-five who loses his job has difficulty in finding another and may well become a human wreck. In a Socialist system the position is better, but in all societies the necessary lowering of the age of retirement, combined with the continuing increase in the life span, creates a class of old people reduced to a minor role in society, when they are still able and willing to share fully in its activities for many years to come. They are alienated in the Marxist sense of the term.

Again, we must not forget that some psychoanalysts think that technical progress tends to create a mechanized, artificial world, completely contrary to man's real needs and deepest desires, to his very nature. On this view, by freeing individuals from the need to work constantly in order to live, material affluence would only make them more aware of this contradiction and cause them to suffer more deeply from it. Thus the conflict between men and society will grow worse rather than better. The increase in mental illness, the reappearance of certain forms of violence, the development of neuroses, anxiety and anguish, the absence of any real joy in life – these it is said are defects congenital to the most modern societies, and they are therefore permanent, not temporary ailments brought on by the change to new forms of existence.

In any case, even if technical progress reduces conflict between individuals and groups, the conflict between authority and citizens does not follow the same pattern and seems to be growing rather than shrinking. Certainly authority is less tyrannical as far as ends are concerned; it acts more in the general interest and is more useful. As far as means are concerned its growth increases its hold over men and the shame with which their bondage fills them. Anatole France said, 'I forgive the Republic for governing badly, because it governs scarcely at all.' The modern state governs better, but it governs more. In ancient societies authority was very remote and men rarely came into contact with it; they dispensed with it for most things. In modern society each citizen depends on the state for a considerable part of his existence; relationships with authority are multiplied and so therefore are the occasions when its rule is felt.

The methods through which authority exercises oppression are becoming more complicated. The tendency for leaders to abuse their authority is not suppressed or restrained by technical progress, but rather increased; to increase the means in the hands of authority is to increase the possibilities of abusing power. Modern methods of communication and propaganda give modern dictators a hold over nations which bears no comparison with the authority of ancient tyrants. When the latter became unbearable they were likely to be dethroned. Today authority has powerful arms at its disposal which make any resistance on the part of citizens more difficult. Revolt by the masses was simple when soldiers and policemen were armed with sabres or lances; against tanks, machine-guns, planes and armoured cars the people are powerless, as the Spanish Civil War proved.

Furthermore, the psychological oppression deriving from the leaders' will to power is paralleled in highly developed countries by a sociological kind of oppression springing from the evolution of the structures of power. The broadening of the state apparatus leads to an increase in the numbers of people making decisions in the name of the state. The circle of rulers, that is the number of people whom citizens must obey, is widened. The single tyrant with his few associates is replaced by a host of petty despots. Each has only a limited field of action, but the pressure which they all exert results in a restriction of mens' freedom of movement, condemning them to the lot of Gulliver, bound to the earth by thousands of Lilliputian strings, each small in itself, but constraining by their very numbers.

Above all, the modern state is gradually ceasing to be simply a collection of leaders, rulers and administrators, each individually abusing their power. It is becoming a huge machine, the overall power of which exceeds the activity of each of its cogs. Its very mechanism is by nature oppressive, independently of the intentions of the men constituting it. This phenomenon that we call 'bureaucracy' is not limited to the state, that is, the power within the nation. It extends to all forms of power in large modern conmunities, huge firms, political parties, mass organizations and so on. Although it may be abstract, mechanical, devoid of emotion and physical violence, and 'hygienic', the tyranny it enforces is no less oppressive than that resulting from the will to power of leaders.

This is probably the essential factor of conflict in highly developed societies. As we approach the level of affluence class war and competition between citizens diminish, with the reservations already mentioned. Conflict between authority and citizens, on the other hand, is increased. The question of liberty tends to return to the centre of political debate once again, as it was for Liberals in the nineteenth century. They had situated it within the microcosm of relative plenty which the bourgeoisie then was, itself at the centre of the mass of the people reduced to penury. Their material problems being solved, for the bourgeoisie the defiance of authority by the citizen became the essential problem, but for the working class the struggle for existence, for equality and dignity were still much more important. Political freedom, which was a real issue for the bourgeoisie who had the means to exercise it, was still a mere formality for the proletariat. The fundamental conflict was the class struggle.

In the affluent society the bourgeois microcosm grows and embraces the whole community. Important divisions between individuals and groups still exist, as classes always have a tendency to reappear in different guises, but these divisions are secondary in comparison with the division between citizen and authority. Firstly, liberty now become meaningful and valid for all citizens, since all have the material means of exercising it. Then, while it develops a state of plenty and thus diminishes conflict arising from penury, technical progress increases the strength of authority and its power of oppression. Thus liberty regains the original meaning attributed to it by Liberals in the nineteenth century. 'Liberty is resistance', said Benjamin Constant, contrasting this modern conception with what he called 'the liberty of the Ancients which consists of active participation in corporate power'.

In fact, this liberty of the Ancients has gradually become our modern liberty, particularly in Anglo-Saxon countries, where democracy is above all the active participation of each individual in collective decisions, such participation being made possible by decentralization and a multiplicity of societies and civic organizations closely involving each individual in community life. At the same time Socialism has shown, contrary to capitalist doctrines, that the state can act as liberator. 'Between rich and poor, weak and strong, it is liberty which oppresses and law which frees', said Lacordaire. The abolition of transfer of property is a step towards liberty and so is the abolition of poverty. Alongside 'liberty as participation' we can thus see the birth of the concept 'liberty as self-development'. Theories of the affluent society and of the higher phase of Communism are based on the idea that every man has the right to develop according to his own nature and to dispose of all means necessary to that end.

While the notions of liberation through the state, of liberty as self-development and liberty as participation were being formed, the idea of liberty as resistance was gradually losing its value. The development of modern societies is tending to resurrect it and probably even to give it pride of place again. Certainly, technical progress and relative affluence allow each individual to develop more freely. Certainly the action taken by the state against private domination and exploitation is generally liberating. Certainly, too, citizens' participation in decisions at all levels is an essential element of their liberty. But the more developed the society, the more powerful and bureaucratic political authority becomes, the more it becomes necessary to resist it. Liberty has always meant resistance and it is becoming resistance more and more. The affluent society does not lead towards the withering away of the state but towards its growth and its bureaucratization. The opposition of citizens to power then becomes the fundamental conflict. There is no evidence for the belief that this conflict will disappear or even diminish. Political conflict in the form of the struggle for liberty has no foreseeable end.

### BOURGEOIS AND PROLETARIAN NATIONS

A Martian who visited the Earth, like the Persians who visited Europe in Montesquieu's story, would not be immediately aware of the differences between western and Socialist countries. The difference between industrialized and underdeveloped countries would, however, strike him forcibly. There are, of course, many nations at an intermediate stage between these two extremes: Japan, for example, is moderately developed; Latin America, the coloured areas of Africa, the Middle East and the Far East are not underdeveloped to the same extent or in the same way. These distinctions apart, all underdeveloped countries share the same characteristics: a predominance of agriculture in a primitive form, food scarcity, a low level of industrialization with a low consumption of mechanical energy, a low level of national income, with excessive commercial activity, outdated social structures, great inequality between the poverty-stricken masses and a very wealthy, very small privileged group, the non-existence of middle classes, a considerable disparity between urban and country modes of life, illiteracy, a high birth-rate together with a high death-rate, and so on. All these phenomena are interconnected, though the relative importance of one rather than another varies according to the particular country. The overall picture which they present is sufficiently characteristic to leave no margin of confusion.

Two worlds face one another, the one rich, the other poor. Whereas the former is anticipating the dawn of an affluent society the latter is nearer to the medieval period with its poverty, its famines and epidemics. In western Europe and the United States the national *per capita* income is between ten and twenty times higher than it is in Asia and Africa. The mechanical energy consumed per head is between ten and thirty times greater. Infantile mortality is, on the other hand, ten times less. In the industrialized nations the illiteracy figure is 3 or 4 per cent, whereas in some Asiatic and African countries it is 90 per cent. The gap between bourgeois and proletarian nations today is as great as the gap between the bourgeoisie and the proletariat in any European country in the nineteenth century.

The gap is increasing instead of decreasing. The nations of Africa, Asia and Latin America are said to be developing rapidly and this is true by comparison with the extremely slow rate of development they have known in earlier centuries. It is false if compared with the development of the industrial nations, which are evolving much more rapidly. Generally speaking, the rate of annual growth in the national income is higher in Europe and North America than in the Third World. The rich are continuing to grow richer and the poor to grow poorer. The share of the industrial nations in the world's wealth is increasing while that of the underdeveloped countries is getting smaller.

This situation creates two kinds of conflict: internal strife within the underdeveloped countries; external hostility between them and the highly developed nations. The proletarian countries are rent by all the divisions which penury creates and these divisions are exacerbated by increased contact and improved communications, by the very efforts made for development. When the Indians of Latin America or the peasants of the African brush and the plains of Asia lived isolated and shut away from the world, poverty and inequality were less of a burden to them than now, when radio, television and the cinema have made them aware of the existence of different kinds of civilization which ease the lot of man. Injustice and poverty are more easily endured in an unchanging world in which they appear to be natural calamities that are impossible to avoid. They are less endurable when the world around begins to change and when it becomes possible to hope for greater justice and less poverty. This transformation is provoked when countries enter upon the path of accelerated

development. However, the very conditions of such development preclude the immediate realization of the hope it engenders and in the short term they aggravate the suffering
which development is aimed at abolishing. These contradictions inherent in the intermediate phase and the divisions which
they bring about have already been discussed.

The disparity between a falling mortality rate and a stationary
birth ratio leads to a formidable growth in the population
which cancels out the benefits of economic development for
the individual citizen. The cake increases in size, but the
number who need a share in it increases faster, so that each
individual's share, which is already too small, becomes smaller
still. The need to direct manpower away from the production
of consumer goods in order to create the infrastructure of a
modern society similarly tends to depress an already low
standard of living. The difficulties attendant on the primary
accumulation of capital which created the appalling exploitation of the working class in nineteenth-century Europe and the
Stalinist dictatorship of the twentieth century now beset Latin
America, the Middle and Far East as well as Africa.

These economic and demographic contradictions are paralleled by political contradiction of similar magnitude. Even
in times of tranquillity democracy can scarcely function in
underdeveloped countries. An illiterate population lacks the
education to understand political problems and makes it sus-
ceptible to every form of persuasion, to every form of dema-
gogy. Moreover, the extent of inequality and the violence of
the antagonisms which it brings about prevent that minimum
consensus of agreement being achieved without which the
machinery of parties and elections cannot function freely.
Underdeveloped countries are therefore condemned to authoritarian régimes. Now, these last tend of their nature to disorder
and inefficiency, even to despotism and corruption. The
educated minority is so small that the creation of administrative and technical cadres is difficult. The gap between the
privileged and the mass is so great and the masses are so backward that the abuse of power is easy and the temptation to
abuse strong. The very nature of underdeveloped countries

makes democratic control impossible and the absence of democratic control leaves their citizens at the mercy of arbitrary power.

Alongside these internal contradictions there is the development of deep-seated antagonism between the proletarian and the industrialized nations. As class divisions dwindle away in industrialized societies the class war is tending to move from the national to the international plane. The growing wealth of the rich nations and the increasing poverty of the poor naturally make the latter hostile to the former. The hostility is made more intense by the fact that rich countries exploit the poor just as the bourgeoisie exploits the proletariat under capitalism. Technical aid is but a mirage which *mutatis mutandis* reminds one of the myth of charity in Dickensian England. In a few individual cases, for political reasons, some rich countries give more, and sometimes much more, to certain poor nations than they receive in return; this is the case for French aid to Africa and American aid to Viet-Nam. Overall, however, and generally speaking the total value of the sacrifices accepted by the rich nations to help the underdeveloped is less than the profits they derive from the low price of the raw materials they buy from those countries. Industrial societies exploit agricultural societies by taking advantage of their economic weakness.

Good intentions are no more capable of ending such exploitation than they were of ending the nineteenth-century exploitation of the proletariat by the bourgeoisie. The driving force in a capitalist society is economic interest and to it all else is subordinate. Western governments can, by invoking the themes of Christian charity and the danger of Communism, get their taxpayers to make some sacrifice to help underdeveloped countries, but they can never bring about a state of affairs in which large capitalist organizations do not seek to pay as little as possible for the raw materials coming from those countries; nor can they prevent these organizations from having the last word. Of its essence capitalism is opposed to any real international aid which would help underdeveloped countries to rise above the contradictions inherent in the intermediate phase.

Nevertheless the conflict between industrialized and proletarian nations is scarcely likely to produce any direct confrontation. The new class war differs in one fundamental particular from the old. In the nineteenth century the privileged classes were literally besieged by the proletariat, against whom their police and military forces were inadequate to defend them. The bourgeoisie was therefore compelled by working-class pressure gradually to abandon part of its privileges. Today under the protection of distance, of the oceans and deserts which separate them, and under the even more powerful protection of their mighty weapons of destruction, Europe, Russia and North America run no risk of attack by the proletarian countries. No underdeveloped country can attack the industrialized nations. On the political level the conflict between rich and poor nations is not fundamental, because the two opponents are unequally matched.

However, this conflict intensifies the antagonisms between industrial nations. The two developed worlds, East and West, are relatively fixed and stable; each has renounced the conquest of the other and the frontiers between them are clear. This particular antagonism has lost its virulence like the class struggle within industrial societies. On the other hand, the underdeveloped Third World is unstable. By leaning towards the East or the West it can give one side or the other an important advantage in their rivalry. The uncontrolled and uncontrollable reactions of the proletarian countries are reviving the struggle between the two industrial empires which otherwise would be at peace. Washington would react strongly if an important area of Latin America became Communist. Thus the proletarian nations may not be able directly to confront the highly developed nations, but they can impel them to confront one another. Such intensification of international conflict revives internal divisions. In the West today the fear of Communism, that is of an external danger, is a basic element in internal political conflicts. So long as there are proletarian nations, the rich will not achieve total integration, even supposing that to be possible.

# Conclusion

Despite the wide areas of disagreement between western thinkers and Marxists, their conceptions of politics have much more in common than they realize.

The former have almost abandoned the idealism which was but a thin disguise for behaviour that was in practice far from idealistic. Today they are prepared to admit that socio-economic factors play an essential part in the development of political conflict. At a primitive level, when techniques are rudimentary, these socio-economic factors are mainly geographical, and depend on climate and natural resources. At the next stage they become technical: the level of industrialization conditions the standard of living, which in its turn conditions political warfare. This western analysis is very different from the Marxist picture, but the divergences bear ultimately on secondary points. Both western and Marxist thinkers agree on the main factor, that technical development is the primary cause of evolution in the social structures, on which developments in political warfare and integration depend.

For their part, Marxist thinkers are beginning to attribute more importance to cultural factors. They still formally maintain the distinction between the foundation and the superstructures, but in practice they are increasingly recognizing the influence and the independence of the latter. They still consider cultural factors as second in importance to socio-economic factors, at least in the present phase of human development, but many western thinkers are of the same opinion, which is doubtless well founded. Even the psychological theories are not convincing in this respect, for temperaments and psychological complexes, and even the 'self', are perhaps more dependent on the social environment than on innate disposition.

Both Marxists and western thinkers probably underestimate the influence of value-systems: disinterested beliefs, ideals, and grand designs are a fundamental driving force in politics, and their importance even seems to be growing, as the rising standard of living makes it possible for all men to free themselves from the *primum vivere* and reach the *deinde philosophari*. This mistake is common to both theories, and unites them more than it divides them.

There is even greater similarity between the theories relating to the transition from conflict to integration. Khrushchev's programmes for Communism in the 1980s show a striking resemblance to descriptions of 'the American way of life' coming from the other side of the Atlantic. The western picture of a comfortable and depoliticized affluent society is very close to Soviet pictures of the higher phase of Communism and the decline of the state. Both show the same excessive optimism. To sum up, though western and Marxist thinkers do not share the same overall view of politics, yet they no longer imagine totally different worlds with no point of contact. Henceforth, the similarities between their respective conceptions of the world are almost as marked as their differences.

Developments which have actually occurred probably show an even greater degree of convergence. We have already said that to all appearances, the two developed worlds – the East and the West – are each firmly set in their positions, with no change possible on either side. But, in fact, a deep change is slowly bringing them closer to each other. The U.S.S.R. and the People's Democracies will never become capitalist, while the U.S.A. and western Europe will never become Communist, but both sides seem to be moving towards Socialism, in different ways: through liberalization in the East, and through socialization in the West. It is probable that this double movement will meet great obstacles, that it will take a long time, and that it will suffer reversals. But ultimately it would seem to be irresistible.

Naturally, each country can see the evolution of the other more clearly than it sees its own. In the West, people have become aware of the liberalization which is taking place in the

Soviet world owing to technical progress and economic de-velopment. In industrial societies, which make material well-being possible, the aspiration towards this well-being cannot be stifled. The citizens of Socialist régimes want to make the best of life, to enjoy themselves, and to taste the fruit of the tree which the Revolution planted. They want to do so in peace, in 'safety', as the French said in 1789, free from the rulers' rod and police control. The desire for liberty is insepar-able from this desire for well-being. People want to travel, to go abroad, and sample foreign cultures. They want to express their own opinions, to say what they think, to discuss the offi-cial line, and hear other points of view. In a word they, want to be able to wander along any road, and even off the road, instead of having to keep to the narrow track of the state railway.

At the same time the demands of technical development make it necessary for many people to be given a high level of culture, which encourages a spirit of comparison and a critical outlook, that is, the idea of liberty. Contacts with foreign countries are essential if scientific research is to be pursued and discoveries developed: Stalinism caused serious delays in several sectors. Opening up the means of communication makes it impossible to maintain the intellectual isolation which dictatorships need. Soon every Russian will be able to get western television programmes on his set, and will want to do so, and the government will not be able to stop him. Liberali-zation will be a slow and difficult process. International crises will cause it to be interrupted and even temporarily reversed. But technical and economic development will prevent the movement of Communism towards democratic Socialism from being effectively halted.

The Afro-Asian countries can do much to speed up or slow down this movement. There is every reason to believe that the proletarian nations, too, will one day enter on the path of democratic Socialism. The problem is whether they will do so directly, or whether they will make a detour via Communism or capitalism, like other countries. If they choose the direct road, they will speed the evolution towards democratic Social-ism; if they choose the other ways, they will slow it down. If, in the coming decades, many African, Asian or Latin-American countries align themselves with China, liberalization will be delayed in the U.S.S.R. and the European Peoples' Republics, first because the Stalinists in those countries will find their hand strengthened, and secondly because the inevitable reactions in the West will make peaceful co-existence more difficult and will reactivate the cold war.

It is impossible to suggest an overall hypothesis about the future behaviour of the underdeveloped countries. A few points only seem certain. The Afro-Asian countries will not be able to achieve modernization by capitalist methods, because their domestic capital resources are insufficient, and foreigners will only invest capital in proletarian countries if it is to their own advantage. That is to say, they will only do so in colonial-type enterprises, which exploit some exceptional natural resource regardless of the general economic balance of the country (bananas in Central America, sugar in Cuba, diamonds in Katanga, petroleum in various countries). However, under-developed countries can help to equip themselves by allowing foreign capitalists to set up this kind of enterprise and operate it for some time, and later nationalizing them. They frequently use this method, if the colonialist enterprises do not control the government through police or military forces.

It seems equally impossible for really democratic Socialism to be established directly. We have said earlier that the social structures of the proletarian nations make it very difficult for democracy to work and freedom to develop. Afro-Asian Socialism will necessarily be authoritarian. The only real choice will be between varying degrees of authoritarianism and differing forms of Socialism. It is uncertain whether the most brutal way is the most effective, and in this respect the Chinese model is a dubious one, though for the moment there is no other. One may imagine a less violent form of Socialism, which would allow some political liberties, and would constitute a first stage on the road to democratic Socialism. Several countries in Africa and the Middle East are feeling their way in this direction. It cannot yet be said that they have been very successful.

The socialization of the West will perhaps be a longer and even more difficult process than the liberalization of the East, but it seems just as inevitable. It will probably not follow the pattern that Marxism predicts. In industrial societies class warfare is lessening rather than intensifying, and a proletarian revolution has become all the more impossible as the revolutionary spirit no longer exists and the proletariat is in process of disappearing. However, three very important facts are becoming apparent, the consequences of which do not seem to be appreciated by western thinkers: the technical superiority of planned production over capitalist production; the impossibility of building a real human community on capitalist principles; and the loss of value these very principles are undergoing.

American economists are themselves becoming aware of the inferiority of capitalism in the third sector. Many services can only be adequately provided by the collectivity, and by abandoning the rule of economic profitability: that is, by Socialist methods. Now, the more highly developed a society, the more important the tertiary sector becomes, and the greater its influence over the rest of the economy. In a more general way, the superiority of Socialism over capitalism is simply the superiority of organization over lack of organization. Capitalist organization within firms and enterprises is sometimes excellent, but by its very nature it is inadequate in the economy taken as a whole. It is impossible to organize the total economy while techniques of forecasting are relatively undeveloped, and at that stage Socialism is inferior to capitalism, because then the attempt to co-ordinate the total production, by a plan which fits every part to the whole, is even more rough and ready, more approximative, and less satisfactory, than the co-ordination which the machinery of competition spontaneously provides. Advances in economic analysis have changed this situation, and however imperfect techniques of forecasting may still be, they are already making it possible to draw up plans which achieve better co-ordination than free enterprise and the laws of supply and demand. And they will undoubtedly gain in precision in the years to come.

Such total planning is not possible in a capitalist framework.

Each firm can draw up plans on its own account, based on analyses and calculations in its own branch of activity. But these plans are bound to go wrong, because they cannot take into account such general factors as the behaviour of consumers, changes in the cost of raw materials and of labour, etc. In the capitalist system planning and organization can, at the most, only reach one product group, through the development of agreements and trusts. But the total planning and organization which would cover the whole society is impossible.

Only the political power, the state, can apply the techniques of calculation and forecasting to the whole community, and draw up an overall plan based on them. Such a plan is meaningless unless the different branches of private activity are forced to follow it. This constraint implies that the freedom of the owners of private firms, the very basis of capitalism, will be restricted.

Evolution thus tends towards Socialism, by a process which could be summed up as follows: (1) technical development makes organization of the whole economy possible: (2) this overall organization is more effective than the approximate adjustments which result from free competition; (3) it cannot be put into effect in a capitalist system; (4) capitalism loses its efficacity as a means of satisfying individual and social needs as a whole; (5) it is therefore tending to disappear, in favour of a system of planned production, the corollary of which is that the owners of firms will lose their power of making fundamental decisions (volume of investment, trend of production). Having summarized thus the trend towards Socialism, there are two conceivable forms which socialization could take: outright suppression of private ownership of the means of production, that is Socialism in the current sense of the term, or a decrease in the rights of owners, who would still keep their positions.

There are two paths which capitalism could follow in its evolution towards Socialism, both analogous to the ways in which autocracy gave place to democracy: the republican way, and the way of the British monarchy. It is possible that one day the owners of firms will have no more power in their own enterprises than the Queen of England has today in that country. This change has already begun to take place in many western countries, where firms are no longer like absolute monarchies, but more like constitutional monarchies. François Bloch-Lainé has written a theoretical study of this 'Orleanist' capitalism. If the movement develops to its logical end, it remains to be seen how the continued existence of owner-monarchs and of their Civil List, that is, their profits, can be justified. However, Bloch-Lainé points out that institutions survive long after they have outlived their usefulness, provided they are not too much of a hindrance.

Overall planning of the economy certainly has some draw-backs. The unavoidable mistakes in forecasting, the decelera-tion caused by co-ordination of effort, and the 'loss of impetus' along the administrative lines of transmission all lessen the efficiency of the system. Excessive centralization gives rise to serious mistakes, many examples of which are offered by the U.S.S.R. and the Peoples' Democracies. Some decentralization is needed, but it presents a problem which is not easy to solve. However, many of the mistakes of planning are a result of its present state of imperfection, and will gradually be corrected. In any case, the losses caused by planning are much less serious than the enormous wastage found in developed capitalist economies. Because we are on the inside, it is difficult for us to appreciate the stupefying absurdity of a system which is coming more and more to depend on the creation of artificial needs by advertisement, so that useless products, from which the con-sumer derives no real satisfaction, can be sold in order to guarantee the profits of capitalists, who are thus enabled to afford a few more similarly useless objects. Planning is better, not only because it organizes the means of production, but also because it defines its purpose. It substitutes a normal, coherent, and purposeful movement for the aberrant behaviour of capital-ist economies, which remind one of animals whose brains have been tampered with in vivisection experiments.

This brings us back to the second element in the evolution of the West towards Socialism, that is, the impossibility of founding a real human community on capitalist principles. By its very nature, capitalism is anti-social: it centres each individual's activity on himself and closets every man in his egoism. To make personal profit the main motive in collective life is to deprive that life of any really collective nature and to destroy the principle of any society, which is solidarity between its members. In the capitalist system this solidarity is simply material interdependence: society simply makes it possible for individual interests to be more amply satisfied and for egoism to fulfil itself better. The 'social service' theory is just a piece of advertiser's blurb. The producer is not concerned with 'serving' the consumer, but with making as much profit as possible. Even if it were true that by pursuing his own profit he contributed to satisfying the needs of all as well as possible, this self-seeking orientation of all human activity would still be contrary to real community life.

This basic vice of capitalism can be well illustrated by the way material well-being and moral loneliness are developing side by side, and by the way men's sense of solidarity grows weaker as their material interdependence grows stronger. The revival of religious feeling in the West is probably a result of this phenomenon. It is caused not so much by a need for transcendence and eternity as by a thirst for communion. It is directly opposed to the very principles of capitalism. There has always been a basic contradiction between Christianity and capitalism. When western societies claim allegiance to both the one and the other they are claiming to serve two incompatible masters; in reality, they serve only one of them, and the other is but a screen. At first they used Christianity to camouflage their capitalism. Now, perhaps, we may be entering a second phase, in which a return to more authentic Christianity will help to destroy the very bases of capitalism, and in which religion will change from being the opium of the people to being an instrument of their deliverance.

The superiority of planning over anarchy, and the impossibility of building a real community on capitalist principles, are already causing the latter to lose their value. In a deeper and more general way, the very basis of the system, private ownership of the means of production, is losing its legitimacy in the eyes of western peoples. One by one the things which justify it in practice are disappearing. Today technical progress is a result of fundamental research which, disinterested in nature and backed by enormous financial resources, can only be adequately undertaken by the state or non-capitalist institutions. Salaried workers, who have no security of tenure, face greater risks than do the owners of firms. As a motive for economic activity, pursuit of personal profit is more or less meaningless now to the owners of large firms. It can be encouraged among salaried directors by profit-sharing. The management system works just as well in branches of state-owned stores as it does in branches of capitalist chain-stores. Giant enterprises are organized in much the same way in both the U.S.S.R. and the U.S.A. In a decentralized Socialist economy public firms can compete with each other just as freely, if not more so, than private oligopolies can in a modern capitalist economy.

Private ownership of the means of production is being challenged even more from the theoretical point of view than from the practical. In the U.S.A. this attitude has not developed as far as in Europe, but already technologists and scientists have replaced entrepreneurs and big businessmen at the top of the American scale of values. In Europe ownership of firms is being seen more and more clearly in its true light, as power, hereditary in nature, over other men. To his employees, the capitalist owner is a boss, a ruler. His works and office staff are more subject to his authority than to that of the state. For more than half their conscious waking life they depend on him directly, and for the other half they depend on him indirectly, since salaries and wages, holidays, and working hours still affect them then. Any enterprise or organization, capitalist or not, certainly needs a boss; but what basically characterizes capitalist firms is that in them authority rests on the same divine right that was thought to be the foundation of power in the state centuries ago.

From this point of view, private ownership of the means of production is essentially contrary to the western value-system. It is no longer accepted that the son should succeed his father in the army, the administration, politics or science, and it is coming to seem less and less natural that he should succeed him in the economy. In industrial societies, where most people are wage- or salary-earners, where there are old-age pensions, and education is economically more profitable than inheritance, private ownership of the means of production is an anachronism. It can more readily be accepted in small family firms than in large firms, because there it is less easy to distinguish from ownership of personal belongings. But these small firms, being less well adapted than the large ones to modern techniques, are slowly disappearing. Even in agriculture and among the peasantry, private ownership is being devalued. Hereditary transmission of economic power, like all other forms of inheritance, is becoming less and less justifiable.

Finally, in the West today capitalism is little more than negatively legitimate. Belief in its fundamental principles is decreasing more and more. But the kind of society these principles create is preferred to the only kind of Socialism which has effectively worked so far: Communist dictatorship. Stalin strengthened capitalism by making Socialism identical with totalitarianism, just as the Jacobins strengthened monarchy by making the Republic and the Terror one and the same. The childhood illnesses of the new régimes are slowing down the processes of evolution which are leading other countries towards Socialism; but they cannot halt them definitively. When the U.S.S.R. and the European Peoples' Democracies achieve true democratic Socialism, then it will be seen that, in the West, fear of totalitarian Communism was the mainstay of capitalism. Of course, before that time comes internal changes may have caused capitalism to disappear, and democratic Socialism may be attained in the West before it emerges in the East. No valid predictions can be made about this matter.

One thing seems certain, which is, that East and West are developing along convergent lines towards democratic Socialism. (The Afro-Asian countries are following the same trend, but with a considerable time-lag.) These convergent lines, however, will never quite meet. The differences between the cultures and traditions of the East and of the West are too deep-rooted ever to vanish completely: new structures never entirely destroy the value-systems and mentalities built up by the old structures. Just as a man cannot escape from his past, so a society cannot free itself entirely of its history. The very fact that the Marxists began by creating a Socialist framework and then liberalized it, while western countries began by political democracy and are now grafting Socialism on to it, is enough to prevent East and West from ultimately developing the same type of régime, although general technical progress tends to force them towards uniformity.

# Index